Sins & Ivy

SINS OF THE SYNDICATE BOOK TWO

LEXXI JAMES

SINS of the Syndicate Book Two
Sins & Ivy
Copyright © 2022 Lexxi James

www.LexxiJames.com
All rights reserved. Lexxi James, LLC.
Independently Published

With Grateful Appreciation to My Remarkable Editing Team
Cate Hogan and Jaime Ryter
and with Special Thanks to Rebecca Mysoor

Cover by Book Sprite, LLC
Image by Wander Aguiar
Wander Aguiar Photography LLC
Model Sam Myerson @sammyerson

This is a work of fiction. Names, characters, places, and incidents are the product of the author's imagination. Specific named locations, public names, and other specified elements are used for impact, but this novel's story and characters are 100 percent fictitious. Certain long-standing institutions, agencies, and public offices are mentioned, but the characters involved are wholly imaginary. Resemblance to individuals, living or dead, or to events which have occurred is purely coincidental. And if your life happens to bear a strong resemblance to my imaginings, then well done and cheers to you! You're a freaking rock star!

Prologue

LEO

Dear Diary,

There are three universal truths of love.
The first truth is when love is present, you know it. You
can feel it. It's tangible. It wraps around you like your
favorite blanket and addicts you like a drug. It's beautiful
and bright, coloring every aspect of your world, even
outshining the sun. It is everything.
At least, it's everything that matters.

The second truth is that when it's gone, you also know it.
Food is bland. Life is gray. And nothing matters. Nothing
at all. Least of all what the fuck I'm wearing.

Today, after an inordinate amount of time staring at my
closet, I managed to get my ass in gear and roll out of
bed. I tore one shirt off a hanger, then compared it to

another. Why I have thirty goddamn shirts in white is truly beyond me. Telltale sign of a psychopath.

I tossed both to the floor, making sure I stomped on them, and decided on a Navy SEAL hoodie I haven't worn in years and a pair of jeans comfy enough to tackle a buffet.

And the third universal truth of love... Drum roll, please... If I have love for even a second, I will royally fuck it to hell and back again because that is who I am.

I sit on the bed, cross-legged like Buddha, as I stare at the page. *Dear Diary*? Who came up with that shit? It's a journal to myself. It should say *Dear Prick—stop writing and get your head out of your ass.*

I imagine tossing the whole damned journal into the fireplace, smiling as it's destroyed in a spectacular blaze.

What do therapists call that? Self-destruction. I call it satisfying.

Instead of torching it like a roman candle, I take a beat and breathe through it like I do after every touchy-feely entry. It's not like anyone will read these rantings. I chuck the journal in the drawer, adding it to the pile.

Whatever demented sicko came up with purging your emotions to feel better, lied.

Ivy, my almost girlfriend, was supposed to be a one-night

stand. I haven't spoken to her in days. And scrawling my feelings out on paper isn't lifting my spirits. If anything, it only serves to point out that I'm nothing more than a colossal shit.

I drag a hand over my face and check the time. It's ass-crack o'clock, and I'm doing what I do every morning: spying on Ivy. Watching through the window has become a habit, and even without looking, I know she's up.

From the lone house hidden behind the tree line, I watch as she finishes the last moves of her yoga routine. I have to remind myself that keeping my distance is for her own protection. Spying on her stalker-style?

That's for her protection, too. At least, that's what I keep telling myself. But when she pushes through her last downward facing dog and my cock clenches, I don't turn away. Watching her is depraved and twisted, but I can't stop. I won't.

Here she is. Four-thirty in the morning—a routine of hers that now begins a full half-hour before she should be up so she can bury her head in some book. And not an electronic book that I can easily hack into. No. With Ivy, there's always something I don't know. A mystery I have to solve. A small secret I'll relish unraveling.

I step away from the window and wonder about the book. Is it a romance? A thriller? It's the little things I don't know about her that feed my obsession. That, along with her delectable lips, magnetic eyes, and fuckable body. She's a walking wet fucking dream. Of course, I'm obsessed.

What's worse is that I broke up with her. So, logically, I should avoid her at all costs. Let the poor girl enjoy her breakfast in the estate kitchen alone.

And for the last few days, I have. But not today.

Today is our day of reckoning. Today is the day Ivy Palmer has to speak to me.

Even if it kills us both.

CHAPTER 1

Ivy

"Any day now." Impatient, my fingers tap out their annoyance. Bagels should be golden and crispy, but perfection takes time, and the wrecked me says *screw that*. I rip the bagel from the toaster and move on with another day jam-packed with anything but Leo.

The broken, desperate side of me craves Leo like a Kardashian craves filler. But the jerk-face is avoiding me like a woman toting a snake saying, *"Try this apple."*

Deflated, I keep one eye on the door, losing myself in a pathetic daydream, wishing those blue eyes and growly demeanor would appear from out of nowhere any minute now.

It's not impossible. Like me, he, too, is an early riser.

I like reading at breakfast.

Leo likes reading at breakfast.

Plain bagel and coffee for me.

The exact same breakfast for him. Every. Single. Day.

It might be considered sweet and cute, but in the post-breakup riptide of sadness and rage and confusion that

7

threatens to drag me under into an abyss of loneliness, it's not cute. It's a reminder that what we had should have been more than a fling. What should have been a rom-com, spiraled into a Romeo and Juliet tragedy playing out before God, country, and two dozen members of Leo's security team.

And I have no idea why.

I scowl at the camera in the far corner of the room and debate flipping it the bird. Or flashing it my ass. I don't even care if everyone witnesses me skywriting my pissed-off heartbreak across the sky of Leo's world. At least he couldn't keep ignoring me.

Screw a plain bagel. I grab the whipped cream cheese and under-toasted bagel and settle into a quiet morning of preserving my sanity and keeping my job.

Two heaping schmears of cream cheese later, I swallow my pride and come to terms with losing Leo—something I do about a dozen times a day.

I'm unraveling at the seams, drowning one deep breath at a time, and Leo hasn't noticed. He's cool. Casual. Emotionless. And as much as I want to chalk this up to him being a total asshole, the truth is, he isn't an asshole. He's been honest with me from the start. He didn't promise me a thing. So, why do I feel so jilted?

Leo isn't interested. Period. And not being interested isn't a crime. Even if it feels like a punishment.

Barely two bites in, and I hear it. "Good morning." The deep growl is as gruff and throaty as it's warm and familiar, but it isn't Leo. It's Smoke.

Mason "Smoke" D'Angelo. Protective. Dangerous. Ruler of the D'Angelo estate. A man with enough power to crush me from my nearly invisible existence with a snap of his fingers. And I've had the insane lapse in judgment to deceive him.

"You're up early," I say to him, suddenly worried. "Is Trinity—"

He waves away my concern. "She's fine."

Technically, I'm Trinity's caretaker and companion. Or, at least, that legitimizes my reason for being here. There's a very real chance that I'm their half-black, half-Italian half-sister. Make no mistake, I'm half-out-of-my-mind for risking everything to con the most notorious mob family in Chicago. They've held court here for generations. Wiping my life from existence would take no more care or concern than flicking a speck of dirt from their shoe.

So, why am I doing this?

Because it's a shot I've got to take to get to know the people who might be my big, fat, Italian family. And it's the only way for them to get to know me. No pretense. No walls. Just them and me getting acquainted over bagels and coffee.

I take another sip, and another step deeper into nestling my way into the warmth of their well-protected nest. I have to do this.

Despite Smoke's granite jaw and princely gait, he looks like hell. His lack of a smile is enough warning for me to avoid asking about his night. He's dressed down—a T-shirt and jeans that are normally paired with his favorite leather jacket. I can't tell if he's just coming in or about to take off, and even in his disheveled state, he's handsome.

Women flock to him like kids around an ice cream truck. Smiling and energetic and ready to tear the wrapper off his popsicle with their teeth.

I'm not sure if it's his model good looks, public net worth, or that edgy bad-boy presence he effortlessly exudes, but his natural mojo works like a super-magnet. Well, it works on all women except me. Thank God. Some part of my genetics must be on high alert. *Warning: Potential Sibling. Step away from the family tree, and no one gets hurt.*

"Coffee?" I offer. Before I can get up, Leo breezes past me, appearing out of nowhere like Casper the ghost. And in true Leo fashion, he beats me to catering to the needs of his boss and BFF.

Smoke sports a lopsided grin as he and Leo exchange a glance. The silence is unnerving.

"Should I go?" I'm really saying that because I'll take any excuse to distance myself from Leo. I stand to leave.

"No. Have a seat." Smoke's authority is unmistakable. I sit. He takes another look at Leo as invisible messages travel between them. Maybe they're mind-melding a mob hit. Maybe they're telepathically gossiping about me and my now third helping of cream cheese. Or maybe, just maybe, they've decided their outfits are too similar, and one of them has to change.

Smoke takes a long look at me, frowning and formulating his words. "I need you to stick close to Trinity today."

His sister. And for all I know, my sister. His request is nothing new. "Of course."

"And keep her away from my office."

I'm used to him speaking to me like the staff—because technically, I *am* the staff—but his words are heavier than normal. Weighed down with something I can't quite put my finger on.

I smile through my nerves. "Why? What's happening in your office?" I probably shouldn't ask that with my outside voice, but let's face it. Thinking before I speak isn't exactly my strong suit.

I take my first good, long look at Leo. There's so much emotion behind his eyes, it's too easy to lose myself in unraveling all the enigmas he's content to hide.

Smoke steals my attention, sitting beside me. "Do you believe some secrets are worth dying for?"

Heat rises up my neck. Guilt suffocates me. "Is that my only option?"

His massive hand lands on my shoulder. I jolt as he pins me to my seat. "One word from you, and it's all over."

"What is?" My pulse thuds loudly in my ears.

He looks sideways at Leo, who shrugs and nods so casually that I'm not sure what to make of it. Was that a mafia *she's cool* nod? Or a mercenary *kill her now* nod?

The stiffness in my shoulders eases as Smoke's demeanor melts into a broad grin. "Our brothers are coming."

"What?" The D'Angelos—*all* the D'Angelos—will be here? My chance to meet them. Their brothers.

Maybe *my* brothers.

A squeak chops at my throat, and Smoke raises a brow. I breathe it back. "Trini will be so excited."

"Maybe half as excited as you." Smoke says through scrutiny and surprise.

I scrunch up my face and shrug. "I'm excited for Trini. She raves about them. I know she misses everyone. This will make her year." It's about to make mine.

Smoke gestures to Leo, who moves to the door, keeping watch. When Smoke leans in, I lean in, too, eager to hear more about the infamous brothers I've heard so much about. But

Smoke washes all happiness from his face, and I recognize the crease that sets in between his brows. He's worried, and his worry becomes my worry.

"What is it?" I ask.

"You know about our father, Antonio."

Antonio D'Angelo. The patriarch who turned his back on the mob. A man who went missing five years ago—now presumed dead. And if the fates are especially cruel, someone I would have given anything in the world to know.

In all likelihood, my father.

He has no idea what it means to hear him say *our* father, and I don't share how close it lands to my heart. I nod, and Smoke continues. "With our father missing, we took desperate measures after the vicious attack on Trinity. We swore an oath to keep our distance. Never have all of us in one location at the same time."

"Never?"

"Never."

The gravity of his story pierces my heart. I grew up alone, wrapping myself around Brooke's family like a foxglove vine, surviving through their strength and warmth as I bloomed in the comfort of their shadow.

The D'Angelos did the opposite. Severing themselves from the tight grip of their family ties—slicing the limbs of their love for only one reason. "Self-protection," I utter.

"Family preservation," Smoke says, correcting me. His voice is steel. Even. Unbroken. "But now we have to meet. There is a family event—a legacy—one which must be honored." Fire heats his words. "The ceremony requires all of us. It's our first gathering in years, but no one can know."

"Not even Trinity?" I ask, confused.

He blows out a breath, his smile and emotions genuine. "For our baby sister, it's a surprise. She doesn't know about the pact we made. And with our busy lives and schedules, it's been easy to make excuses. Work. Life. Too busy. No time. Trini needed to focus on recovering. Not worrying about us." He sips his coffee, smirking. "Trinity—the old Trinity—tends to be a bit of a mother hen."

Leo cuts in, speaking for the first time since entering. "It might have something to do with the lot of them always being at each other's throats."

Smoke doesn't hide his growing smile. "We sometimes have differences of opinions."

"That you enjoy settling with your fists." Leo rolls his eyes.

Smoke gives a careless shrug. "Distance makes the heart grow fonder." He stands. "You've been a godsend, Ivy. We're all glad you're here."

My smile is shy. He said *we*. Does that include Leo?

Don't look at Leo. Do not look at him.

Smoke gives two brisk pats on my shoulder before he heads out. "There are a lot of preparations. Keep Trinity distracted." Again, I nod, and he leaves the room. I expect Leo to join him.

He doesn't. Flutters awaken in my chest, and in one deep breath, I calm them.

Leo stands at the counter, doing something sophisticated with a bag of coffee beans in a grinder that makes a whirring sound.

With his back to me, I debate leaving. My eyes wander over him in a way that's not psycho-stalker-ish at all. In comfortable jeans and a hoodie that manages to hide his ripped muscles and tattered scars, Leo is dressed to travel. Is he leaving again? His holster is noticeably absent. Like, all of a sudden, it bothers him to wear it around the house. That, or he knows it bothers me.

After rummaging through a cupboard, Leo turns to me. All my good senses abandon me. I don't run like I should. Instead, I stay in place, a deer basking in the glow of headlights.

Our eyes lock, and a trace of energy swirls between us until three chimes ping. His coffee is done. The connection we have is clipped like the wings of a bird, killing any hope for flight.

I take another bite of my bagel and slip back into reading the latest gossip about this season's bachelor when Leo slides a cup front and center before me. Next to the one I already have.

The cup is fancy with gold filigree along the rim. A far departure from my *I* ♥ *Barbeque* mug or the tattered cup he keeps in his left hand. The black mug he holds carries an eagle across the front. The large bird clutches an anchor, a trident, and a gun. Despite the chip in it, it mirrors everything Leo is. Tough. Broken. Beautiful.

The military cup is his favorite, and I know it'll be glued to his hand for most of the morning. I want to know why it's so important.

He fills the fancy cup in front of me. "What are you doing?"

"Pouring you coffee."

I stare at him. "Why?" I take a sip of my own coffee for effect.

"Consider it an olive branch. You and I are going to be circling each other for a very long time."

I hold my stare, and mentally flick him in the forehead. He crushes my heart, gets crazy dramatic with moving out, but thinks coffee will superglue all the broken pieces of me that Hurricane Leo left in his wake? He can't be this dense.

Though, compared to the jet fuel I'm drinking, it does smell good.

"We have to communicate, and I don't want you not speaking to me." Angst twists his face as he continues. "I want us to be...friends."

"Friends?" Does he mean friends-friends? Or friends-with-benefits friends? I study him suspiciously.

Instead of meeting my eyes, he focuses on the steam rising from his coffee. He doubles down on his statement, though his eyes avoid mine. "Yes. Friends." His words are platonic and professional. Pure bullshit at its finest. Before I say a word, he carries the conversation to a more manageable minefield. "And this isn't just any coffee. It's extremely rare."

"Rare? As in expensive?"

"Knowing Smoke, it probably costs a thousand dollars a pound. It's known throughout the world, and there isn't much left." He pulls the bag from the counter and sets it next to the fancy cup before me. "*Geisha Hacienda La Esmeralda*. Smoke got it for me a few months back. It's cultivated along the sides of Mount Baru."

"Panama."

Curiosity quirks his lips until a small smile emerges. "You know it?"

I hand him back the bag. "It's written on the label." I tap a finger at the word. "I wouldn't have pegged you for a coffee snob."

"Me neither. But when it's homegrown in Panama beneath

the shade of guava trees, how can I refuse?" He points to the caption on the label that says exactly that.

"What a beautiful image." I take a deep whiff. Rich chocolate notes wrap around me, reminding me of a decadent Italian espresso Trini made for me last week.

Would Trini accept me if she knew who I was? Would Smoke?

"Where'd you go?" Leo notices that I've stopped short of drinking.

"Nowhere," I lie.

That deep blue of his gaze always threatens to sweep me in. My phone pings with something irrelevant, and I ignore it. I don't want to lose this moment.

He takes a sip of his coffee and leans closer. "Is this okay?"

My heart leaps to my throat as his aftershave melts my defenses. "Okay?" I whisper.

His face is inches from mine before he looks past me. He's reaching for today's paper and clears his throat. "I wouldn't want you to lose your place. I just wanted to grab—"

"The sports page," I whisper, flustered as the reality of *"friends"* hits me square in the chest.

"Aren't you going to get that?" He glances at my phone, then at me.

The text message is meaningless, though I'll give them credit. The tactic is original as it flashes on my screen.

Call me: I'll make it worth your while.

I shake my head. Telemarketing and phishing scams have hit a new low. Loser.

Leo frowns. "What is it?"

"Hmm?" His stare hasn't lifted from the phone. Is this his way of being polite? Carrying on the conversation?

Or maybe that's just me. Wanting him to look at me. See me. Acknowledge that I was more than a one-night stand.

I'm fine. I don't want this to get awkward, so I force a smile and shove the phone aside. "It's nothing."

He straightens the paper, snaps it in half, and sips his coffee. The awkward silence I was hoping to avoid creeps between us. He extended an olive branch. Now, it's my turn. I clasp the fancy cup with both hands. "Leo, I'm not exactly sure how to say this, but tell me the truth."

"Okay," he says with another casual sip.

I inhale the aroma. "This isn't one of those coffee beans that has passed through an animal's ass, is it?"

Coffee nearly flies out his nose. "What?" His lips stop short of another sip.

His twisted expression meets mine. I'm enjoying this way too much. "Is this one of those super expensive coffees that some animal has to eat and poop out for it to be worth the price tag?"

It takes half a second for my question to fully process through his stoic head. His cup lands on the paper, coffee sloshing over the sides. Hands clasped and eyes shut, he exhales through his nose. "Tell me that's not a thing."

"Oh, it's a thing. Some of the most expensive products in the world have passed through an animal's butt. Hair products. Skin products. Coffee—very, very expensive coffee. How expensive did you say this one was?"

His brow furls as he pinches the bridge of his nose. "Expen-

17

sive," he chokes out. "It would be just like Smoke to give me that as a gift. I wouldn't put it past him to hand me a bag of shit coffee just so he can laugh every time I drink it."

"That's a really expensive gag gift."

"Yes. And it's exactly what that fucker would do." He holds out his hand. "Give me your cup."

I hoard it protectively. "Why? World-renowned, expensive poop java? Not on your life. I will drink every last drop and like it." Without asking, he whips the cup from my hand. "Hey!"

"Your lips are not touching a drop. Not until I look into it. It's one thing for Smoke to have a laugh at my expense. You are entirely off-limits."

"I am?" Somewhere between breaking my heart and throwing me an olive branch, did Leo just become protective? Over me?

Or is it just all in my head?

I shake off my stupid sentiment and watch as Leo buries himself in Wikipedia on his phone. It gives me the excuse I need to take a closer look at him. His rugged, square jaw is tightly clenched. It reminds me of our last night together. When nothing existed but us and the moment his armor vanished away. When he was mine, and I was his.

"Crisis averted," he announces. I smother a laugh at his exaggerated, relieved sigh. "I am happy to report that the coffee beans used to make this expensive cup has in no way, shape, or form, passed through the asshole of an animal." His shoulders relax, and he slips my cup back into my hands. We both ignore the charge of our touch. He enjoys a bigger sip of his coffee, and I do the same.

"So, tell me..." he begins.

His eyes are bluer than ever, and his half smile is dimpled and charming. I kick myself repeatedly for wanting a man so completely unavailable. "What?" I ask.

"I'm curious. How the hell does any person in their right mind look at what came out of a critter's butt and say, *I wonder what that would taste like roasted and brewed*."

We both crack up laughing. And the awkwardness fades away. For the next hour, he relays all the details of the days to come—when each brother is coming and how the security teams will be diverted from D'Angelo Tower to the estate. I give him all my attention and try to imagine the grounds with twice as many people.

It troubles me to wonder if it's enough. I can't lose the family I'm just getting to know.

When he's done, Leo tosses back the rest of his coffee and stands. "It'll be fine," he says, reassuring me as he reads my mind. "Guarding the D'Angelos is the one thing I do well."

His words are iron, reinforcing the barricade he manages to hold up between us.

"I'd better get to work," he says, placing his mug in the sink.

"Leo?"

He pauses before he reaches the door. His turn is slow as he pockets his hands. "Yes, Ivy," he says tenderly as if whatever I'm about to ask might loosen the wrong Jenga piece and shatter us both.

I clear my throat. "Why do you drink out of a chipped cup?"

He's thoughtful for a moment, considering his words before he speaks. "It's a reminder."

"Of what?" As soon as the two little words come out, I wish

I could scoop them back in. Maybe it's from his late wife? Or reminiscent of another equally traumatic period of his life? It's wrong of me to ask. We're not in a place to chat about anything deeply personal. "I'm sorry, I didn't mean to pry."

"No. It's all right." He thinks through my question and finds the right words. "It's important that I see it every day. It reminds me that no matter how strong something appears, it may be more fragile than it looks. If I'm not careful, all the things I care about will break."

Between his open-hearted words and the honesty in his eyes, I feel like this is less about the cup and more about me. Us.

My cell pings again. Another random, meaningless sound that tells me it's no one important.

Leo's expression hardens as he glances at the phone. "Answer it."

"What?"

Two steps closer, and he repeats himself, seething and insistent. "Answer it."

His glare is daunting. I glare right back. But Leo's sudden mood swing is a force to be reckoned with, and I haven't had enough thousand-dollar-a-pound coffee to deal with his pop-up PMS. I pick up my phone. "Fine." *Psycho.*

I click on the message.

Pharmacy Notification: 1 prescription is ready for pickup.

It takes me a second to realize he's hovering over my shoulder, attempting to read the text as I do. I whip it to my chest. "Why are you acting like this?"

"Like what?" He steps back.

"All weird and hovery...and jealous."

He shakes his head. "I was not acting weird and hovery." He noticeably bypasses the accusation of jealousy. "I thought it might be..." he begins, then stalls.

I look up at him, suddenly interested in whatever it is he has to say.

He straightens one sleeve and then another, coming up with some imaginative excuse for getting all helicopter parent on me. "Important," he finally blurts out.

"Mm-hmm. It took you all that time to come up with the word *important*."

He holds out his hand. "Show me the text."

"What?"

His expectant fingers wiggle, waiting for me to hand over my cell. I stare up at him as if he were some random nutjob on the L-Train asking for cash, food, or sex.

He doesn't waver. "Don't play games with me, Ivy. Show me the phone."

"Are you out of your delusional mind?" By the indisputable fury in his eyes, it's apparent he's not kidding. He very much *is* out of his delusional mind. I clasp it tighter.

Sweet and sentimental Leo has vanished into thin air, making way for his moody, broody twin. "The contract you signed is iron-clad. You will hand over any and all property when requested by the chief of security. Me. I won't ask again. Hand over your phone."

What the ever-loving fuck?

Any concern or confusion I feel is plowed under a lava flow of rage. "No. The contract I signed says that I will cooperate with any and all investigations and provide information upon request. I will hand over any and all D'Angelo property when requested." His nostrils flare. I tap the phone to my lips. "Exactly what information from my phone would you like to see?"

"Your last text," he says, without a trace of amusement.

There is a dangerous side to Leo. The one he keeps buttoned up to preserve his public persona. A side of him that fights to be loyal and kills to protect. The side of him I probably shouldn't taunt on a whim, but I do.

"My last text? But you're not weird, hovery, or jealous, right?"

"I'll tell you what I'm not, Ivy. I'm not asking again. Show me the message. Now." His words come out calm, a dark threat that assures me his last shred of sanity is three seconds from snapping.

I open my phone and produce the message, watching as he reads and rereads it. His expression falls from irritation to dismay.

I take another long sip of coffee, then glance at the screen. "Well, Leo, you caught me red-handed. My secret love affair with the pharmacist is exposed. Next Tuesday, he's about to celebrate his seventy-fifth birthday. Would popping out of a cake be too much? Perhaps I should check with his wife."

Unamused, he huffs. For a brief moment, our eyes lock, and I can't read him at all.

"Perhaps you should," he says as he taps a single finger on the face of the phone. "And perhaps you should program in his number so there's no mistaking who's calling."

I blink at Leo. He's dead serious.

I'm at...a loss.

I look into his eyes, then down at my coffee, then back up at him again. I shove it an arms-length away. "Are you sure this ultra-expensive coffee isn't laced with acid? Exactly how much have you had?"

His face is a clusterfuck of confusion. It's probably mirroring mine.

With a shake of his head, he moves to the door, looks back at me once, and leaves.

I take my coffee and pour the questionable liquid straight down the drain.

Maybe there's a book on the subject. *Loose cannons and the women who love them*.

Did I just say love? Where the hell did that come from?

And what the hell just happened?

CHAPTER 2

Leo

*W*hat the hell just happened?

In long, desperate strides, I bolt from the kitchen, creating as much space between me and Ivy as I can. *Fuck, I need some air.*

Ivy has me so wound up that I feel like I'm losing my mind. Between her soft skin and that intoxicating scent of citrus and vanilla that follows her damn near everywhere, my chest is tight, my dick is in knots, and I can't think straight.

Focus.

That first text on her phone—the **Call me, I'll make it worth your while** text—I know that number. Or... was it all in my head?

My reaching around wasn't to get closer to Ivy—at least, that's what I keep telling the incessant throbbing in my pants. I needed a closer look at the screen. As luck would have it, the damned thing timed out and went completely black.

When the second text came in, I lost my shit. A premature act, considering all I could see was the area code. A

Chicago area code is common enough. But I know what I saw.

Think. I recall the number from Ivy's phone. What if I wasn't imagining it? That first number.

I race to my office, tearing open one desk drawer after the other. "Where is it?" I mutter, rifling around for my old notebook.

Jesus, I've got a lot of crap in here. Pens. Post-Its. Scraps of surveillance notes and a few receipts. Handcuffs. A pack of mint gum from who knows when. Magazines on cars and firearms and, of course, Rachael Ray.

A ruler? A goddamned ruler? Where the fuck is Marie Kondo when I need her?

Knock. Knock-knock.

The distinctive knock is Hunter. The lethal mercenary I put in charge of Ivy. Mostly to keep her at arm's length from me, but also because I know that if I can't be the one protecting Ivy, Hunter is my next best option. "Come in."

Hunter enters, closing the door behind him. "You all right, boss?"

My frustration peaks out by drawer number three. Playtime is over. I dump the largest drawer onto the floor, drop to my hands and knees, and rummage through the unruly mountain of contents. "Fine, Hunter. Why do you ask?"

He squats down beside me. "Um...Ivy said you didn't seem like yourself."

"I could say the same about her." I mutter under my breath. "Where is it?"

"Where is what?" he asks as he pilfers the pile alongside me, shuffling its contents from one side of the rug to the other.

He tugs a small blue notepad from the pile. I stare at him as if he's a Hobbit who just discovered a ring. "Open it," I snap. "Look at the first page."

"O-kay," he says, confused but playing along.

"Look at the first number." He does. I close my eyes, praying for the first time in my life that I'm wrong. "Is it 224-555-0116?"

"No," he says, and my shoulders relax. "But it's the second one."

"What?" I snatch the notepad from his hands and stare in disbelief. There it is, in black and white. The number. The one that texted Ivy.

Fuck-fuck-fuck-fuck-fuckety-fuck-fuck.

Fuuuccck.

"Boss, what is it?"

I wipe a hand down my face as a heavy ball of dread sinks into my gut. *It's Uncle Andre D'Angelo's private fucking line.*

I only think that. I don't say it. It's not that I don't trust Hunter. The son of a bitch would take a bullet for me, and I would take one for him. He's on my team because I do trust him. Implicitly.

But things aren't adding up. Nothing makes sense. I suck in a needed breath, then ease it out to clear my head. I have to get to the bottom of this before Ivy becomes an enemy of the state.

At one point or another, we've all speculated that Andre had a hand in Antonio's disappearance and probable death. Andre's been public enemy number one—battling the D'Angelo children over the fortune and estate for years. If the family caught wind that Ivy might be mixed up with Andre, all hell would break loose.

They're not exactly the *hash-it-out* types. I know their M.O. Shit, I wrote the book on it. Unleash the wrath of hell first, ask questions later...as we commence with a wet cleanup, and make plans for the disposal of her body.

Mercy is not an option. They'd crush her. And for reasons I can't explain—not even to myself—I can't let that happen.

"It's nothing," I manage to say. Hunter quirks a brow. It's hard lying to a man you trained in interrogation, so I elaborate. "It's private. Something I need to figure out on my own. That's all."

"Fair enough. Can I help?"

I rise to my feet and hold out a hand, helping him up to his. "No." My better judgment kicks in. "Yes. Stay close to Ivy."

"Close?" His brow ticks higher. "How close?"

I let out a long breath through my nose. "Close," I repeat, mentally building a wall between what I want to do and what I have to do. Hunter is a chameleon. He'll do and be whatever Ivy needs him to be: captivated, adoring, a good listener who sees the *real* her. A manipulative fuckhead who will go to whatever lengths needed to gather the necessary information.

Trust me, the last thing I want is Hunter Walsh turning up the charm. But, fuck. I need the truth. And he's in a prime position to get it for me.

In that regard, he's perfect. A presence in Ivy's life who can worm his way into her trust. Investigate without it seeming overt or suspicious. And after my little tantrum this morning, let's face it; clearly, I'm the wrong man for the job.

"Are you sure?" His question is obvious. He knows I've slept with Ivy. Hell, everyone working under this roof knows that. I have a vested interest in her, and I can't deny it.

But Hunter isn't looking out for Ivy's well-being. I could be half a step from chaining her to my bed, forcing her to be my sex slave, and asking him to set up the video equipment. He's not asking for Ivy's sake. He's asking for mine. He needs an assurance that whatever he does, he won't be crossing a line.

I swallow my hesitation, the taste of regret bitter and hard. "I'm sure."

He nods once. "That shouldn't be a problem." Is he smirking?

I shake off the urge to throat-punch him and continue. "She reports to you. That gives you enough excuse to chat up a storm and pry into her day, but I want more than that. I want a full report."

"A full report?" He pauses, treading carefully before he speaks. "But a full report requires—"

"I know what it requires, Hunter. Wire her room. Clone her phone. Track her car. Do it."

"But it'll take more than just me. Anyone she talks to. Anyone she sees. It's a three-man team."

"No. Just you. If she leaves the estate, stay on her heels. If she sneezes, I want the time and place. Anything that looks like a message. Code. No matter how the picture ends up looking, lock every puzzle piece in its place."

"Yes, sir." His two words are unyielding and definitive.

The good thing about working with someone you've been in combat with is they know when not to question your orders. Or intentions. No matter how batshit crazy you sound.

"Anything or anyone, in particular, you want me to look out for?"

It takes me half a second to think it through. "No. A detailed report is enough. I'll take it from there."

He takes his orders and heads for the door.

"And Hunter," he turns, facing me, "this stays between us."

His nod is serious and assured.

CHAPTER 3

Ivy

Staring out the kitchen window, it's easy to lose myself in the landscape and forget why I'm here. A scattering of rich yellows and vibrant pinks bloom along the path leading down to the first of three serene lakes. All the while, my finger circles lazily along the rim of Leo's mug. It's careful each and every time it skips over the sentimental little chip. And each time it does, its significance tugs at my heart.

It's a warning. A big, blaring yellow light nudging me to proceed with caution. *Be careful.*

I'm keeping a secret—the longer I hide it, the more I can feel it chipping away at the trust I'm beginning to build.

I take a long look around the empty kitchen. With Smoke and Leo both gone, the space is unnervingly quiet. An all too familiar state of my life I've always loathed.

Loneliness.

What if Smoke and Trini are the beginning of a new life? My long-lost brother and sister. The first in a long line of siblings I never could have imagined. A family that only existed in my loftiest dreams. A beautiful swan family welcoming a tattered, little lone duckling into their fold.

But what if I'm not one of their flock? I have no proof that I'm their sister...other than a photo and a hunch. Considering that the photograph with my mother and Antonio D'Angelo has been MIA since I arrived, that leaves me with a whole lot of nothing more than a deep-rooted hope that this is my family, and they want me.

I want them. Does that count? I want to be part of them so bad it hurts.

But this isn't just about Smoke and Trinity and the rest of the D'Angelos. It's about Leo, too. This time, when my finger skims that tiny little chip, it doesn't skip over. It stops. I take a long, hard look at it, noticing the fracture that branches down the rim. It's small and fine and nearly invisible, but it reminds me how much Leo is right.

If I'm not careful, everything I cherish could break.

Something beautiful broke between me and Leo, but it's fixable. I can feel it in my gut. But what if I keep this from him? Me being a D'Angelo. The man whose world is layered in loyalty and trust. Could he ever look at me the same?

Not telling them isn't a lie. So why does it feel like one? Like every time we speak, and I don't tell him who I might be, it's a deception.

But I can't tell Leo first. And I can't tell Trini. I don't know all the fragile points in her history or her triggers. I can't break the precious bond that's been forming between us.

Smoke. It has to be Smoke. The boss. The patriarch. And the man whose bad side I never want to be on. Nerves rattle my soul at the thought of approaching him. If I don't say a word, I can keep this precious time we're all sharing together.

But what if in Smoke's eyes, a lie by omission is still a lie? A deceit. A betrayal. Smoke only needs one reason to cast me aside and never look back, and this would be it. I can't not tell him.

And there's no time like the present.

I steel my resolve and make my way to Smoke's office, using the length of the hall to rehearse.

I could be casual. Start with, *"Hey, you. Did you ever want another sister?"*

Or, *"What a coincidence. We both like Italian food."*

Perhaps I could try, *"I know we haven't known each other long, but we have a lot in common. Like... genetics."*

Deflated, I shake my head.

This is a hardcore mafia family, not a Hallmark movie. Direct, straightforward, and to the point. Leave the gun. Take the cannoli. Avoid horseheads in the bed at all costs.

I pass a large mirror on the wall and glance at the scared girl staring back from it. In every family photo, the D'Angelo children are tall, beautiful people with noble features and glowing olive skin sun-kissed by the gods. My frame is petite and insignificant, easily dwarfed by all of them—even Trinity.

My dark brown curls are frizzed and wild, and so out of place I can't help but smooth them down. Epic fail. Is it possible to will my hair to be tame for once? And we'll all ignore the fact that my skin is about, oh, I don't know, seven shades darker.

My nerves prick along every ounce of bravery on the verge of fleeing. I suck in a breath and focus on the lone silver strand that falls from my temple. A reminder as to why I'm here. Antonio D'Angelo. His splash of silver graced his temple at exactly the same spot. A ribbon of silver that binds us by heritage if not by name. A genetic lifeline that fills me with hope.

I practice once more, muttering five crazy, little words softly to myself. "I think I'm your sister."

Shoulders squared and back straight, I step up to the carved wood double doors. Butterflies flit along my insides as I bite my lower lip. Palms sweaty, I close my eyes and posture my fist for a knock.

Deep breath in. Slow breath out.

Knock-knock-knock.

I rap at the door so softly I'm not sure the little sounds could be heard until a deep baritone voice breaks through. "Come in."

My steps are timid as I enter the large, opulent office. Smoke's enormous frame easily fills the space. He makes his way around the desk, and despite the casual shirt and laid-back jeans, everything about him is no-nonsense and intimidating. His hard lines and muscular build are the epitome of strength and power. Wealth. Privilege. The heir to the D'Angelo estate. And a man who shouldn't be fucked with under any circumstances. "I bet I know why you're here."

My heartbeat flutters. "You do?"

He scoops an envelope from his desk, and hands it to me. Nerves frayed, I open the flap and take a look. It's a check. I look up, confused. "What's this?"

He arches a brow. "Payday. Unless you've decided you'd rather volunteer your time here."

My paycheck. Right. "Thank you." I fiddle with the envelope, but don't move to leave.

Smoke takes a seat on the side of his desk, giving me full view of the larger-than-life image that hangs behind him. A portrait of Antonio D'Angelo. I've never met him, yet I feel him. His presence. His absence. I can't explain the loss that burrows a hole within me. The pain. A wave of sadness drags me ten feet under. It hurts.

"Ivy?" Smoke motions for the chair, nudging me to take a seat. "Is everything all right?"

My nod is weak and unconvincing. Still, I smile, not wanting to taint our conversation with sentiments I have no right to. "Thanks," I say, sinking into the large, oversized chair. The entire office holds notes of leather and bourbon and faint wisps of cigars. A masculine swirl that may be as much Antonio as it is Smoke.

Several unwieldy strands of hair pester my face, and I slide them behind my ear. My lips are tight, and my throat is as dry as a desert. And those tiny, little words that, moments ago, seemed so easy to say are suddenly gone.

Smoke notices me staring off—a million miles away. He turns, pointing to the small table in the corner that holds my glance. "Did you want a drink?"

"I don't drink," I manage to squeak out. When I notice the clock, I have to laugh. "And it's ten o'clock in the morning."

He shrugs. "It's five o'clock somewhere. What's on your mind?"

Just say it. *I'm your sister.* Is that what I was going to say? Or was it, *I think I'm your sister*? As soon as his big, blue, expectant eyes meet mine, all I can do is point to the makeshift bar he thought I was thirsting for. "Is that a flask?" I ask. *Stupidest question ever.* Maybe that single sip of poop-free papaya hillside coffee was one sip too much.

To my surprise, Smoke beams, nodding and proud. "It was a gift from all of us to our father. With each of our signatures engraved into the silver."

I step over to it. "May I?"

Nodding, he jumps from the chair to hand it to me. It isn't delicate, but I handle it as though it's made of the thinnest glass.

The autographs wrap around the curve, each one beautiful and precious. The signatures of every D'Angelo child. Every one except mine.

I ignore the way the shiny memento claws my heart from the inside out and focus on the one signature that grounds me. My finger traces it, looping the letters with love. "Trinity." Over each 'I' is a tiny heart that tugs at mine.

"The Princess," Smoke shares.

"Enzo."

"The King," Smoke announces before correcting himself. "Or the villain if you ask anyone who's ever met him." He laughs. "Enzo runs D'Angelo Holdings."

I continue with all of them. Dante's signature has an extra-long tail after the E, ending in something that looks like a Devil's tail. Hence his nickname *The Devil.* Mateo's letters are tall and no-nonsense. He's *The Saint,* though I can't imagine any of them being entirely good.

Dillon's handwriting is carefree and fun, with a happy face in the 'O.' He is *The Player,* and by Trini's disapproving account of his legendary conquests, it's easy to see why. And last but far from least: "Mason," I say with a smile.

Smoke waggles his brows. One of these days, I'll have to find out more about how he came into a nickname that suits him as much as his leather jackets and deadly scowl.

"So, we have a Princess, a King, a Devil, a Saint, and a Player...what do they all call you?"

Coyly, he offers a boyish shrug. "The Beast." I stare at him, unsurprised.

"Because you lock yourself away in a castle, waiting for your queen?"

"Because no one else would be in Trini's dumb little play. One role, and I'm typecast for life." He growls, loud and boisterous, with eyes bright. His laugh grows to a big, hearty belly laugh as he reminisces, and I latch on to that laugh. It's filled with visions of an idyllic childhood. Of all of them together. "You must miss them," I say sadly.

He nods. "I do. But by the end of next week, I'll be happy to have their asses gone. They all have a fucking opinion on everything. How I run the estate. How I care for Trini. How my life will change when I settle down—as if that will ever happen." He returns the flask to the corner table, taking a minute to set it in the perfect spot. "But our brothers are very excited to meet you."

Tension builds just below my skin. "They know about me?" I bite my lip.

Smoke notices. "Don't be nervous."

"I'm not," I lie, fidgeting with my fingers.

"If they even look at you sideways, I've got a size fifteen boot going straight up their asses."

I laugh off his protectiveness. "It's not like they're all

coming to meet me." They think I'm Trini's caretaker. Just another staff member in a hive of worker bees.

"Don't be so sure. Trini has been singing your praises." Smoke slips both hands into his back pockets. "Listen, the past few years have been hard. The brothers have barely spoken." Smoke struggles to find his words. "But we need to come together."

"Why?"

"The D'Angelos have a tradition—one that goes back generations. This year, I turn thirty-five. And because I'm the eldest and agreed to take the mansion and keep it as a home for Trini, that puts me in the position of *Erede al Trono*."

Shyly, I repeat, "*Eh-ready al torono*?"

Approving, he nods. "That's good. In the most direct translation, it means *heir to the throne*. For the D'Angelos, its meaning is more significant. You know about our history?" he asks, lifting a brow and hesitating until I've answered the question.

I nod. When his brow pinches, uncertain if I really do know their family history, I verbally respond. "Grandfather Vito D'Angelo was in the mob."

His lips pinch with the knowing smile. "Our grandfather *was* the mob. He owned Chicago."

"But that was forever ago."

"No, Ivy." He lowers his voice, though it's just the two of us in the privacy of his office. "If you're going to be in our inner circle—holding our trust—it's important you understand. Enzo runs our business. So does Dante. And they embrace the ways of our grandfather. I don't. For a long time, I rejected it. If I could, I'd pass on this *honor...*" He says the word with disgust. "Hand everything to Enzo. But he's too much of a wildcard—drunk with power. High on wealth. I have to be the one to accept it. Be the family protector."

"That's why they're all coming."

"Normally, we wouldn't have outsiders at the ceremony." He places a paternal hand on my shoulder. "But Leo will be there, and I hope you'll be there, too. What you've done to bring Trinity out of the horrors that happened to her is nothing short of miraculous. This is my formal rite of passage, where my word is law. A tradition that's handed down from firstborn to firstborn. Trinity wants you there, and I want you there, too."

"Smoke, there's something important I have to tell you—"

Knock-knock.

He smiles an assurance to me and squeezes both my shoulders. "Hold that thought." He hollers to the door. "Come in."

Leo enters, followed by Hunter. Hunter flashes a warm grin at me, and I can't help but smile back. When I smile at Leo, his attention turns to Smoke. "You wanted to go over the security details for the event."

Smoke ends our discussion with a smile. "Duty calls."

And just like that, I'm dismissed.

CHAPTER 4

Leo

A few jabs in, and Smoke hammers me with a powerful kick to my thigh. I think I hear a bone break. "Stop going easy on me," Smoke insists, his tone of admonishment totally lost from the throbbing pain in my leg.

"Cut me some slack. I'm getting old. My joints literally creak when I get out of bed like the fuckers are made of wood."

He chuckles. My words distract him for the half-second I need to sock him hard in his smug-as-shit face. His annoyed growl is an angel's song to my soul.

He spits blood on the floor, clears his throat, and speaks. "I invited Ivy to *Erede al Trono.*"

Stunned, I dropped my arms. Smoke lays me out with an uppercut to the jaw. It throws me back—both the punch and his invitation.

The sucker punch knocks sense into me—instant clarity. None of us really knows who Ivy is, and every last one of the D'Angelos, other than Uncle Andre, will be at this event. After our last night together, I never followed through with completing her background check. I should kick my own ass for that one.

Smoke mirrors me, dropping his hands. "Did my punch land you in the concussion zone? Or was me inviting Ivy that much of a shock?"

"If I'm totally honest, a little of both." I look at him, formulating the words I'm about to say. "Ivy hasn't been fully vetted."

Smoke's gaze lasers on mine, the way it always does when he attempts to read my mind. *Poker face up.* "Let me get this straight. You've unveiled the deepest, darkest, most intimate secrets of Chicago's underground, known terrorists, royals, and heads of state. You can no doubt tell me which of my brothers is viewing porn at this very minute, and which of them is plotting my demise as we speak."

"Dante for porn. Enzo for your demise."

"Exactly my point." His eyes narrow. "Is there something about Ivy you don't want to tell me?"

Technically, no. Because, *technically*, she didn't take a call from Andre D'Angelo. And *technically*, saying that with my outside voice would only draw out my death.

Instead, I broad-brush the truth. "I was in the middle of investigating her the night Trini disappeared." I could say the last night Ivy and I fucked like a giant asteroid was seconds from colliding with Earth, but Smoke already knows that part.

And it isn't just that Ivy and I fucked, which we did in spades, but we also made sweet, tender, passionate love that both satiates me and has me ravenous for more.

It also happens to be the night that I decided to kill our relationship for good, so for argument's sake, let's just say I fucked up all around. But when it comes to the D'Angelos and their protection, fucking up is not an option.

Smoke gives me that brotherly look. That tender, sympathetic stare of pity with *you poor, dumb bastard* written all over his face.

"I'm taking care of it," I assure him.

"I'd give you more time, Leo, but you don't have it. Trinity wants her there, and so do I. Unless you've got a reason why she can't be there, she's coming."

I nod, eager to stop pining for Ivy like a lovesick puppy and start seeing her for what she is. A stranger. A wildcard.

A potential threat.

"You can count on me, Smoke."

"I know I can," he says in return. "And actually, I need you to do me a favor."

"Anything."

"There is a part of the ceremony where the D'Angelo dagger is handed down. An antique laden with the blood, sweat, and tears of every D'Angelo who has held it. If my father were alive, he would perform the ceremony. But I want you to do it."

"Me?" That doesn't make any sense. Smoke has nearly half a dozen brothers. Even if he had a falling out with Enzo or Dante, Mateo and Dillon are still behind. And not to get all women's lib about the subject, but Trinity would be next—should be next—if no one else was left. "I'm flattered, but I can't stand between you and your family."

"That's just it, Leo, you are our family. You will always be there for Trini, just as we would. In the eyes of every D'Angelo standing, this makes us brothers."

"But Enzo—"

"Enzo doesn't have a say. You're more than a spectator in our world, Leo. I want you there."

There are no words that can express what I'm feeling. We smile as a long, sentimental silence builds between us. So much so that it becomes awkward. I clear my throat. "As much as I appreciate the sentiment, Smoke, don't expect me to kiss you or anything."

He deadpans. "I'm wounded. Really, I am." A hopeful smile lifts from his face. "You'll do it?"

Humbled, I reply, "Yes. But if any of your brothers object—"

"They won't," he assures me. "And it's a black-tie affair."

My face falls. My last tuxedo was from my wedding. The thought of wearing another one has me reaching for an EpiPen.

Smoke pats my back. "It's just one night. You won't even need a tie."

"Doesn't that defeat the purpose of black tie?"

"I know for you wearing a tie is as appealing as matrimony or death, so I'll do you this small favor if you do me a big one."

"Here it comes..."

He takes one last look at my throbbing jaw. No doubt relishing in his handiwork. "Figure out where you stand with Ivy." I roll my eyes. "And don't roll your eyes at me. Whenever you're around her, you're like kerosene around a fucking flame thrower. Bottled up and ready to explode."

"Spare me the lecture. Ivy and I are professionals."

"Uh-huh."

"Platonic professionals," I assure him.

"Whatever you say."

"But I appreciate the reprieve on the tie."

Smoke pats me on the back as we head out of the gym. "You put Don Juan Hunter on Ivy. The less rope you have to hang yourself with, the better," he chuckles.

Fucker.

※※※※

It's two in the morning, and I'm barely three-quarters through Ivy's background check because every time I see a goddamned picture of her eyes, I pause. Their darkness captivates me because her every thought and emotion is on constant display. Contentment. Joy. Sorrow. Grief. This woman is no more a manipulative succubus than I am a man of the cloth.

Her life is far from a mystery, with loose parallels to mine.

My mother was a garden variety alcoholic with random fits of smacking kids around. Compared to Ivy's mom, mine was vying for mother of the year.

Samara Palmer took bad parenting to a whole new depth of hell. Booze was merely her gateway to a lifestyle of gambling and cocaine. Prostitution. Abusive men. And on more than one occasion, child abandonment. If the local sheriff hadn't stepped in, Ivy would've been trafficked to the highest bidder.

Yet, as I did with my mother, Ivy took care of hers to the bitter end. Knowing this makes me want to hold her, steal her away from here.

Love her.

Fuck. This is why my investigation keeps stalling out. I'm standing on the sidelines, admiring Ivy like she's a pretty pink marsh flower trapped in the knee-deep Carolina wetlands. My job isn't to rescue her. My job is to nail her to the cross if there's even the faintest chance she's here to fuck over the family.

I stare down at the five-year-old faking a smile for the camera. As much as I want to ignore her past or the way it makes my blood roll to a boil, I can't.

Where the hell was her father in all of this? Mine is in jail. I smile, recalling that it was me who sent him there.

Hmm...

Maybe it's time to track down hers.

CHAPTER 5

Leo

What's she doing?

I move from my Ivy files and step closer to the window, seeing that Ivy veered from her usual routine of Trini, yoga, and reading. I watch as she makes her way past the east lawns and down to the lake.

I check my watch. By now, she should be elbow-deep in a Trini cooking lesson. Instead, she's traipsing through the tall grasses, making her way to the only hillside with no camera coverage.

I flick away my one working brain cell that should be sending a message to Hunter to check it out. Instead, I do the worst thing possible. I stalk her.

I know, I know. Once is chance. Twice is coincidence. Three times is a pattern that's considered a Class 4 felony by the great state of Illinois and is punishable by one to three years in prison and up to a $25,000 fine.

Whatever.

I don't know what it is about Ivy. Half the time, I want to

protect her. Half the time, I want to interrogate her. And half the time, I want to slam her up against the nearest wall and fuck her into next week. And, yes, I'm painfully aware that Ivy Palmer has driven me to a world where it takes three halves to wrap my head, heart, and dick around every aspect of her.

She ambles along the path, losing herself in all the wonders of a bright, sunny day, oblivious that I'm keeping pace thirty feet behind her.

I shed my jacket. Between the unusually hot day and high humidity, I'm sweating my balls off during what's become a two-mile hike. I'd almost think Ivy was heading to the largest pond on the property for a refreshing swim except she doesn't swim. I'm both intrigued and suspicious.

In many ways, I've overlooked the beauty of the property. It's not that I don't see the lush gardens and serene backdrop that canvas the estate. I'm usually preoccupied with monitoring it. Surveillance. Wide range proximity detectors, 1080 resolution cameras with infrared LED night vision, and listening devices that can detect a fart from a fly from 900 feet away.

I know better than anyone, that when you're on the D'Angelo estate, privacy is as real as a tea party with the Tooth Fairy. No doubt, my men are watching me. Monitoring my every move as I monitor every move of Ivy's.

So, why am I following her?

Because over the expanse of the hundred-acre estate, there's one blind spot. The lake on the east lawns. And Ivy's heading straight for it.

It would be so easy to believe Ivy is the sweet, southern girl she portrays herself to be. But what if she isn't? What if she's a conniving con artist—covering every secret and lie like a blanket of wildflowers over a steaming pile of manure.

When Ivy disappears over the hill, I hurry to catch up. She meanders toward the old, creaky dock that I'm not entirely sure will hold her weight. There's a wooden tackle shed that has seen better days, and my curiosity is piqued when she opens it.

The shed has to be at least a quarter of a century old, withered and dilapidated. There are no plans to replace or remove it. Antonio D'Angelo built it with his bare hands and the hands of every one of his children—a three-dimensional model of family at its finest.

I've heard the stories of their lazy Sundays at the lake. Enzo and Dante competing to see who could dive the best or swim the fastest. Mateo torturing Trinity, chasing her with wriggly worms. Dillon capturing everything in photos and video. And Smoke...fishing with his father—wanting to do and be everything he was.

So, why is Ivy here?

Ivy fights with the rickety door before wrestling free a fishing rod. The bass pro enthusiast in me cringes as she drags the tip along the ground.

She moseys to the end of the dock, kicks off her shoes, and sits, letting her feet swing aimlessly in the water as she casts her line. Content to have scared off every fish for miles with her careless foot dangling, she pulls out a large book and proceeds to read.

"Rookie mistake," I say as I loosen my tie and roll up my sleeves.

She looks back, rolls her eyes, and flips the page. "I'm not hoping to snag a blue marlin. Just enjoying some alone time."

Hint of the century.

I remove my shoes and socks, pull up my pant legs, and sink into the soft grass and damp soil. She snaps her book shut, annoyed. "What are you doing?"

Blades of grass are damp and cool under my feet. "Your fishing expedition is missing something." My fingers bore into a particularly moist spot of ground, unearthing a prize worm in no time. I dangle it proudly.

She winces in disgust. "Ewww."

I move to the dock and sequester her fishing pole to properly bait the rusted hook.

"I know how to bait a hook," she says, underwhelmed.

"I'm sure you do," I say, sardonic as shit. "By the way you were using the pole to scribe your name into the deck, I can see you're a real natural." I finish and hand her back the pole. She accepts it with a frown. "What?" I ask.

Her words are timid. "I didn't really want to fish."

I scratch my head. "Then why did you risk a tetanus infection to get the fishing pole?"

"Trinity told me the family used to come out here on Sundays. It sounded..." She trails off, nibbling the uncertainty from her lower lip.

"Like a Norman Rockwell painting come to life?" I ask, taking charge of the pole again and casting the line far into the lake.

She shrugs and hugs her knees to her chest. "I wish I could go back in time. For just one second, see them—all of them—at their happiest."

Her statement squeezes my heart—what little of it I have. Somehow, I'm not surprised by Ivy's sincerity. There's a closeness she has with the family. One that rivals my own. It's the reason they've fallen for her.

The reason I fall for her...over and over again.

For a while, we sit in silence, me with my fishing line, her with her book. It's not awkward or standoffish. It's peaceful. Maybe my first taste of peace in years.

I look out on the gentle, rippling water as it leads to a forest of sycamores in the distance. I've mapped every square inch of this land. I know every building. Every hillside. Every lake. Every camera, sensor, and motion detector. But in all the years I've memorized the landscape, I'm not sure I've ever looked out and simply enjoyed it.

Ivy breaks the silence with a question. "What's your greatest fear?"

I puff air into my cheeks. "That's easy. That I won't be able to protect the people closest to me."

"You can't control everything. Even Superman can't save everyone."

"The man was faster than a speeding bullet, could fly, had x-ray vision, and was made of steel. If he couldn't save everyone, the fucker was just lazy."

Amused, her mouth falls open, and I try not to stare at her lips. "Superpowers don't exist. I keep my wits about me. Stay focused. I do what I do best by leaving my fears, doubts, and heart at the door."

Her eyes move to mine. She studies me for a long beat. "And what is it that you do best?"

Her tone isn't suggestive. She genuinely wants to know. I hold back my knee-jerk reply of *plowing to the center of your vagina,* and answer her question. "Protecting the D'Angelos."

She nods half-heartedly as her smile wanes. I ask her original question back to her. "What about you? What's your greatest fear?"

She pauses for a long stretch.

I encourage her. "It can be anything. Spiders. Men with horrendous breath. Tiny penises. Lay it on me. I won't judge."

Thoughtfully, she answers. "I'm afraid when people get to know me, they'll reject me."

Her words are jagged arrows, cutting straight to my heart. "Ivy, I'm sorry about what happened between us."

She rolls her eyes. "I didn't mean you."

"Ouch," I exclaim, grabbing my chest as if wounded.

Her shoulder bumps mine as she laughs. "I mean...I found out I have a family. On my father's side. A family that, up until a month ago, I had no idea existed."

There's something she's leaving unsaid. I speculate the reason for her frown. "Let me guess. They have no idea you exist."

She nods. "I want to get to know them. And I want them to get to know me. Does that make me selfish?"

"I'd call it cautious."

"They're very...private. And I know me showing up out of the blue would be a shock." She faces me. "What would you do? If you knew you had a family out there, but you weren't sure they'd accept you?"

I rub my neck, thinking it over. "I'd probably do what I always do. Investigate. Observe. Strike when I think the time is right." Her nod is slight, but my words do little to console her. "A wise man recently told me you can't be all things to all people. The ones who matter most will always love you."

SINS & IVY

"Using my words against me."

"It's what I do."

She's quiet again, turning her attention back to her book. I pretend not to notice the title, *The Psychology of Pain*, and look off into the distance. "What's that you're reading?" I ask casually.

"Nothing. Just an old textbook."

I recast my line. "A no-kidding hardback textbook. They still make those? Who knew?"

I can feel her smile. "I found it at a local bookstore."

"A little light reading?"

Her posture straightens. "I've always wanted to help people."

"Is that why you became a caretaker?" She gives me a cross-eyed glance. "It was on your resume." And I've been investigating her like the discovery of a yeti is at stake, but that's neither here nor there.

"I sort of fell into that when my mom became sick. Traded services for her care."

"I didn't know anyone worked on the barter system."

"I needed my mom taken care of, and they needed someone willing to work nights, weekends, and holidays for pennies on the dollar and tip money in the form of Coca-Cola. Win-win."

"Hopefully, employment with the D'Angelos is a little more appealing."

"A little." A reflection of sunbeams lights up her face as she smiles. "In some ways, I feel like I was always meant to meet Trinity. Like every step of my journey was leading me to help her. But..." she trails off.

"But what?"

"When Trinity and I talk, I feel helpless. I want to do more." She flips another page in her book. "Each page gives me hope that I can."

It's clear that Ivy is hard on herself. "Hey." I wait until her eyes meet mine. "You've done more in a few short weeks than we've been able to do in years. What you've achieved is extraordinary." Ivy smiles, and the wider it grows, the more the iceberg wrapped around my heart melts. I lean in. "It's little wonder that the family wants you at *Erede al Trono*."

Her sigh is heavy. "Smoke invited me, but I feel like it's something too important. Like maybe I'm overstepping. I—" She cuts herself short. And I'm not in a hurry to hear what she has to say. I slowly reel in the line and set the pole aside, patient as I wait for Ivy to release whatever's swimming around her beautiful mind.

Instead of sharing more with me, she changes the subject. "In your line of work, you probably have to keep information to yourself. Carry so many secrets inside you, you find it hard to breathe."

"Sometimes," I say, wondering where she's going with this.

"Does it tear you up? Not being able to tell all of the truth all the time?"

I swallow my hesitation. "There's a fine line between protecting the interests of others and withholding the truth. It isn't that I don't want to share. When I was a SEAL, I had a lot of secrets. Where I was. What I was doing. How long I'd be gone. But if I shared any of that with anyone, no matter how trustworthy, my men, my mission, and my own life were at risk. Maybe even the person I shared the information with." I don't look at her when I ask, "If you need to run something by me, or unload what's weighing on your mind, I'm a vault, Ivy. Your secrets are safe with me."

It's the first real lie I've told Ivy. If she reveals something—anything—that pits her against the D'Angelos, I will assume my role as the enforcer.

Like tearing the wings from a butterfly, my punishment will be swift and unforgiving.

I swallow the lump of guilt forged in my throat, moving my hand to hers. I need her to trust me. Almost as much as I need to keep touching the warm softness of her skin.

She stares aimlessly across the lake, and I push her a little. Just to test the waters.

"Is there something you need to get off your chest?"

Her shoulders slump in defeat. "It has to do with my future here. If I have a future here."

Her cryptic little riddle disturbs me. I turn to give her my undivided attention and to ensure I have hers. "What do you mean?"

Her head shakes slowly.

Did Smoke say something to her? Or Trinity?

Again, she says nothing. The devil on one shoulder has no patience for this and is ready to interrogate her. The annoying angel on the other coaxes me to give her time. I flick that fucker away like a bug.

She needs to open up.

"I'm listening," I say from out of nowhere, repeating the very words therapists have hurled at me year after year.

They'd have better luck cracking open a bank vault with a vibrator.

When her big, brown eyes turn to mine, I know she's about

to say it. Whatever secrets she's held captive have outgrown their cage, wild and edgy and eager to escape.

Ivy's show and tell time shouldn't mean more to me than the sum of the information. She is a Pez dispenser, relaying some precious nugget of intel that I'll chew up and spit out into one of three categories: important to her, important to her and me, or important to her, me, and the D'Angelos.

But the longer she takes, the more my chest tightens with discomfort. It's important to her. Really, really important to her. And she's sharing it with me. It shouldn't mean anything to me, but it does. I want this to be the first of many secrets she shares. Her dreams. Her hopes. Her desires.

Her lips begin to part. "I—"

"I hope I'm not interrupting," Hunter says from out of fucking nowhere. I swear to God, the man has goddamned cat feet.

And yes, he was interrupting, and at the worst possible time. Annoyed, I scowl at him the second Ivy scoots away. And his Hollywood dimple isn't helping his cause. "What?" I seethe.

"There's something we found. You need to take a look at it."

Ivy hops to her feet, using Hunter's piss-poor timing as an excuse to flee. "I need to get back," she says, clinging to her book, composure, and secrets as she rounds the hill and disappears from sight.

I narrow my eyes. "Look, when I said stay close, I didn't mean when I'm—"

"Canoodling?" he says, smirking. My death glare wipes the dimple from his face. He clears his throat.

I ignore his comment. "What do you have?"

He hands me a shriveled piece of paper that once passed as a photograph.

"What the hell is this?"

"A photograph of Antonio D'Angelo."

I inspect the front and back. It takes me a minute to realize that the face beneath the muck is indeed Antonio D'Angelo. A much younger version, but unmistakable with his big, blue eyes and square jaw. "Where did you find it?"

"Not too far from the location we found Trinity's phone the night she went missing." My jaw tightens. I hate that it happened. Trinity was missing for two hours on my watch. And it killed me.

I think about that night, and I hate *this* more. The Ivy factor. Losing Trinity was fleeting. Losing Ivy was everything. I barricaded my heart against her that night because I have a job to do.

I examine the small photo, wondering how it ever managed to survive a thunderstorm. It's beginning to yellow. How old is it?

The mud is caked hard onto it. "Is this a tire mark?" I ask.

"Yes, sir," Hunter replies. "It, uh, must have been run over by an ATV."

That would be my ATV. The one I used on my frantic search for Trinity that night. No matter. "I'll take care of it."

He nods. "There's something else. Ivy has received eight more contact attempts. All from the numbers on the list you had."

I breathe a long exhale through my nose. "And?"

"And nothing. She hasn't answered a single one. If they call or text more than once, she blocks them."

I play with the photo, deep in thought. Why is Andre trying to contact Ivy? And why isn't she answering? Is she returning his calls and texts another way?

My nail digs into a smudge of mud from around Antonio's face, snagging off a small bit of the photo in the process. "Shit," I huff.

"Did you hear me?" Hunter asks.

"Of course, I heard you." My words are even. "He calls. She ghosts. What else?"

"Maybe I could get you more if I had more men on my team."

We engage in a small stare-off. The son of a bitch is right. He can't watch Ivy 24/7. At some point, he has to eat, sleep, and pee. Like an infant. "Fine. One more."

"Two," he counters like it's a fucking debate.

"Two. For one week. And I want results." I hand him back the photo before I destroy it any further. "And get Sam on this."

"The counterfeiter?"

"Photo restorationist," I correct him. "Same timeline. One week."

CHAPTER 6
Leo

Hours later, and a long drive across town, I get my ass in gear and give in to my needs. Not *those* needs— the needs that bring me closer to Ivy. No, I squash those like a bug beneath my shoe and opt for the hard way. Option B. A plan that will drive a wedge between us like a stake through Dracula's heart.

Parking nearly a block away is a trivial security precaution, but it gives me time to take note of my surroundings. The quaint area on the outskirts of Chicago is a smattering of cozy, little houses, joggers, and dog walkers, and it has just enough green space per capita for raising a family and playing catch. Suburbia at its finest.

I double-check the address and knock on the door.

Footsteps close in from behind it. "Be right there," she hollers in her soft, southern drawl. The familiar sounds of rattling have my ears perking up. Even in a middle-class sanctuary like this, a five-dollar chain lock is hardly protection.

A point in my favor if I ever need to bust down the door.

The door swings wide, and I'm greeted with big, green eyes and a cheery smile. Identical to her photograph.

"Good afternoon, ma'am. Are you Grace Everly?" The fair-skinned redhead, affectionally referred to as "Aunt Grace" by Ivy, nods.

"Why, yes I am." Her natural sweetness is charming. "Are you going to tell me that I just won the Publishers Clearing House? Because if there's a camera crew coming, I need to fix my hair." She runs her fingers through her hair, tugging an errant roller from her red locks with genuine concern.

Amused, I smile back. "I wonder if you might have a moment for some questions. I'm doing an employment background check on Ms. Olivia Ann Palmer."

She stares blankly, her face void of recognition. I double-check my notes. Out of nowhere, she smacks my arm, her eyes wide with delight. "Oh, you mean Ivy." Worried, she frowns. "Has something happened?"

I shake my head. "No, not at all. This is all part of a very routine background check." The lie rolls off my tongue easily. I fish out my wallet and hand her my card.

"Chief of Security...Z.?" she reads aloud. "Is that your actual name?"

"It's what I'm called." By most of Chicago, anyway. "I'm part of a private security firm." I flash a boyish grin.

"So, it's like a callsign or a codename?" She sounds impressed.

"What can I say? I guess that makes me a diva. But the phone number under it is to my direct line. You can call or text me there any time, day or night."

"Night?" she asks, giggling. "Well, with your good looks and sense of style, that's quite the offer. Though I'm a little old for you." She winks. "Ivy's the one you should hand your card to. I'm sure the two of you would have a lot to talk about during the night."

"I'm sure we would," I agree, though the last thing Ivy and I would do alone all night is talk.

"May I come in?"

Cautiously, she plants herself in the door. "How long will this take?"

"I'll only take as much time as you're willing to give me. And if this is a bad time, I can always make an appointment and return."

"I'll let you in on three conditions."

Conditions? What possible conditions could this woman have? "All right. Name them."

"You have to stick around for at least an hour and a half."

A ninety-minute hostage situation? I check my cell. It's not like I have anything better to do for the next two hours. Plus, I'm not used to this. If anything, most people do their damnedest to get rid of me. The thought of someone wanting me around, asking questions to my heart's content, is oddly refreshing.

Thinking it through, I rub my chin. "You drive a hard bargain, Ms. Everly, but I'll give you my time unless work calls me back."

Her arms cross tightly. This must be her serious look. "Ninety minutes or nothing, security guard."

That's chief of security for a multi-billion-dollar global conglomerate, but correcting her would be a waste of time.

Time that I need to spend charting every square inch of Ivy's past.

My smile stands pat. "Agreed. And your second demand, Ms. Everly?"

She opens the door wider, waving me in. "That you call me Grace."

Easy enough. "Grace, it is. And your final demand?"

"That I get to read your palm before you go."

"Read my palm?" I ask, now scouring the room for assorted crystals and voodoo dolls. "I don't really believe in... that."

She ponders my words, a finger tapping her chin. "Then there's no need to share the premonitions I see, correct?"

I frown. "Whoa. Hang on now. If you're going to go through all the work anyway, you might as well let me in on my future. Just because I didn't buy the ticket doesn't mean I won't enjoy the carnival ride."

"Deal," she says, quickly ushering me in and closing the door. The chain lock I was so concerned about is barely hanging on by a screw, but thankfully, she secures it diligently. I make a mental note to fix it before I go.

The home is tidy with well-loved furnishings that are well-blended with touches of Ikea. A living room window is in desperate need of repairs, and the overloaded power cord makes this shack one charge away from a five-alarm fire. Everywhere I look is a reminder that whatever this woman does for Ivy has nothing to do with money.

"So, other than Ivy, what will we be talking about for ninety minutes, Grace?"

"Oh, I just wanted to see if there was enough time for me to bake us a pie while we chat. You look like a city boy who could use a little down-home cooking."

"You had me at pie." I loosen my tie. "How can I help?"

On the way to the kitchen, I notice a picture on a small table next to the couch. Their family is huge with five-or-six-year-old Ivy front and center. Her bright eyes and sweet smile are radiant. And that streak of silver stood out even then. Grace notices me staring. "She and Brooke have been best friends since the first grade. She's always been part of our family."

Grace beams with pride, lifting the photo and handing it to me. Brooke and Ivy are holding hands, Ivy's dark skin a striking contrast to the sea of fair redheads and blondes surrounding her. "She looks loved," I say honestly, handing back the frame.

"How could you not love a girl like Ivy?" she muses, sentimentally and almost to herself. My heart squeezes. Her innocent question hits me like an archer's arrow straight through the heart.

The small kitchen is immaculate with fresh wildflowers from the garden in a cheap vase centered on the table. It brightens the unassuming space with splashes of yellow and pink.

Grace begins removing bowls from the cupboard. "How can I help?" I ask.

"You can make yourself comfortable for starters. And feel free to ditch the blazer. I already know you're packing." Her comment catches me by surprise. "My family is all military and law enforcement. And I'm no priss around a double-barrel shotgun."

My eyes widen. "A woman after my own heart."

She pulls down an assortment of ingredients from the

pantry, readily handing them off as if I were her child. "Set these on the table, will you?"

I do as I'm told. "And what are we making?"

"Had I known I was having company, I might have tried to whip up something extra special. But as it is, I think we're going to settle for a good, old-fashioned apple pie. You all right with that?"

I slip off my blazer and toss it to the chair. Holstered weapon and all, I roll up my sleeves. "Perfect. I might have made an apple pie or two in my life."

"You bake?"

"My girl and I do. All the time. Maybe you know her."

"What's her name?" she asks excitedly.

"Rachael Ray."

"Oh, she happens to be my girl, too. In fact," she taps a finger to a magazine, "this is her recipe."

We get to work, naturally sinking into our divided roles. Grace works on the dough while I take ownership of the apples, peeling and coring with ease. "How long have you known Ivy?"

"It feels like all my life. I met my little Ivy-vine forever ago."

"Ivy-vine?"

A warm smile rises high, twinkling her eyes. "Ivy and I got along right from the start. She would cling to me like a vine. An ivy vine tangling herself around my heart. That little girl was so starved for love, you wanted her to never go without. Lucky for me, I had plenty. Whenever I'd visit my brother and his kids, Ivy was the shyest among them. Every time I left, I hated letting her go." Her smile twists with sadness. "I tried to adopt her."

Her admission is almost a whisper. "Does Ivy know?"

She shakes her head. "My husband and I were rooted in

Chicago. I could only get back to North Carolina every few months. Her mother agreed to let us adopt her, then changed her mind. Demanded the kind of money we didn't have. I even tried to raise the money. I got close, and I let her mother know."

Grace trails off, concentrating harder on working the dough, slicing it, then losing herself in weaving the inch-wide strands into a lattice pattern.

My hand goes to her arm. "What happened?"

Her eyes stay down. "Her mother demanded the funds in cash. Like idiots, we gave it to her. That's when she upped the price. It took us two-and-a-half years to try to raise that kind of money. We never did get Ivy. In the end, we got a heaping pile of debt that served to feed Samara Palmer's addiction."

"You said you come from a family of law enforcement. Why didn't they do something?"

"Because if we did, Samara threatened to do things to Ivy. Unconscionable things."

I don't pry. Samara's rap sheet had enough to fill in the blanks. She was probably days from outright selling Ivy when her liver failed.

Grace pats my hand. "She's in my life now. And living close by, though I haven't been able to see her since she started her fancy, new job." Hopeful, her face brightens. "Do you ever see her?" I nod. "How's she doing?"

I tell her the truth. "I just saw her today, actually. She's impressive. She has a way with people that we've never seen before." I'm diligent not to mention Trinity's name. Her privacy and the privacy of all the D'Angelos is always at the forefront.

Grace relaxes her shoulders, sighing with relief. She butts her elbow into my ribs. "I knew she'd kick ass."

"She's an amazing ass-kicker. And absolutely everyone adores her." Myself included, though she doesn't need to know.

Talking with Grace is effortless. In the time it takes to stage, assemble, and bake the pie, I've learned more about Ivy than I probably know about anyone on the planet. From her favorite books, food, and movies to her favorite color—a distinct shade of purple common to passion vines. Grace even dishes the dirt on Derrick, the asshole who cheated on Ivy. Or Daredick as her niece, Brooke, aptly named him.

Luckily for everyone, he just moved to the top of my shit list.

As Grace fixes me a cup of tea, I pry further. "What was it that brought you and your husband here?"

"My husband was offered a job. It was a few months after I first met Ivy at my brother's place of work." She takes a nervous sip from her own cup, and I instantly connect the dots.

"What was a child of Ivy's age doing at the county jail?"

Grace is taken aback. "How did you know it was at the county jail?"

It's my turn for a long sip of tea. The sweetness coats my throat, the combination of peaches and sugar or honey or— what is that—agave? Whatever it is, it's surprisingly refreshing and gives me a moment to think.

"Lucky guess," I finally say. "You said military and law enforcement. In North Carolina, that puts her at either a base or with the local sheriff."

My explanation seems plausible enough that she continues. Grace lowers her voice as if sharing unsavory town gossip. "Ivy was just a child. Her mother would leave her for days, and it was reported to my brother—the sheriff. That little girl made the best of it. The first time my brother found her, her mother picked her up right away, not wanting trouble. Ivy didn't have any bruises, so he couldn't keep her. She was lean but not entirely malnourished. He did keep an eye on her, though."

She trails off, and I probe for more. "Each time got worse?"

Her brow pinches, pained. "The next few times, Ivy explained it away, making it look like everything was fine. *Nothing to see here, folks.* When my brother found the cereal, he knew he had to do something."

"The cereal?"

Grace twists her expression. "Do you know what a dime bag is?"

"Yes," I say slowly. In the literal term, it's a small plastic bag that holds a gram of drugs and sells for ten bucks. The fact that the sweet homemaker before me knows what it is surprises me. Even if cannabis is her thing, I imagine she'd be into gummies and lollipops. Hell, she'd have a nice little side hustle with edibles. Brownies, cookies...I take a sideways glance at the half-eaten slice of pie and the over-the-top sweet tea. "How do you know about dime bags?" I ask

She takes a deep breath. "Ivy had separated an entire box of cereal into dime bags."

"Why?"

"So she wouldn't eat too much of it at once. Three of those a day is what she held herself to."

A lump forms in my throat. Ivy wasn't denied a childhood. She survived one. "Why didn't your brother do something?"

"We tried. Ivy was bright beyond her years. She didn't want

to go. She'd do anything to stay exactly where she was."

Realization hits me like a battering ram to the chest. How similar Ivy and I really are. Covering for the sins of our parents to preserve the only thing we cherished.

Family.

My brothers and I told any lie to keep from being reported. We wouldn't be separated. *Couldn't* be separated.

I don't share my background, though, on some level, Grace expresses her understanding. "Ivy was an only child." I square my jaw. "Why would she cover for Samara, trying not to get reported?" I ask, confused. "What was she clinging to?"

Grace heaves a sigh, shaking her head. "From an outsider looking in, maybe. But Ivy had Brooke. From the very first time my brother took her in, those two were inseparable. Like sisters. She snaps her fingers. "Instant connection. The way Ivy is with everyone."

It reminds me of her and Trinity. And her with me. Is it a survival mechanism—a chameleon doing and being what others need her to be? Or is it just who she is?

"You took her in?"

Her nod makes me wish we'd had an Aunt Grace. "As best we could. Sending her through the system crossed our minds. How she'd end up on the other side was a crapshoot. Most of the time, we just took her under our wing. She was the easiest child. Never wanted anything but love."

Guilt chokes me. The one thing I refused to give her.

Ding.

Grace removes the pie from the oven and sets it before us. The smell is otherworldly, surrounding my senses and reminding me that I haven't had a thing to eat today.

I'm ready with a knife, prepared to dive into my first slice, when she smacks the back of my hand. "You have to let it cool. It tastes better that way."

I scowl playfully. "You said ninety minutes. Your time's almost up, and I'm starving."

Her lips purse to one side. "Fine." She snatches the knife from my hand. "Cutthroat it is." She retrieves two large, unmatched spoons from the drawer and hands one to me. "Dig in."

"Caveman style? Don't mind if I do." The first bite is hot and satisfying. I sink into it like a starved man ravaging a Christmas feast. *"Mmm,"* I muffle through my mouth full of apples and cinnamon. "Ivy's cooking skills must come from you."

Her head tilts to one side. "She cooks? Is that part of her job?"

"More like a perk. There's an impressive chef's kitchen there. She loves it."

Her spoon taps mine. "I'd love to see where she works. Any chance you could make that happen?"

Grace bats her thick eyelashes and clasps her hands. I don't give in, enjoying another bite without a word. That's when her tactics turn dirty.

She produces a pint of Ben & Jerry's Whiskey Biz ice cream.

This woman means business. "Maybe," I concede. "In exchange for information."

She pops open the lid. "Deal."

Grace and I take civilized turns with each spoonful of ice cream. "What do you know about Ivy's father?"

"Nothing much." Her tone is honest and matter-of-fact. Disappointing, to say the least.

Grace thinks it over and takes a long time to wipe her mouth with a napkin before finally speaking. "Samara blew every penny she had on drugs. But about twice a year, she'd be rolling in the dough."

"Like how much? Enough for food and rent?"

"More like a new car. Which did her no good. She'd blow through it and end up selling the car a few months later to keep her head above water. We all wondered if it might not be from Ivy's father. We tried finding him. Maybe sway him to help us adopt Ivy. We never found him." At this point, my spoon criss-crosses over the crumbs remaining on the pie tin. Getting to know Ivy's Aunt Grace? Nice. Coming up empty on more of her history? Epic fail.

"But I think Ivy had a lead on finding her father. That's why she came out here."

"Ivy didn't move out here to be with you?"

"No. Her roots were firmly planted in North Carolina. In fact, I had planned to go and see her in a few months. It was such a relief when she decided to come up here. My blood pressure has been acting up, and my doctor recommended not traveling.

The glint in her eyes is telling. "You would've gone anyway."

"Damn straight, security guard. I'd never let my Ivy-vine down."

"So, what was the lead?"

Elbows on the table, Grace leans in. "You'll have to ask her that one yourself. I'm pretty sure *23 and Me* isn't part of an employee's background check."

She's got me there. I nod curtly and notice the time. Two hours. "I better get a move on before I end up napping on your couch." I gather our dishes and stack them neatly in the sink.

Before I can slide my jacket back on, Grace pipes up. "Not so fast." She motions for the chair.

I pat the roundest part of my newly formed Buddha belly. "Have mercy. One more mouthful, and I'll pop."

"Well, that's what you get for treating my pie like an eating competition," she scolds.

I chuckle. "It's not my fault. Apple pie is my favorite, and it's the only thing I've had to eat all day."

"Then you need to take better care of yourself." Her tone becomes solemn. "Now, give me your hand."

I forgot about the third condition. Palm reading.

I return to my seat and roll my eyes. With an outstretched hand, she wiggles her fingers expectantly, waiting for mine.

Reluctantly, I lay my right hand in hers, palm up. "Don't you need a crystal ball or exotic headdress to do this right?"

"*Shh!*" Deep in thought, she traces the lines with a single finger, chasing the unseen trail of my life.

She lifts my hand closer to her face, carefully inspecting the horizontal line near the top for who knows what. My past. My future. The innermost secrets of my soul. A rogue freckle that seemed to pop out of nowhere. She goes over it again and again as if analyzing the details of a treasure map.

I yawn.

"You care for a lot of people," my psychic friend surmises.

I play along. "Correct," I say, nodding ceremoniously. I'm not placating her because her knack for the obvious astounds me. But I might need to drop by again, and I wouldn't want to ruffle the feathers of the best damn baker this side of Chicago—psychic or not.

Her hand hovers over mine. My pulse ticks up just a hair. Her voice is an omen. "Oh, dear."

What the fuck does that mean? *Oh, dear.* Am I about to get a colossal case of the runs or get shot? Fuck, don't tell me I'm going bald.

She bites her lip thoughtfully. "You're coming to a cross-roads," she announces.

I deadpan. *Who isn't?* "You don't say," I reply, monotone.

Her nod is grave as she clasps my hand with both of hers. "Your fate is not yet decided."

"So free will prevails." I look at her blankly. "Can you tell me anything more?" I ask, trying not to sound too under-whelmed.

"You have a decision to make."

"Is this where you hand me a red pill and a blue pill? I already know my answer."

My wit is lost on Ivy's poor Aunt Grace. Her trance-like state continues. "At a fancy affair. Elegant. A small gathering. Black tie, I think. But not a wedding…"

"Thank God for small favors."

Her face contorts as she continues the reading. "You are of importance. Best man comes to mind…something about a throne…"

Erede al Trono… Could she mean *Erede al Trono? Heir to the Throne?*

Holy shit, is this woman for real?

Stunned, I mutter. "Yes." Wide-eyed, I lean into the table,

searching my palm for whatever it is she seems to see. "What else?" I demand, alarmed and impatient.

Is something going to happen at the event? Is it Trinity? Is someone in danger?

For the love of God, woman, talk!

Unhurried, she takes her sweet, southern time, a trait some find endearing. I find it aggravating and irksome, and I swear to God, I'm about to lose my shit all over the place.

Hmm escapes her tight lips, and fuck me, but I think she's dragging this out on purpose.

Before I can threaten to rip every Rachel Ray magazine she owns to shreds if she doesn't get on with it, she finally speaks. "Your heart..."

My hand lunges to my chest. "What about my heart?" Goddamnit, I knew it. My blood pressure is shot to hell, and the sugar, fat, and cholesterol brought on by her decadent apple pie sure as hell isn't helping.

I wince, suddenly noticing a pain I never felt before.

"It's...divided," she says prosaically.

"Uh-huh. Okay." I nod several times with a sigh. "My heart is divided into four chambers. Thanks for the reminder. I think I can live with that."

Her head shakes with reticence. The small pinching in my chest returns as the psychic that I don't believe in once again speaks. "You will have to choose between your sense of duty and your heart."

"With me, they're the same thing."

"Not this time, Leo." She gives my hand several motherly pats. "Choose wrong, and you risk losing the only thing that matters."

"Which is?"

"Your heart."

I stand and button my blazer, flashing her a confident smile. Her charlatan tricks are over. "That's where you're wrong." I pull back my hand, pocketing it. "That's impossible."

"What do you mean?"

I give it to her straight. "I have no heart."

I decide to take the long way back to the D'Angelo estate. It's been a solid half-hour of me processing my time with Grace. It isn't until I'm halfway home that it hits me.

She called me Leo.

How did she know my name when the only name I gave her was Z? I take another look at my palm and focus on the line that stretches across the width of my hand. My heart line.

I ball my hand into a fist. There is no free will. If duty is at a crossroads with love, duty wins. It isn't a decision. It's history repeating itself.

The phone chimes once before I answer. Hunter. Right on time. "What do you have?"

"Nothing but a string of calls to North Carolina. Brooke Everly."

"Her best friend," I reply unenthusiastically. What was it Grace said? Brooke and Ivy are like sisters. I pump my fist on the wheel. Sisters tell each other everything. "Do you have an address?"

"Yes, sir."

"I need an overnight bag and the jet ready. Meet me at the

airport now. Let the pilot know the destination, and have a driver on standby."

"Do you want any of the team with you? Or any weapons?"

"Nope. It'll be quick." Unless I find something.

"And if Smoke asks?"

I puff out an undecided breath. "Just tell him I'll speak to him tomorrow. That should buy me some time."

"And Ivy?"

I take another look at my palm. I told Grace the truth. I have no heart. Determined to prove my point, I make a preemptive strike against the merciless fates, and fuck destiny in the ass. "Do what you do best, Hunter."

Hunter pauses. "You...don't mean that."

"You heard me."

Another pause. "I just want to make sure I heard you right. You...want me to kill Ivy?"

"What? No. For fuck's sake." I take a breath. "I want answers about Andre once and for all. Do what you have to do to get them."

The uncertainty in his silence is fucking annoying. I don't wait for his response. "Just do it!" I disconnect the call before I change my mind.

At the next four-way stop, I hang a left and head north. By the time I arrive at the airport, the pilot has my bag on board and the jet ready.

It isn't until I'm seated and we begin to ascent that I take another look at my hand. There's a clean cut across the inconsequential love line and a fork in the road at its tail.

"See?" I mutter like a madman. "Duty fucking first."

CHAPTER 7
Ivy

Am I'm paranoid, or is Hunter following me?

We've bumped into each other five times in the hall. When Trini and I were rolling meatballs, he offered to help. And in the middle of my mid-day stroll by the lake, Hunter Walsh just happened to be jogging by. Shirtless. Smiling. Sheening.

Is sheening even a word? Well, it should be. His ripped chest and glorious six-pack are borderline ridiculous, glistening like a homing beacon for panties everywhere. Grade A, southern girl crack.

I knew the signs. A sin-laced smile. Dimples. A hand through his sweat-drenched hair to show off his pecs...

Red flags up. The man wants something.

"Hey." Hunter slowed to a stop, his muscles on full display at military parade rest.

I shook my head, smiling back. "What do you want?"

His smile widened. "How about dinner?"

"Dinner?"

He picked a small, yellow wildflower from among the reeds, handing it to me. I take a sniff of its light perfume and wave it at his face. "Leo lets you have dinner? How unlike him."

"Don't let him fool you—" Hunter says, matching my casual pace. "Leo is hard on the outside. Soft in the middle. Like a dark Lindt truffle."

Now, I've heard it all. "Did you just compare a lethal enforcer to a delectable chocolate?"

He thinks on his feet. "Maybe. He was sweet enough to assign me to you." I fling the little flower in his face. "What?"

"I'm sorry, I just swallowed a little vomit in my mouth at you calling your boss, 'sweet.'"

"We both know if Leo were here, I'd be hard at work."

I call him on his bald-face lies. "First of all, like Leo and the rest of you ex-military macho machines, you're a workaholic. And second, the only reason you're cuddling up to me like a Maine Coon is because you've been told to do so. By your boss. And I get it. I'm an outsider creeping in, and no one has a reason to trust me. You don't have to pretend to be my friend. It's cool."

"Maybe I want to be more than your friend."

I take in all six-foot-four inches of him. Wavy hair. Boyish grin. A killer bod desperate to be ridden until the wee crack of dawn.

The problem is he's not Leo.

"You're a perfect specimen." I say, suddenly in the market for a perfect specimen.

His Elvis impersonation is spot on. "Thank you, thank you very much."

"How do you feel about redheads? Strawberry-blonde to be more precise."

Skeptical, he glances at my hair. "I can't quite picture it on you."

"That makes two of us."

I pull out my cell and select an image of Brooke in all her shot glass toasting glory and show it to Hunter. His long whistle is all the validation I need. Nailed it.

"Wow," is all he can seem to say.

"This is Brooke. She can wield a shotgun and a shot glass with the best of them, and her hobbies include horseback riding and raising hell. She wants Christmas with the family, a houseful of kids, and a man who spanks her at poker but doesn't play games."

He expands the image and zooms in on her face. Breathless, he stares, seduced and smitten. "Is she dancing on the table?"

"Yes, but not professionally."

He lets out a small, *aww*. "Look at those freckles."

I roll my eyes and snag back my phone. "This is it, Hunter. You are the bachelor. You only have one rose." I hold Brooke's sassy image against my cheek. "Will it be the girl you're fake asking out because your boss told you to or the girl with all those adorable freckles?" I wiggle the phone suggestively.

His brow furrows, heavy with indecision.

"We can still have dinner. I can tell you more about Brooke."

He still doesn't budge.

My hands fly up in defeat. "You can still stalk me."

His hand locks with mine. "Deal."

My cell chimes with the familiar ringtone of "Mamma Mia" by Abba. It never gets old. "Hi, Aunt Grace."

"Hi, Ivy. I wanted to let you know I got a visit from a hot guy with some security firm. Asking about you in your new job. Said it was for a background check."

I cut my hand over the receiver and ask Hunter, "Is someone on the team asking around about me? In person?"

He shrugs. By the boyish innocence of his non-answer, he knows, but he won't say.

"Did they leave a name?"

"Let me get his card." She takes a moment, and I hear her mumbling in the background. "Where did I put that card?" Relieved, she shouts, "Found it! Okay. It's a little unusual because there's no last name. Just an initial. Z."

"Leo," I say, perturbed, as I give Hunter the stink eye. He raises his hands in surrender. "Sit tight. I'm coming over."

"But he already left."

"That's all right. I wanted to see you anyway, and this gives me the perfect opportunity. Then you can fill me on absolutely everything that was asked."

"Oh, if you're going to be dropping by, do you mind picking up my prescription? I'll call and pay for it so all you have to do is pick it up."

"Sure. I'll head over there now."

"You know," she says, mischief in her tone, "that Leo sure is a good-looking man. Do you work with him?"

"We'll talk when I get there," I say, turning sharply away from Hunter. From the smirk on his face, he heard.

Giggling, Aunt Grace agrees. "Great. See you soon! I'll get working on the second pie."

"The two of you ate an entire pie?"

"Do not give me that tone. He gobbled it up like it was his last supper. Besides, at the very most, I ate a quarter."

I smile widely and look straight at Hunter when I ask, "Leo ate three-quarters of an apple pie? By himself?"

"Apparently, nobody's been taking care of that boy."

"Apparently." I shake my head because it's not like I didn't try. "See you soon." I hang up and pin the six-foot-four Hunter with my glare. "Do you plan on following me?"

He rubs his chin. "It's for your protection."

"Could you protect me closer?" He stares back, confused. "I need a ride."

"Done."

A small bell chimes as I push open the door to the pharmacy. Hunter makes his way to the magazines, giving me privacy with the pharmacist.

The elderly man looks down at me with a smile as I request the prescription for Grace Everly. "You must be Ivy. Grace called ahead to let us know you'd be heading over. One minute."

He flips through several containers of pre-bagged medications until he finds the right one.

The pharmacist frowns. "She was very specific to only request half of the pills."

"Half?" I unwrap the small paper bag and pull out the bottle. The name of the medication is a hundred letters long and impossible to pronounce. "What's it for?"

"High blood pressure. And the prescription is written for a full dose each time."

"Then, aren't you required to fill it?"

He shakes his head, matter-of-factly. "For most medications, I can adjust the quantity based on the leeway with the insurance provider and the request of the customer. Especially if they're trying to cut back on costs." His grave eyes meet mine. "Please make sure she's taking at least one pill a day."

Worry pricks through me. "What happens if she takes less?"

"With this medication..." He shrugs. "It's dangerous. Her blood pressure may creep up unexpectedly. A heart attack or a stroke isn't out of the question. She should really speak with her doctor. It's risky."

"Isn't there a cheaper generic?"

He checks his computer. Within a few keystrokes, he shakes his head. "There are plenty of generics. But with all her allergies, this is the only one she can take."

"How much is this medication?"

"She paid ahead," he answers flatly.

"But filling the full amount. How much would it be?"

The pharmacist does the math in his head. "If she purchased the entire amount now? It comes to fifty-five."

Fifty-five dollars? She probably spent more than that in the fixings to make her homemade pastries and blue-ribbon apple pie for Leo. I fish three twenty-dollar bills from my wallet and lay it on the counter.

He pats my hand. "I should have said it clearer. Five thousand, five hundred dollars."

Stunned, I repeat the price loud enough for everyone to

hear. "Fifty-five hundred dollars? That's...preposterous. Her insurance—"

His voice lowers. "Her insurance is a widow's insurance. For some medications, it'll cover nearly all of it. For this one, it covers none of it."

I proceed to lose my shit. "There's no way she can afford that. It's probably twice her mortgage. There has to be another medication available. A cheaper one."

Hunter sidles up to me. "Is everything okay?"

I nod, despondent. Nothing is okay, but the last thing I need is Hunter running this information to Leo. Because if Leo's involved, the D'Angelos aren't far behind. I can't exactly build their trust with a hand out, begging for cash.

This isn't their problem. It's mine.

I open my purse and come face to face with my saving grace. The check. It's for nearly three thousand dollars and signed by Mason D'Angelo. "Smoke," I say sentimentally under my breath. I hadn't yet set up a local bank account. For once, procrastination pays off. I give the pharmacist a hopeful grin. "Can I sign over a check to you? And pick up what I pay for?"

"Sure."

If I'm living at the mansion, my expenses are nil. The five hundred dollars I came here with hasn't been touched. And I'm not exactly a shopaholic. Books are my retail therapy, and the estate has more books than Barnes & Noble.

Without another thought, I hand over the entire check. That way, Aunt Grace has a cushion. The pharmacist gets working on the remainder of her prescription. If I'm frugal and stick with a budget, I can cover Aunt Grace's prescription and take care of her the way she's always taken care of me. Showing me how to cook. How to read. How to love. Effortlessly. Naturally.

By the time everything is sorted at the pharmacy, I make my way to Aunt Grace's on foot. It isn't far, and I don't want her getting all starry-eyed and grilling me about Hunter. Never mind that he's trailing behind me like a shadow. At least I'm not stepping out of his car.

The house is quiet when I walk in. I find her napping soundly on the sofa. Considering her nickname as the Energizer Bunny, her deep, slumbering breaths worry me.

I tiptoe beside her, unnerved. What if she isn't sleeping? What if she's passed out and needs medical attention? I lower my face until it's practically touching hers. Her eyes fly open, and her scream pierces the air. I fall back, my ass landing on the table. Hand over her heart, she pants heavily. "Child, you nearly gave me a heart attack."

"Ditto." I shake the bag of medication at her. "Maybe you shouldn't be skimping on your pills."

She waves away my concern. "I'm fine."

I open the bag and shake the little, orange bottle full of pills. I let one slide into my hand and hold it up to her. "If you haven't taken one today, you'll take one now." Her brow lifts warily. "There's a...new program at the pharmacy. You're actually eligible for free medication."

That has her sitting up. "I am?"

"Yes, it's all taken care of."

She snatches the pill from my open hand. "Gerald never told me about free meds."

"It's a new program. New to the pharmacy, too." I look around, handing her a half-finished cup of tea as she pops the pill. "Why don't you let me fix you a fresh cup of tea and some lunch."

"I should be fixing you lunch. You're the one who picked up the meds and made some miracle happen with the insurance." Skepticism stretches across her face as she studies me.

Rather than cross the threshold with a bald-faced lie, I about-face straight out of the room. Normally, Aunt Grace would be hot on my heels, going a hundred miles a minute with taking charge of her kitchen and spearing me with question after question about everything going on in my life. But today is different. I'm left alone to prepare her meal in peace. The quiet feels strange and unsettling.

I whip together a sandwich and grab some chips from the pantry. By the time I've returned, her head is resting back on the sofa pillow with her hand over her eyes. "Are you all right?" I sit beside her and check her pulse, a habit I'd fallen into while working at Sparrow Assisted Living. Her pulse is weak. Weak enough to make me want to throw her in Hunter's car and cart her off to the nearest urgent care.

Her hand slips from mine to cradle my cheek. "It's nothing. Just a little dizzy spell. They come and go. It's no big deal."

It's true. She has had dizzy spells for years. Had she had problems with her blood pressure all this time? Was that why they moved to Chicago? Uncle Jerry said he found a job with good pay and benefits. "Can you sit up?"

With a little assistance, she does.

"Moment of truth." My eyes lock with hers. "When's the last time you took your medicine?" I ask.

Her nose wrinkles as she blows out a thoughtful breath. "I don't know. Yesterday, maybe..." Childlike, she hangs her head.

"There were only a few pills left, and I wasn't sure when I could make it to the pharmacy. They last a lot longer if I don't exert myself, but when that hot chief of security came by—"

I stop her, practically shoving the sandwich down her throat. She takes a welcome bite. "Why didn't you call me? I can be here in forty-five minutes."

She swallows. "Because I don't want you to worry. And I can't drag you away from your important new job." She sips her tea, her eyes full of wonder. "Any news on your father?" Opening the chips, I slide several to the plate before grabbing a handful for myself. "Nothing to report." I can't tell her everything I've discovered. Not yet. Not until I know without a doubt that I am a D'Angelo.

Her finger taps my knee. "And what about this security guy?" Her voice is full of excitement and romance.

My eyes roll in avoidance. "Leo is all business. Someone I work for."

"Ohhh." She elongates the word suggestively. I don't dignify her whimsy with a response. It's too hard to explain how my one-night stand became my boss.

Instead, I turn the interrogation spotlight back onto her. "What did you two talk about?"

Her shoulders raise and lower. "A little bit of everything."

"How long was he here?"

She chews as she thinks. "After all was said and done, almost two hours."

"Two. *Hours*?" What kind of background check was this? I calm down, mindful of her blood pressure. "I'm sorry he was here so long."

"Oh, I insisted."

"What do you mean you insisted?"

"Ivy, it's the southern way to be hospitable."

"He's the chief of security for a billion-dollar corporation, not a houseguest."

"In this case, he was both. And you know it takes at least a good, solid forty-five minutes to bake a pie."

My face falls into my hand. "I still can't believe you baked him a pie."

"And read his palm, too," she says with way too much enthusiasm.

I cringe at the thought of Leo—former Navy SEAL and no-nonsense mob enforcer—sitting idly by while Aunt Grace reads his palm. "Please tell me you didn't wear the headdress."

"He was in a hurry."

Mortified, I shake my head. "Did you find anything noteworthy?"

"Oh, Ivy," she scolds. "You know as well as I do that all palm readings are strictly confidential."

"Are they? Wasn't it you that stood up in the middle of Brooke's birthday party and told half the freshman class that I was destined to become royalty?"

She munches another chip. "I might've been bragging just a little."

"Which, by the way, happened to be totally untrue."

She yanks my hand, rereading my fortune. Her finger points hard to my palm. "I still see it. Clear as day. It's in your past and in your future."

"What is?"

"A throne."

A throne. *Erede al Trono*. Can she see that? I squint,

studying each line of my hand as if a holographic crown will magically rise from my palm.

Her finger traces one line in particular.

"Tell me more about Z."

"Leo? What about him?"

"What kind of relationship did you say the two of you had?"

Two words come to mind. "Platonic. Professional."

Aunt Grace releases my hand and bites into her sandwich, chewing around a big, cheesy grin. "Mmm-hmm."

Hiding anything from Aunt Grace is like hiding an iceberg from the Titanic. She'll find out sooner or later. Might as well brace her for the impact. "Don't get your hopes up. I might be into him, but he's definitely not into me. He's made that extremely clear."

"Oh." She reads my cues, swallows her mouthful, and switches gears like a NASCAR driver. "How's your new job?"

A wide smile overshadows my heartache. "I love it. I care for Trinity. She's been through a lot. Leo said she's really taken to me. That I'm the first person to break through to her in four years. Being able to help makes me feel good. Like this is what I'm meant to do."

"It's just like I told Leo. People can't help but love you."

Her hand pats mine. My heart clenches at the thought of her saying that to him. If only she knew how wrong she was.

CHAPTER 8
Leo

When the wheels touch down at a small private airport outside of Raleigh, North Carolina, a black SUV with dark tinted windows waits, idling. My driver gets out to greet me. "Good afternoon, sir."

The petite brunette is dressed in a pencil skirt and cream blouse with her hair secured in a tight bun at her nape. Her cheerful smile is deceptive, not your typical run-of-the-mill chauffeur. She's part of an elite team I've hired across the country to do any number of investigative services. Background checks. Surveillance. All veterans. All cleared with advanced accesses. And all lethal and proficient in a wide array of weapons.

I greet her with a nod. Her name is Denise Daniels, though she goes by Deedee. Deedee prefers vodka to gin, rocket launchers to firearms, and men to women, though she often indulges in both. She also prefers to let her blown ACL heal in the comfort of her hometown before she goes back into the field. Fair enough.

She opens the back door, but I wave her hospitable pleasantries. Instead, I climb into the front passenger seat and wait until she's behind the wheel to discuss the agenda. "You know where we're going?" I ask.

Her nod is no-nonsense. "I've got the itinerary. Three stops today. Sheriff Everly is expecting us first followed by a visit to medical records at the hospital Miss Palmer was born. And finally, a trip to Sparrow Assisted Living facility."

"I'd like to get back before midnight."

Her mouth twists, amused. "If you're in a hurry, you've come to the wrong state. We're a little more laid-back in these parts."

"Be laid-back on your time."

"Yes, sir." Her foot slams the pedal. I nod in approval.

Our first stop. Sheriff Wade Everly. Stepping into his office feels like I'm the one under investigation. Small talk lasts as long as it takes him to pour me a cup of coffee. "What's this investigation about?" he asks, handing me the mug.

That's North Carolina for you. Hospitality with a stiff dose of cut the crap. "The usual background investigation."

"That so? Well, city boys aren't the only ones good at investigating." He smirks and opens a folder. "Leo 'Z' Zamparelli. Decorated vet. Honorable discharge." His fingers air quote. "Chief of Security for D'Angelo Holdings."

I sip my coffee, peering over the rim in interest.

He narrows his eyes as his hands clasp tightly on his desk. "I've got a question. Why is a Chicago syndicate interested in Ivy Palmer?"

I could lie. Or tell a half truth. The problem with law enforcement is that pissing them off isn't smart. All he has to do is breathe the words *mob investigation* to the FBI, and half our funds will be frozen overnight.

Not all our funds, mind you. Just the half that the public is privy to.

I cradle the mug in both hands and level with him. As much as I level with anyone. "Ivy's important to the D'Angelos. I understand she's been trying to track down her father. We'd like to help."

He squares me up for a long moment, and I'm reminded of how I should never be in a hurry in North Carolina. Instead of checking my watch, I sit back and sink into another mouthful of the diesel he calls coffee. It's actually pretty good.

"There's someone you should talk to," he offers.

I already know where he's going. "I've spoken with your sister."

"You did?"

"Apple pie, palm reading, and all."

With a chuckle, his shoulders relax. "She told me I'd have five children." He waves all five fingers at me. "It wasn't until we adopted our youngest, Nathan, that I realized she was right. Which is nutso, considering she told me this when I was eighteen. Trust these words." He pounds his finger to the desk. "Best birth control ever."

We both laugh at that one, and he opens up, sharing the contents of a folder hidden in the bottom of his cabinet drawer. "We searched for years."

I flip through the notes and printouts, focusing on a deposit slip. "What's this?"

He shook his head. "No idea. When Ivy's mom passed away, it was tucked inside her purse. I checked the bank. She'd been making large deposits every year. Never less than ten thousand dollars, never more than twenty. Always in cash."

There's no name, and nothing distinguishing on the bank slip. I inspect it, confused. "So, why'd you keep it?" He points to the date. I recognize it. "Ivy's birthday."

"Bingo."

We chat on and on about Ivy, exchanging a mishmash of stories from her trying to split her first tooth fairy quarter with her best friend Brooke to me witnessing her encounter with a fishing pole. I do what I always do: Chat him up to win his trust. But with each page of Ivy's history he shares, she's winning mine. My trust. My loyalty. My heart.

My fist wraps around that damned love line. I'm falling more for the girl by the minute. If I don't get out of here before he shares one more whimsical anecdote from her childhood, I'll be shutting down Hunter and going ring shopping.

I stand, ready to end our meeting and get some fucking air. "Thanks for your time."

Instead of taking my hand, he hands me the folder. His *Ivy File*. "Use it for as long as you need."

I thank him and promise to keep in touch. "I'm heading to the hospital next," I say as we exchange numbers.

He nods. Another smirk. "Good luck with Vera."

Vera, the records manager at the hospital Ivy was born, is a ball of warm hospitality behind a curtain of steel. Vera's friendly and polite as she reminds me that no record would be released without a fully executed subpoena. But she did it with a smile and offered me my pick at her bowl of saltwater taffy. My consolation prize.

I took three in vindication. "You're very hospitable to the men you boot out the door."

The elderly woman smiled endearingly. "At least you have manners. I hid my candy from the last guy."

I unwrapped a chocolate one. "I'm honored. This last guy ... what did he look like?"

I chewed the delicious morsel as she thought it over. "Your height. Older. Had a fancy, black car. Chauffeur, too."

"When was that?"

She thinks it through. "A few weeks back. I remember because I was running a double shift and was way over my hours. Thought the man was with corporate and was about to write me up."

On a hunch, I show her a picture of Andre. Vera studied it closely, zooming in on his face. "Right age. Wrong guy. The man I saw was a stone-cold fox. This guy?" Her face contorts with disgust. "Straight up serial killer if you ask me."

"They say that the eyes are the windows to the soul..." I mutter.

"Well, his must be filled with tar." Vera shivers and finds relief in a cherry taffy. She offers me more for the road, and I'm on my way.

I'm left with a file of mostly nothing, a pocketful of candy, and the disconcerting feeling that another man is trying to find Ivy. For all I know, the guy could be her real father.

I shouldn't be this invested in what comes out of my investigation, but I am. There's no denying it—Ivy Palmer is important to me.

I don't expect too much from our final stop. We round a corner of bright yellow birch trees and roll up to a single-story building surrounded by patches of flowers and native pines. I picture Ivy here and wonder how happy she was.

Her mother was here for a year and a half, shackling Ivy to her debt. Had she paid it off? Is that why she left?

If it weren't for the large sign that read, SPARROW ASSISTED LIVING, I would have thought this was a small hotel or large bed-and-breakfast. The landscapes are trimmed and maintained with small, pink primrose shrubs and vibrant yellow lilies scattered throughout. From every angle, it's inviting.

I enter. Notes of lemons and vanilla float through the air. The furnishings are warm and cozy with rich drapes and tasteful area rugs. There's a grand bookshelf just beyond the concierge desk, and the magazines on the counter are new. It feels well-kept. Homey. So different than the cold tiles and sterile atmosphere I imagined.

An older woman in a pale pink dress and knit sweater comes to greet me, extending her hand. "Welcome. I'm Daisy."

"Leo," I say, taking her delicate hand for a quick shake. With the sheriff and the hospital, I'm above board, giving them my identity as chief of security for a multi-billion-dollar firm. Here, I'm just Leo. Being less forthright means fewer speed-bumps and quicker access to information. "I appreciate you taking my last-minute request for a tour."

"Of course," she says enthusiastically and nudges me down the hall. "Right this way." We meander through the facility as she leads me through a vacant bedroom, the dining room, the rec center that doubles as a gym, and finally, to a courtyard where several people are enjoying the sun.

A frail woman struggles to take down her canvas and easel. I give her a hand and notice the mocha-skinned beauty centered in the frame. Her hair is soft, wavy, and raven black with a single silver strand that graces her face. My heart squeezes in an instant. "Ivy," I whisper.

The painter nods, and Daisy tilts her head in question. "Do you know Ivy?"

"No," I lie, shifting my gaze. I point to the corner. "That small gold leaf. Ivy, right?"

The artist nods, then struggles for a moment to speak. I smile patiently. Finally, she strings together several stutters until the words finally form. "I mmmm-miss h-h-her," she says, her lips twisting in sadness.

I stare at the big, beautiful dark eyes of the woman in the frame. God, I miss her, too. "Can I buy it?" I ask from out of nowhere, not really sure what the hell I'm doing.

The artist ponders it for a moment, opening her mouth, then closing it again.

Daisy steps in, speaking on her behalf. "I think she was hoping that Ivy would be back. It was meant to be a birthday gift, but it wasn't quite ready on her birthday."

"Her birthday?" What was it about Ivy's birthday? It spins around over and over again, like the prettiest horse on a carousel, begging for attention.

Daisy nods. "Her twenty-fourth. Oh, to be twenty-four again," she says, romanticizing the thought.

Twenty-four. Why is that familiar? Hmmm. When I was twenty-four, I was dumb, broke, and too young to care. Thank God for the military.

"Y-y-yes," the artist says, definitively.

I stare at her blankly.

"H-h-how m-m-m-much?" she asks, suddenly eager to hear my offer. I look it over. The dimensions are large, and the details are exquisite.

I scrutinize it carefully. I know diddly-squat about art. Monet and Michelangelo are as familiar as Playtex and Pampers. Seen them around but never had a need.

As Ivy's painted eyes gaze into mine, the piece speaks to me. And I'm not letting it go. "Five hundred dollars?" I offer.

"Five?" the artist repeats without a single stammer. "Higher," she says, clear as a bell. Her eyes light up, and I imagine Ivy's bright smile if she ever discovers how her sweet friend haggled over the sale. I smile, amused. She's got me by the balls, and she knows it.

"You drive a hard bargain. One thousand dollars. Take it or leave it." *Please take it.*

She nods. I pay.

I take Ivy off her hands, careful not to smudge the fresher strokes of paint. Now that I have it, I scratch my head, wondering what I should do with it.

I check my watch. It's getting late. "Where's your bathroom?" There's one more stop I need to make before I go. But I need to ditch Daisy.

She points in the direction of the bathrooms. I walk that way and make a detour to the one person I can't wait to meet.

Derrick. The cheating lowlife that once referred to Ivy as his girlfriend.

He also happened to be her boss. And the fuckhead who'd been skimming off the books for years, driving Sparrow Assisted Living straight into the ground.

A demented thrill runs through me as I step up to his door and knock. I don't wait for his response and enter.

He jumps from behind his desk, scrambling with his keyboard as he hurries to zip up his pants. I'm pretty sure I interrupted the douchebag during his afternoon porn surf. Note to self: Do not shake his hand.

"Excuse me," he says with a half-inch of authority. "You can't barge in here."

I close the door behind me and lock it, careful as I lean the painting against the wall.

"Who are you?" He notices the portrait. "And what the hell do you think you're doing with that?"

I unbutton my blazer and take a seat. "That?" Casually, I point to the painting. "I just purchased it from a resident. It will look amazing in the grand entry, don't you think?"

"What?" He grabs the phone. "I'm calling the cops."

Before the receiver makes contact with his ear, the barrel of my Glock lodges at the base of his throat. He frowns, shaking as he drops the receiver. I give his cheek two baby smacks. "Very good."

The asshole cheated on Ivy for nearly a year. The alarmed expression on his face is remarkably satisfying, filling me with a sick sense of glee.

Instantly, his hands raise in surrender. "Fine. Keep the damn painting. I swear to God that bitch is more trouble than she's worth."

Rage boils over. I sock him square in the jaw so hard it sends him flying across the room. He lands on the floor; all his pathetic begging falls on deaf ears. I set my foot just above his throat as I train my weapon straight at his head.

"You weren't taking Ms. Palmer's name in vain, were you?"

He trembles and shakes his head. "I didn't think so. Now, get up." I wave the gun over to his desk, directing him behind it. He scrambles to his feet. "Pull up everything you have on her. Including what's on your phone. You're gonna tell me everything you know about Ivy Palmer."

He rushes to a drawer and produces a folder. Dismayed, I stare at the two sheets of paper in it. Her original application along with a copy of a certificate. "Art Therapy?" I question Derrick. "She's an artist?"

His head shakes. "It's some special type of counselor that uses anything available to help work with people who can't speak. Whatever interests them. Drawing. Sculpting. Poetry. She's tried to take college courses here and there, but the costs were high, and her hours here didn't help. That certificate is as close as she got to a degree. Personally, I thought the whole damn thing was a bunch of mumbo jumbo horseshit."

I flick his face with a pamphlet. "And yet it's on your brochure." He looks away. "Let me guess. Your clients pay big bucks for all that mumbo jumbo horseshit, right? Is that why you were paying Ivy pennies while charging your residents a premium for her services?"

Derrick's eyes widen in fear. "How do you know that?"

"Because I know everything about you, Derrick. I know about your parents living in a small apartment about two hours from here. I know your credit score ranks in the mid-five hundreds. I know your computer sees more porn than a Hustler Hollywood. And I know the corporate credit card you've been using includes charges for car maintenance, booze, and whores."

He recoils, stunned.

"Oh, and I also know more than I want to about your fascination with ferrets." I shake my head in disgust. "Seriously, knitting them sweaters crosses some weird fucking line."

"What are you? CIA?"

"Because the CIA has a vested interest in Derrick the dick fiddler?"

I fold Ivy's paperwork and slip it into my pocket. "What else?"

"There is nothing else."

There has to be something else. "Show me your financials."

"Why?"

His idiocy astounds me. "Because I have the fucking gun." I wave it around for effect.

Derrick nearly shits his pants and manages to retrieve every last transaction for the past two years. What do you know? The man does have a working brain cell.

Profit and loss statements. Balance sheets. Annual reports. Derrick's outdone himself. Skimming off the top was just the start. He's shorted the wages of every member of the staff while simultaneously up-charging all the residents. He's damn near added surcharges for Q-tips and squares of toilet paper.

Even then, he's managed to keep his job despite Sparrow Assisted Living swapping owners at a rate of once a year. Even now, the current owners are ready to dump the place at fire sale prices. Which means more of the same for dumbass Derrick, and prompt evictions for some of the residents, including Angie, but gets me no closer to what I came here for. I've got more information on Derrick Landon, this place, the owners, and every resident past and present...

But nothing more on Ivy.

I drop the aim of my Glock to his pants. "This is everything?"

His hands fly to his crotch. "Yes. Yes! I swear to God, that's everything. Ask your friend if you don't believe me?"

I narrow my eyes. "What friend?"

"The guy. He showed up just like you. Fancy car. Nice suit. Not from around here. Handed Ivy an envelope and got grabby with her shoulder before he disappeared."

"When?"

"The day she quit."

With my free hand, I flip through a few images on my cell, then hold it up. "This guy?"

Derrick takes a good, long look. "Maybe."

"Look. *Harder.*"

He shrugs, waving his hands wildly. "I don't know. It could've been. I remember thinking he's too old to be hitting on her."

"How old?"

"I can't be sure. Maybe sixty. They were outside. I was in my office. I wasn't paying much attention."

The more Derrick talks, the more I realize the guy's fucking useless on every level, and putting him out of his misery might be best for all involved. Except that Derrick the douchebag might come in handy down the road.

Fine. He lives. I check my watch and holster my weapon. "I was never here. Our little talk never happened. Got it?"

Eyes closed, he nods.

I straighten my jacket and head for the door. "And one

other thing. Let the staff know Sparrow Assisted Living has just been sold."

The hour-long drive to the airport gives me time to think, so I type a note to Smoke.

Ivy and Andre know each other

Then, I delete and rewrite it.

There's a *chance* Ivy may be working with Andre.

Fuck, no.

Delete. Delete. Delete.

I can't say anything. Not without proof.

Frustrated, I blow out a breath as my head sinks back on the seat. I stare out into the darkness. It's pitch black. Like the world is at peace.

Or the calm before the storm.

CHAPTER 9

Ivy

Loud, clanking sounds wake me from my deepest sleep in weeks. It takes me a moment to remember where I am. Frilly curtains. Purple flowered sheets. I yawn with a grin. Aunt Grace's home.

I check my cell and roll out of bed. The little clock says 9:00 a.m. Which makes this my personal record for the latest I've ever slept in.

In a plain grey sweatshirt and some comfy pants Brooke left behind, I stretch and make my way to the kitchen. "Morning, sleepyhead," Grace says, handing me a sinful-smelling muffin.

I hold it to my face, enjoying a deep whiff. The aroma is heaven. "Mmm. Banana."

"Banana chocolate chip. Though I also have plain banana as well as banana with chopped up candied pecans."

"Not gonna lie. I will probably have one of each. Maybe two." I take a seat, and Aunt Grace brings a large platter of assorted banana muffins, centering the yummy goodness between us. My coffee is already on the table, though hers is noticeably missing.

"Where's yours?" I ask. Her shrug confuses me. If she's low on coffee, too, I'm busting out my emergency fund and hauling her ass to the store.

"I thought I'd try a day without it. Enjoy the whole caffeine-free lifestyle."

Her words are half-hearted at best. In solidarity, I do the unthinkable. "Oh, thank goodness," I say, pouring my cup of coffee straight down into the sink. "I'm not much of a coffee drinker," I lie. "I was drinking it to be polite." I stick my head in one cupboard, then another. "Didn't you used to keep lemon-ginger tea? It's amazing with fresh banana muffins."

Aunt Grace puts a kettle of hot water to heat on the stove. Her hip bumps mine. "I know you really wanted that coffee," Aunt Grace says.

"And I know that when I was nine years old, you really wanted that apple fritter in the big box of donuts at Christmas. But you gave it to me anyway."

She wraps an arm around me, squeezing me so hard I squeak. We giggle into a moment I wish would last days. Then, the kettle whistles, and I drop a teabag into each mug as she pours. "As I recall," she says while dunking her tea bag up and down, "you did give me a colossal bite."

I rest my head on her shoulder. "And you gave me a childhood."

After breakfast, I tidy up and make sure Aunt Grace has everything she needs. Her fridge and pantry are adequately full.

"Swear you'll call me if you need anything and that you'll take your medicine as prescribed."

"I swear." She crosses her heart to take a whole pill every single day. "I'll be fine. You have a new job and a family that needs you," she says, popping a finger to my nose.

Hunter is waiting for me bright and early with coffee in his hand as he holds open my door. Mortified, I make my way to the passenger side. "Tell me you didn't sleep in your car because of me."

His boyish shrug levels me with guilt.

We make our way back to the estate, and I can't stop imagining this mammoth of a man squished inside the sportscar like a sardine. "Aunt Grace had another room. I would've invited you in."

"It's no big deal." He notices me staring down at the Styrofoam cup. "Hey." I drag my eyes to his. "How about you make it up to me?"

I scoot an inch further from him. "How?"

He chuckles. "Not like that."

His thumb taps the steering wheel, and I slowly sip the coffee, waiting out whatever it is he's about to say. Could Hunter be nervous?

Determined, he clears his throat. "Your friend, Brooke. I'd like to meet her. The sooner, the better."

I turn to him, deadly serious. "If you hurt her, I will have you killed."

He shakes his head. "Wow, Leo's really rubbing off on you." My glare turns menacing. "You have nothing to worry about. I noticed her Facebook profile."

I put two and two together and sock his arm. "You checked her out."

"It's sort of my job." I sock him again, lightly to avoid

hurting my hand. It's enough to shake loose his intentions. "Fine. I wanted to find out a little more about her." This isn't news. Brooke Everly is head-to-toe stunning. Smart. Sassy. The kind of girl men fall all over. I've seen it a million times, and not once have I been jealous. I was too busy picking up the pieces when they broke her heart.

I pull up her profile and laugh into my hand. The caption reads, "Me and Hunter." She and Hunter-the-Shepherd are filtered in tiaras and bright red lipstick .

"She has a Belgian Malinos shepherd named Hunter. So, she already likes the name." His smile is endearing before curling down in sadness. "Do you know where she got him?"

I think for a moment. "He was a K-9 rescue. Her family is all cops and military, and they love dogs." I leave out the part about Brooke needing an assistance dog for her epilepsy. "You must like them, too, if you know the breed."

He nods, and we sit in silence as he gets lost in his thoughts. After a while, he speaks. "In one of my last tours, I was assigned with a dog—certain breeds are ideal for working with the military because of the strength, versatility, and ease of training. Resilience." He trails off. "My dog, Pax, suffered a bullet to the hind leg. I took two in the chest." He sucks in a breath. "But I was patched up and sent back out."

I swallow hard as instinct takes over. I squeeze his hand. "I'm so sorry for your loss."

He casts me a sideways glance. "What loss?"

"Your...dog?"

"Pax didn't die." He points to his chest. "*My* dog was patched up and retired. *My* dog was a Belgian Malinos shepherd whose paperwork had my name on it as well as his. Pax.

New owner: Hunter Walsh. My dog was supposed to be adopted by me. My mom and dad were ready to take him until I returned." He takes a breath. "But there was a mix up with the paperwork. His name read Pax Hunter Walsh and was adopted by a young woman in North Carolina."

My chest constricts. "You can't take Hunter from Brooke."

"Ivy—"

"You don't understand. Brooke needs Hunter." I'm about to tell him why when he interrupts me.

"Ivy, stop. If I wanted to take Pax, I would've done it years ago." He keeps his eyes on the road. "By the time I tracked down Pax, the young woman who adopted him had already started his training. In seizure response."

He knows. I stare in disbelief.

Hunter taps the face of my phone, and a thoughtful smile emerges. "Like I said. I'd like to meet your friend."

For the remainder of the drive, Hunter shares stories of life with Pax. A hero and his hero dog. He doesn't want to take Pax from Brooke. He just wants to meet her.

"I don't want her to know who I am," he adds.

"Why not?"

"From everything I've learned about Brooke, she's the kind of person that would want Pax back with me."

He's right. Brooke would never keep him if she had even an inkling of what they'd been through together. A Hallmark kind of warmth swirls around me. Hunter really is a great guy.

And I'd love to dive head-first into a cupid outfit and get these two matched already. Love should be in the stars for someone...

"Well," I start, "if I'm keeping secrets for you, I might need you to keep some secrets for me."

He rolls his eyes with disapproval. "You want me to keep things from my boss?"

"Leo doesn't have to know everything. Our conversation, for example. Or anything that has to do with Aunt Grace. She deserves her privacy."

He thinks through my proposal and nods. "Deal."

When I arrived back at the estate, Leo pulls in at the same time. "Good morning," he says all growly and hot. Why does he have to be so good-looking this early in the morning?

Who cares if he's in a suit with his mussed-up hair looking freshly fucked? Or that I'm in a sweatshirt and yoga pants and probably look like I just slept on a park bench.

He eyes me, then Hunter. "Same outfit as yesterday?" he observes under his breath.

"Yes, sir." They exchange several glances before Hunter excuses himself and makes himself scarce, leaving me with Leo and his cedar-scented cologne.

"Where were you?" he asks with enough ownership it strikes a nerve.

"Where was *I*?" I say, sarcasm pricking my words.

His patience takes a nosedive. "Answer the question." Not answering Leo is juvenile. But I want all of Leo. His anger. His emotions. His rage. His heat. And if getting under his skin is the way to get it, game on.

My arms form a tight knot in front of my chest as my heels dig in. "That's none of your business."

His scowl emerges.

I welcome it and step into his space. "What's the matter, Leo? Jealous?"

"I'm not jealous. But I am concerned. You have a job to do. Your job includes being at this property twenty-four hours a day, seven days a week."

"No, my job *may* require me to be on-site *as much as* twenty-four hours a day, seven days a week. My absence was approved by Hunter since you were busy. Hmm, gone all night? Where were *you*, Leo?"

He huffs under his breath.

I begin to make my way into the house. "If there is anything you needed to know about me, you could always ask. And stop badgering my aunt."

"Badgering?" He catches up to me, his anger melting into a smirk. "Ah. You were with Grace. I'm pretty good at reading people, Ivy, and the last thing your dear Aunt Grace would ever say was that I was badgering her. If anything, *she* was badgering *me*. Taunting me with her North Carolina charm and seducing me with baked goods."

"She forced you to eat your weight in pie?"

"Hogtied me to a chair is more like it. Shoved every last spoonful in my mouth," Leo says, exaggerating. "I'm seriously traumatized. I had to walk around the rest of the day with the top button of my pants undone." He leans in, whispering, "She invited me back for banana muffins. I might make my way over there now and"—he air quotes—"'badger her' some more."

At this point, I'm fuming. But I'm also trying really hard not to smile. I bite the inside of my lip. "Too late," I snap in frustration. "I ate them all this morning."

We glare at each other, frozen in a moment of unspoken words and heat. And regret. And then, Leo *Badass* Zamparelli does something I never thought he'd do.

He apologizes. "I'm sorry. Background checks are part of my job. I can't give you a pass because—" He cuts himself off.

"Because what, Leo?"

He lets the sentimental moment between us pass. "I can't give you a pass because you have an in with the pie baker from heaven." He unbuttons his blazer and exposes his shirt. "Yesterday, I was all kinds of glorious Buddha belly. You missed out on some serious sexiness." He waves a graceful hand along his abs, which, from here, still look rock hard. He's witty and charming and impossible to stay mad at.

We make our way to the house. "Leo, I know you have to do a background check. But if there's something you need to know, just ask."

"And if you have something to tell me, just say it." Leo steps closer. The air crackles between us for a long beat, and I want to tell him. It would be so easy to say the words. *I think I'm a D'Angelo.*

Face to face, he crushes me with a whisper. "Goddamnit, Ivy, I'm trying to protect you."

I study his eyes before shutting mine. That's just it. He can't protect me. Anything I say, won't stay between us. It can't. He's made it very clear that between me and the D'Angelos, he'll side with them. Every time.

"You can't have it both ways, Leo. You handed me off to Hunter. You told me in no uncertain terms that when I need you most, you won't be there. You don't get to break my heart, then ask me to bare my soul. It doesn't work that way. You wanted Hunter between us. You've got it."

CHAPTER 10
Leo

Leave her alone. Now there's some great fucking advice. So, why can't I do it?

I watch her walk away, and I let her. It takes every last ounce of self-control I have not to follow her inside.

With Ivy, I've seen every shade of schemes and conspiracies. But maybe that's just all in my head.

Fuck, I've got to stop stalking the poor girl and get back to work. I spent the past two days chasing down the phantoms of her past, finding nothing but shadows. If anything, Ivy Palmer is a wholesome human being who deserves a thousand times better than the likes of me. But the thought of not having her kills me.

Frustrated, I head to my office and work through a mountain of waiting intel reports. The number of threats we have against the D'Angelos rival that of royalty or a head of state. With the brothers collected in one place, we have to be ready for anything.

Knock-knock.

Smoke enters without waiting for an acknowledgment. He shuts the door and strolls to my desk. His smile is telling. "The jet. Your noticeable absence. And Ivy being gone at the same time." His words linger in the air.

I swat them away. "Ivy and I didn't see each other."

"Then where were you?"

"North Carolina."

I'm unusually quiet. Noticing my discomfort, Smoke puts me out of my misery and fills in the blanks for me. "You've obviously resumed your investigation. What I can't seem to wrap my head around is whether you're suspicious of her or enthralled with her." He takes a seat. "Are you minutes from nailing her to the cross, or to the wall?"

I throw my hands up in frustration. "I wish I knew."

He considers me and frowns. "You want to talk it through?"

The offer is tempting, but I shake my head. In some worlds, there's a presumption of innocence. In this world, no one is innocent. But it's up to me to determine whether the weight of their guilt warrants their execution.

As far as Ivy Palmer goes, my head is less certain than my heart is, and my heart is an untrustworthy fuck. Fool me once. So, rather than laying out all my cards and being straight with the man I consider a brother, I go with my gut.

"I've closed the investigation on Ivy. Her background seems like an open and shut case, but I had to be sure with your brothers coming and with her standing in the midst of the ceremony."

His fingers steeple to his chin as he studies me. Smoke knows me better than most, but even he can't read minds. Until

I'm ready to tell him something, he's not going to know. That's for his benefit as well as mine.

He takes a long minute before asking, "So, your investigation of Ivy is closed?"

I swear to God the man lives to make me sweat. I stare down the human lie detector and paint on a mask. "For now."

It's true. Or, true enough. Her background investigation is over. The investigation of her father is personal. Just something I have to do.

I see the doubt creep up behind the hardened steel in his eyes and remind him of the good Ivy's done. "Trinity's made remarkable progress..."

He nods.

"In the years since her attack, the number of words she spoke each year could be counted on one hand. We owe that miracle to Ivy. How she splintered through Trinity's darkness, I have no idea. But I won't overlook that, and neither should you."

"But you're still looking into her."

"I have a job to do, Smoke. It doesn't mean she's a suspect. It means she's been granted access to the circle of trust whether she's earned it or not. That's why I'm here. Your enforcer."

Smoke stands. "If something comes up with Ivy, she won't be your problem, Leo. She'll be mine." It's not a question. Smoke has given me a command.

"Understood," I say definitively.

With both palms pressed against my desk, he leans down until we're eye to eye. "You can fool everyone else, Leo. Maybe you can even fool yourself. But you can't make your feelings for Ivy disappear."

I turn away. "It doesn't matter. This is the life I choose."

"Do you?" He thumps my chest. "In case you haven't noticed, that hardened shell of a heart has started beating again. You can't ignore it."

"I can try," I bark back.

Grimacing, he shakes his head. "Don't you know I'd sell my soul to feel something again? I'm chained to this world. You're not. Don't give up on living only to spend the rest of your life protecting ours."

His words are tiny daggers to my soul because if anyone should know why I'm desperate to sprint from this hamster wheel, it's him. Smoke heads out the door, and I curse across the room. "Goddammit, Smoke. She deserves better."

He turns back, sharing a lopsided grin. "So do you."

So do I? How can he say that to me?

With a buildup of force, I explode. My laptop. My cell. My precious coffee mug. I send them flying across my desk.

I can't believe he actually said that to me. Me, the enforcer to the D'Angelos. I'm not even mildly exaggerating when I say there's a two-story condo in the hottest part of hell carved out for people like me. I have more blood on my hands than the county medical examiner, and believe me, the only form of torture that should be off limits is putting early morning children's shows on repeat.

And Smoke thinks I deserve better?

I scoff to the room. He couldn't be more wrong if he dropped a bar of soap in a prison shower. News flash: I don't deserve anything at all. My late wife, Lori, was evidence of that. If anyone deserved more, it was her.

Smoke can keep laying a brick path of good intentions, but

where my love life is concerned, I won't make the same mistake twice. Ivy deserves to find happiness with someone a thousand times better than me.

And I deserve to serve out this death sentence of a life without destroying hers.

CHAPTER 11
Leo

For the next twelve hours, I comb through one intel report after the other, bouncing between reports about Uncle Andre, the Bratva syndicate, and every so often, the bits and pieces I manage to unravel about Ivy. If she is mixed up with Uncle Andre, she's more covert than Evelyn Salt. Hunter's reports were about as eventful as watching the tumble cycle on a dryer. Nothing ties Ivy to the most hated man in the D'Angelo bloodline, save for his persistent need to keep calling her.

The other thing that's noticeably absent is the lengthy drive from Aunt Grace's house back to the estate. Not a single reference to their conversation. Hence the reason I have Hunter front and center and reporting to me now.

"Is this everything?" I ask.

For two days, Hunter has been Ivy's shadow. I scan through the document on my laptop. Hunter's report is thorough. Fifty-pages. I've finished my review and can't shake the nagging feeling...

I'm missing something.

"Yes, sir. That's everything from what she ate to when she flosses."

"What about the text?"

He rubs his jaw. "It's weird."

My eyes narrow. "What exactly makes it weird?"

"There doesn't seem to be anything to it. She received two texts from the same number. And I verified that the number definitely belongs to Andre D'Angelo. Or, at least, someone on his books."

Hunter stalls. My patience wears thin as a razor. "And?"

"And nothing, boss. No reply text. No calls back. No emails. Unless she's using homing pigeons or telepathy, they're not in contact."

"But Andre is trying to contact her... Why?" We exchange blank looks. "Andre wouldn't be circling her if he didn't have a reason." I stare at the end of his report. "What about the car ride back? You drove for nearly an hour. What did she talk about?"

He thinks about it for a minute before answering. "She really didn't say much." Hunter stands in military at ease position, a habit drilled into the heart of his muscle memory. I raise a brow, and he elaborates. "You always said that a report has to center on the subject of the surveillance. Ms. Palmer. The conversation had almost nothing to do with Ms. Palmer."

"Because it had to do with you?"

His throat bobs as he swallows. "Yes, sir."

"I see."

"I told her about Pax."

Pax was a part of Hunter's life he never wanted to discuss.

The bond between a military handler and his dog can be stronger than one with a spouse. That bond was severed, and not by him. Revealing a detail so personal isn't like him. At all. Hunter usually holds women at arm's length, even with his dick inside of them.

I stare at the lethal killing machine before me, perplexed. Is this more of the *Ivy Effect?* Is the woman a freaking voodoo queen? Or a shaman? Or a witch?

Hunter unlocks from his stance without my permission— *finally*—and offers me his head on a platter. "If you need to remove me from this case, or my duties entirely, I understand."

I steeple my fingers and tap my chin. "Why? It's not your fault that Ivy's the worst surveillance target ever. A good listener is our fucking kryptonite." I stand to connect eye-to-eye. "Are you slipping at your job?"

"No, sir."

"Then enjoy the free therapy."

Unmoving, he blinks back. "You sure you're okay with this?"

I crack my knuckles. I hate the idea. "Positive," I say. I watch as he rubs his neck and notice the bloodshot eyes behind his waning grin. "When's the last time you slept for more than an hour?"

He shakes his head. "I don't know. A few days? Creeping on a week."

And I wonder why he turned into a Chatty Cathy doll with Ivy. "You and the guys get some rest. I'm on Ivy the next two days."

"You got it, boss."

Three knocks sound on the door, and Hunter and I both know who's on the other side. Ivy.

"Come in," we say in unison because someone forgot whose fucking office it is. Hunter smirks, I glare, and we both turn our attention to the woman who steals my breath a little more every time I see her.

Ivy pokes her head in. She notices Hunter, then faces me. "Sorry, I was hoping to speak with you, Leo, but I can come back."

"No need. Hunter was just leaving."

On cue, Hunter begins to head out the door, stopping short of it as Ivy asks, "Are we on for later, Hunter?"

He glances over, uncertain. When the slightest blush rises up Ivy's cheeks, I step in. "What's happening later?" I ask.

Ivy slips her lone silver ringlet behind her ear. A habit she does when her confidence shies away. "Hunter's going to teach me to swim."

Annoyed, I glare. I'm the one who insisted he get close. He couldn't get much closer without a condom. A small nuclear explosion erupts in my head, which I control with white-knuckled fists.

Hunter shrugs, trying and failing not to smile. "I was a SEAL," he reminds me. As if I wasn't. I was his goddamned commander, for fuck's sake.

"You don't say," I let out. "Well, I'm sorry to disappoint you, Ivy. Hunter won't be teaching you to swim today." *Or any other day*.

"Why not?" Her lips form a pout. A full-lipped, delectable pout that my body craves like heroine.

I mentally command my dick to play dead and try to answer

her question. "Because..." I try to think up an excuse. "Because Hunter has more pressing matters. I'm sorry he can't be at your beck and call. That's all, Hunter." I dismiss him, waving him away.

He leaves, shutting the door behind him.

Ivy stands there, unaware that I've taken inventory of all of her. Her snug denim jeans. Her pale pink peasant blouse. No makeup. Hair carefree. The colorless lip gloss she only glides on after each meal.

And a crumb of biscotti at the corner of her mouth I'd like to remove with my tongue.

With Ivy and I, privacy is our anti-Christ, seconds from slaying me with an onslaught of sin.

"Have a seat." I gesture for the chair.

"No, thank you." Her arms remain across her chest, and there is that luscious pout again. I swear to God, I'm beginning to sweat.

"Something on your mind, Ivy?"

She frowns, upset.

I frown, enraged, wondering how glorious it would be to have her in the midst of angry sex.

"Why did you treat Hunter like that?"

"Like what? Like I'm his boss and he works for me? Because I am. It's efficient."

"It's rude."

I tap a finger to my chin and cut to the chase. "Did you come here to give me a lesson on manners, or is there something else weighing on your mind?"

I stand beside the chair and urge her, once again, to sit. She does. I scoot a chair beside her, and pull her feet to my lap, removing her shoes. "What are you doing?" Her question is fair. *What am I doing?*

I sink both thumbs into her arch. Her moan is tight and controlled and barely noticeable, but it's there.

"Nothing you'll object to. You've been on your feet for two days. My hands go no higher than your ankles."

"How do you know that?"

"How do I know you want a foot massage? Because you're a woman."

She points her toe at my torso. "How do you know I've been on my feet for two days."

"Because it's my job to know." I screw my thumb in harder. Her eyes flutter shut as she slumps in the chair. "What I don't know is what you came in here for." She doesn't answer. I slide a feather-light tickle down the center of her foot.

"Eek! Leo!" Her foot tries to kick away from my hand. It's all I can do not to kiss it.

"You know that torture is my middle name. Now spill. What's on your mind?"

I begin working on her other foot as she opens up. "Have you ever felt like you don't fit in?"

I shake my head. "Never. Except for the days I wake up in my own skin."

I give her all the time she needs to confide in me. Eventually, she does. "How fancy is *Erede al Trono*?"

"As fancy as they come. Black tie. Evening gowns." Ivy's expression falls. "Is something wrong?"

She frowns as she works through something in her head. "No," she finally lets out. "But it's just the family, right? Not a huge event."

I nod, not sure where she's going. "The brothers and any guests they invite."

Her brow pinches with concern. "What about Uncle Andre?"

"Definitely not. In case you haven't noticed, he has the uncanny ability to make those around him trigger happy. I'm sure Dante has wet dreams about chopping him up as shark bait, and Enzo probably buys a new set of Loro Piana gloves just in case the opportunity arises to strangle the man." I watch as she processes what I've said. I don't like that she's unsettled. "Is that what was worrying you? Andre?"

She straightens in the chair and sucks in a determined breath. "I'm not worried." Her tone is far from convincing. It hadn't dawned on me that Ivy might be apprehensive or even afraid of him. Considering the son of a bitch had her thrown in jail for the sport of it, it makes sense.

"No one will hurt you," I assure her.

"And you know this because it's your job."

My eyes capture hers. "It's a promise, Ivy."

When she nibbles on her lower lip, my dick throbs. Either I'm fucking her here and now or getting back to work.

I take her shoes off the floor and place them back on her feet. "Thank you," she says.

I return to my desk as she makes her way to the door.

"Will you be there, too?" she asks. "To the big D'Angelo shindig."

"I have to be."

Her mouth lifts with the slightest smile. "Best man?"

"Dragonslayer."

From behind the wheel of my armored Audi, my finger hovers over the start button. Ivy is leaving the house in a pretty, white blouse and tight jeans that I would love to tear off with my teeth. I focus on the box in her hand. It's medium-sized and just big enough to carry all the belongings she came with.

Fuck. Is she quitting?

Ivy can't quit. Trini needs her. And Smoke. And maybe me, too, if I'm completely honest with myself.

She takes a long, mournful look at the estate before getting in her beat-up Honda Civic and driving off.

I slip into stalker mode. The role is warm and familiar and fits with perfection like a custom-tailored Brioni suit. For the rest of the day, I follow her.

She's heading in the wrong direction for Aunt Grace's house, which is a shame. Grace's apple pie has been a siren's song in my sleep.

Ivy attempts the worst parallel parking job ever and then gets out of the car before stopping at the local college bookstore and hauling the box she carried out of the house inside.

From across the street, I watch the cashier pull out the contents. Textbooks. And I recognize the one from Ivy's fishing expedition. Was she finished with it?

The transaction ends quickly, and Ivy counts her cash. Confusion unsettles me. We pay her three times what she was making at Sparrow Assisted Living, and all her expenses are covered. Why is she acting like an intern hard-up for cash?

She continues with her errands. Every step of the way, I'm her shadow. Her next stop is a thrift store. The old red brick building has been on the south side of town forever. Saint Andrews. I went there as a kid. It had little to offer a tall, scrawny boy whose legs were too long for his build.

I follow her inside. The place reeks of bubble gum—a sanitizing agent used to freshen the clothes and make the place smell less poor and more fun. With a lifetime of memories rummaging through these very aisles, trust me, it was never fun.

I keep an eye on her as she meanders from one aisle to the next. She takes her time scrutinizing one hanger after the next. Evening gowns. The selection is sparse, and every dress has to be roughly twice her size. There isn't a single article of clothing that would satisfy her lean waist or seductive curves. And yet, she carefully considers them.

There's a simple black cocktail dress that lures her interest. Her mouth twists with uncertainty as she removes it from the rack. Horrified, I watch as she lines it up against her body and cinches it to one side.

I pinch the bridge of my nose. *Is she fucking kidding? The thing is a tent.* I rub the scruff on my chin and stare in shock. By the way Ivy fusses with it, it's obvious that this one is a contender.

For what seems like enough time to plant the summer harvest, Ivy scrutinizes the dress in the full-length mirror, taking in every square inch. Of course, it has to take this long to take it all in because the goddamned thing is approximately the size of a catamaran sail. Eventually, sanity prevails, and she returns it to the rack.

What kills me is that, even from two aisles away, I can see how returning it to the rack causes a small part of her to deflate.

CHAPTER 12

Ivy

After trying—and failing—to find a gown that was *passably elegant,* I work with Trini on her look. Trini might be shattered on the inside, but from the outside, she's beauty pageant perfection. Her lean, tall physique is crowned by wavy blonde hair and a fair shade of skin that looks good in anything.

"You're stunning," I say, tugging the zipper all the way up. Trinity does a small twirl. She's in an off-the-shoulder blush gown with a cinched waist and chiffon skirt. By the way it fits, it had to be custom-made and probably one of a kind. She does a small curtsy to her reflection, and her smile widens, warm and bright.

"Thank you. It was my mother's," she says as her smile twists with sadness. "I've always wanted a reason to wear it."

"And now you have one. *Erede al trono.*"

Her eyes light as she hops on the bed and urges me to sit beside her. "Our family has a tradition. When an heir wants the keys to the kingdom, he—"

"Or she?" I ask cheekily.

Trinity plays along. "Or she—has to announce it. Formally. Before the family. And if anyone objects, they fight over it."

My mouth falls open, stunned. "Are you serious? A knock-down, drag-out fight?"

She giggles. "No. Well, maybe. I mean, Enzo's a bit of a wildcard. It's more for ceremony." Her hand clasps mine. "This will be the first time we've ever had someone outside the family attending. And I'm so happy you're going to be there, Ivy."

"It's important to you?"

"You being there? Of course." Trini has an uncanny way of peering into my thoughts. The way I sometimes can see into hers. "You are coming, aren't you?"

Her big, blue eyes are hopeful and expectant. Maybe this is the right time to tell Trinity the truth.

But which truth do I start with?

The truth that I might be her sister? Or the truth that there is no way this Cinderella is getting to the ball without a bunch of sewing mice and a pumpkin or two. My paycheck is set aside for Aunt Grace's pharmacy fund, and the little I was able to scrape together from selling my old textbooks has all the buying power of a toilet paper wedding dress.

Her brow pinches with worry. I take her hand and squeeze. "Of course, I'll be there."

"Do you need something to wear?" Trinity floats to her closet—the location of her couture collection, aka, the cave of wonders. Even from here, I can tell there is no way my ass is gliding into any of those dresses without a tub of Crisco and three pairs of Spanx.

Trinity moves an armful of gorgeous gowns to the bed. "Try them on."

I give her a warm hug and decline. "It's all right. I've got it," I say because, at this point, I'm so knee-deep in deception, another inch won't drown me. My gaze moves to several shelves in her closet, and I gear up to beg. "But is there any way I could possibly borrow a pair of shoes?"

Trini claps excitedly and rushes me to the Louboutin shelf. "Anything you need."

Because I gaze at a sparkly pair for more than two seconds, Trinity has them on my feet. The stiletto heel is ten feet tall with dainty straps and bright red bottoms. From what I can tell, they've never been worn. When I slide them on, they feel like clouds of heaven under my feet.

"They're...oh...I don't know what to say." I stand, and for half a second, I let myself imagine a different life. Where shoes fit like a glove, and I feel like I belong.

I take several steps. "We wear the same size?"

She nods, and I'm not exactly sure how to feel about that because Trinity is tall and slender, and on her frame, this shoe size is elegant and small. How my Barney Rubble feet fit into them is a mystery, but magically, they do.

"These are great. They complement any outfit. What color is your dress?" she asks while holding a crimson gown against my body. It's beautiful enough to make me want to shoehorn my backside into it.

"The color?" I ask, trying to think fast on my feet. "It's... uh..."

A small ping chimes on my phone. Saved by the bell. I read the message, underwhelmed.

Call me: Now!

"Unbelievable." I show Trinity the message.

"Who is it?" she asks.

"No one I know." I shake my head dismissively. "Possibly the pushiest telemarketer ever."

She scrunches her face. "Why not block them?"

I shake my head. "Because they're like Hydra."

Trinity tilts her head. "Hydra?"

"In Greek mythology, Hydra was a monster. If you chopped off her head, two grew in its place. I'm finding it's the same with telemarketers. Block one, and two return with a vengeance." I scowl at the screen.

Trinity grabs my phone and blocks it for me. "Now you've got your own Hydra."

Or my own sister. Before I ruin them, I wobble out of the shoes. Trinity frowns. "Don't you like them?"

"I love them. But I don't want to break them before the big event."

She grabs a bag from the closet. "Here."

I can't believe what I'm looking at. The bag is bright red with the name CHRISTIAN LOUBOUTIN and PARIS in black letters across the front. "Oh, my God. Your shoes have a bag?"

"No, *your* shoes have a bag. It's called a dust cover, and they're yours." She places the delicate stilettos inside the bag.

Shoes that have a dust cover probably cost more than a refrigerator. I hand them back. "I couldn't."

Her eyes roll with amusement. "Yes, you can. I have another pair. In pink. It'll be our connection during the ceremony."

I blink back, stunned. I'm not sure which is more surprising. That she wants to gift me her exorbitantly expensive pair of shoes or that she wants to connect us like this.

As if we really are sisters.

Emotion overwhelms me, and I make an excuse to go. "It's late."

"Too late to catch up on your studies?" she asks, nudging me with her elbow. "I saw the box of textbooks. Are you enrolled somewhere?"

I shake my head. "Just something I've always been interested in." Not that it matters now. The books are gone.

***

For a long time, I sit on the windowsill alone in my room. The striking pair of high heels sit across from me, asking me what I'm going to do with them. I seat Mr. Whiskers at their tips.

I hug my legs and look longingly at them. "I'd love to take you out, girls, but pairing you with jeans and a T-shirt would be a crime."

Phone in hand, I consider calling Aunt Grace. Maybe she's got something I can wear. There could be couture in her closet, hidden behind stacks of posh velour tracksuits. Besides, there's no way she's letting me near her closet without telling her why, and *why* would lead to a shopping spree. One that neither of us can afford.

My thumb hovers over her number for a second before I give up. A trickle of rain drums against the window as I stare out into the dark.

Somehow, I got it in my head that if I got to know the D'Angelos, and they got to know me, my life would magically fall into place. All my insecurities and doubts would evaporate away. I'd be home.

But I know them, and they know me. So, why are all those feelings still there? I'm on a massive estate with dozens of people roaming about at any given time, and I feel...alone.

What am I saying? I'm not alone. I snatch Mr. Whiskers and hold him in my hand. He's just a toy—but stroking his soft faux fur makes me feel less alone. A shrink would say I need to ditch the security blanket and face my fears head-on.

Screw that. I say, do what feels right. If I want to embrace a harmless childhood indulgence to feel less insignificant, I'm doing it. Freud be damned.

I dot a finger to his nose and flip him to his backside, unzipping his bottom to remove the contents.

The emergency fund I came here with is untouched—for the moment. I unfold the cash. Five hundred dollars. What if Aunt Grace needs more meds? Between a gown for the ball and Aunt Grace's meds, she wins. Every. Single. Time. I tuck the money back into Mr. Whiskers. My priceless photograph is noticeably absent, and I frown and wonder what could've happened to it.

It should be enough that I'm here, even if the photograph is gone. But it was the only image of Antonio D'Angelo with my mother and is the entire reason I'm here. My eyes close, and I try to reimagine it. The dashing Antonio D'Angelo and the cheerful version of my mother. A version I never knew. It's strange to miss something I managed to lose in under a week, but I do.

My furry, little Mr. Whiskers stares back with a persistent

smile, reminding me that I'm a grown-ass woman who cuddles toys for comfort.

But maybe that's the point. I can't change who I am. Fitting into fancy shoes is a world away from fitting in.

I'm amongst the rich and powerful D'Angelos. Titans of the underworld. Rulers of Chicago.

And I am...nobody.

CHAPTER 13
Leo

"Tell me you're fucking kidding." I stare at the two men who are supposed to be watching Ivy. Hunter is still on a break, but these two numb nuts had plenty of time to recoup.

And yet, here they stand, clueless.

I remain calm as irritation bleats hard in my neck. "What do you mean she's gone?"

They fumble with the monitors and bring up the video feed. "According to the schedule, she and Trinity were supposed to be doing yoga out on the north lawn."

I eye them slowly, one and then the other, assessing the situation. I roll my eyes. "You got uncomfortable watching them."

"I have a wife," Evan says.

"And my girlfriend would kill me," the other guy explains. The new guy. What's his name?

I pinch the bridge of my nose as the nameless one yammers on. "It's the downward-facing dog. And the angle of the cameras—"

"Get out." They stare at each other, confused. "Get. Out!" I shout forcefully as I point to the door.

They scurry like mice, and I second-guess myself for not exterminating them on the spot. *I can't be goddamned everywhere.* I rub my temples and remember the tracker in Ivy's car.

I follow the dancing dot. Her car is heading toward the city. "Now, where's Trinity?"

"Right here." Her voice is angelic, and she pokes her head around my office door. "Looking for me?"

"No. I mean yes. I mean—"

"What happened?" she asks with an innocent grin. "Did your men freak out again during downward-facing dog?" Her voice is mischievous and sarcastic. The old Trini. The one we've all missed.

I give her a playful scold. "Yoga is not a weapon."

"Tell that to Evan and Jim." Jim. That's his name.

Trinity takes a chair, the same one Ivy did, and slumps into it in almost the exact same way. I take a passing glance at the monitor. Goodie two-shoes is barely tapping the speed limit, so there's time for me to catch up to her.

I pull up a chair and sit down. "Something on your mind?"

She shrugs. "Maybe I'm making a big deal about nothing."

"I doubt that."

Her lips press to a tight line, and I'm careful not to rush her. The fact that she's talking again is monumental. For all I care, we can baby step through every conversation from here on out. "You can tell me anything."

"I thought Ivy and I were close."

I don't like the sound of that. My hackles tick up. "Did something happen to make you think otherwise?"

She nods. I listen. It takes a few breaths before she continues. "Ivy isn't going to make it."

"Make...what?"

"Make it to *Erede al Trono*."

Our chat. Did I frighten her off? Me and my aggressive foot rub. I duck down to meet Trini's eyes. "Did she say why?"

"No. Just that she wasn't sure she'd be able to go." Trinity hits me with puppy dog eyes the size of dinner plates, and I melt. "Could you—"

"Find out why she's backing out?" I stand, buttoning my blazer. "I'm on it."

CHAPTER 14

Leo

In under half an hour, I've caught up with Ivy. Which wasn't exactly hard, considering she drives a hair below the speed limit, and I enjoy a comfortable cruise at twice the speed.

It's a route she takes often. The pharmacy. She goes there a lot. Her Aunt's house. A candy bar and a fill-up at the local gas station if she's feeling extra adventurous—all courtesy of the D'Angelo fuel card.

As soon as she leaves the pharmacy, I duck inside and head straight to the man in the white coat. "The woman who was just here. Tell me about the prescription she picked up."

"Are you a relative?"

"Yes," I say without hesitation. "I'm her husband."

The pharmacist looks me up and down, skeptical as he raises a brow. "She wasn't wearing a wedding band."

I flash a grin. "I'm going to ignore the fact that you were trolling my wife's finger for a wedding ring." He doesn't move. I pull out two crisp hundred-dollar bills and slide them across the counter.

After looking around the store, he palms the cash. "Can I get the address and the last four digits of the phone number on file?"

Hmm. A trick question. Chances are Ivy isn't picking up meds for herself. There were no meds in Hunter's report, which means no records on her would exist. I recite Aunt Grace's address and phone number from memory.

The pharmacist checks his computer and nods. He recites a name and dosage. The name means nothing, and I stare back blankly. "Heart medication," he says, clarifying.

I consider how often Ivy's dropped by. "Why has Ivy come by so often if there's just the one medication?"

"To pay. She pays a little at a time."

"How much does that cost?"

He punches a few buttons on his keyboard as he checks the computer. "For a full dose once a day? Fifty-five hundred dollars."

"Every two weeks? What are they, laced with cocaine?"

He smirks. "Cocaine would probably be cheaper. It became an issue when her insurance ran out."

"How does insurance *run out*?"

"In her case?" The pharmacist looks around, ensuring no one is in earshot. "I shouldn't be saying this, but Ms. Everly's late husband used to work for Shelby Petroleum. Last year, the company declared bankruptcy. The news said all the employees got a one-time settlement, but their insurance dried up."

I lose my cool. "Are you telling me that this woman is

condemned to a life of figuring out how to pay to keep her heart fucking going?"

His shoulders lift warily. "She was. Until her niece showed up."

Anger simmers below the surface, but I refrain from drawing my gun. "How do you sleep at night?"

"Xanax." He's joking. I deadpan. His hands raise in surrender. "Don't look at me. Blame big pharma. And it doesn't help that Gracie is allergic to everything but air."

I fish out a credit card and hand it to him. He taps it, skeptically. "You sure you want to do that? Gracie's doctor just upped her prescription to twice a day."

CHAPTER 15

Ivy

It's late afternoon, and I'm drained. Mentally. Physically. Financially. The costs of Aunt Grace's meds went from manageable to bankruptcy in less than thirty days. Under the circumstances, my last resort emergency fund is laughable. Is there a way to buy a lotto ticket without paying for it?

Trinity's last text message makes me want to avoid the house. At least for now.

Please come.
You're like family.
xo, T.

The thought of disappointing Trinity is so unbearable, I can't breathe. But I can't fuss over dresses while worrying about Aunt Grace.

And if I ask the D'Angelos for money, they'd never be able to look at me as if I were one of them. As if I were actually their family. I'd be the girl who betrayed their trust while doing it with my hand out.

I stare up at the elegant mansion, suffocating beneath its weight. I don't want to go in. I want to do the impossible. Find answers to every question I have. Weave solutions to every problem I face.

The setting sun gives me an excuse to go for a walk and clear my head.

I can't ask Smoke for a raise. Hell, I just started. But what if I ask for a loan?

Or, what if I tell him who I am? That should go over like a turd floating around his champagne.

I *what if* myself to the far reaches of the property until I reach the maraschino cherry on this nightmare of a day. I am lost.

I search along the tree line, praying I'll recognize anything along the trail. "Where am I?"

As soon as I round the corner and break free of the thicket of trees, my pulse settles down. I'm not lost. I'm on the far end of the property. The back of the mansion is a welcome sight before me. I can just make out my bedroom window from here.

"I'm not arguing about this, Hunter. Swim lessons are out."

Huh?

I hear the deep, familiar growl, and look around. Leo's voice carries over the rustling leaves and wind. He's somewhere behind the overgrowth of trees and shrubs. I shove aside several branches to get a closer look.

It's a house. I stare in awe, realizing the estate is larger than Disneyworld, and it's nothing to have entire houses scattered along the land. I'm not sure why I'm surprised. Hell, a few more yards, and I'd probably trip over a landing strip.

The large cottage of stone and brick stands practically invisible behind the wall of leaves and branches. I watch with keen interest as Leo comes into view, pacing along this side of the porch. As usual, he's yelling into his phone.

Hunter's chuckle blares from the other end. "You said get close."

What the fuck? Leo told Hunter to *get close*? To me?

Why?

"Close enough to get information, Hunter. Not to perform a pap smear." Red-faced, Leo's head looks to be about six seconds from exploding.

Good. Serves him right.

"In the morning, let her know she'll be reporting to me again. I want to keep an eye on her myself."

I don't even know what that's supposed to mean. I lean deeper into the mass of shrubs, listening intently and praying to the Good Lord above that all the pesky spiders are sleeping.

"I'm just fucking with you, boss. I'd never make a move on your girl."

I am not his girl.

"She is not my girl," Leo says in haste. A little too hasty if you ask me. His words set my fuck-off-o-meter to a rolling boil, even if I did say it first—in my head. I'm two seconds away from giving Leo a piece of my mind when I step before I look.

Crack.

The twig I step on breaks, and Leo reaches for his weapon.

I hold my breath and duck.

"I'll call you back," he says in a hushed tone before he disconnects.

Soft footsteps take noticeable strides in my direction. I cover my mouth with both hands and slow my breath to almost a stop. I send silent prayers in the dark. *Please don't let him see me.*

Eavesdropping on the private conversations of a mob enforcer? Dangerous. Realizing he and his henchman are talking about me? Mortifying. In situations like this, death might be the better option over being discovered, and I tighten my body into a ball.

A minute or two later, Leo finally walks away, and the exhale whooshes from my lungs, and I gasp. I'm about to tiptoe away when I notice it. The hole carved out in the center of a shrub.

The one side stares straight at my bedroom. The other side to Leo's house.

Realization hits me like an arrow to the chest. Leo broke up with me only to watch me all this time.

Well, if he wants to spy on my private life, I'll give him something to binge.

CHAPTER 16
Leo

Dear Diary,

My soul is reaching for a star.
Her name is Ivy.

She's beautiful and kind. Always looking out for others before she looks out for herself. She's about to drive herself into financial ruin to save the only mother figure she's known. And still, nothing in the world will stop her.

She loves with all her heart. All I want to do is shove a grenade in mine.

Some of us are destined for love. And some of us are destined for pain.

And some of us will spend the rest of our lives barricaded from what we want.

. . .

T toss my pen down with force and slam shut the book. I don't care what the therapist says. This, ladies and gentlemen, is not helping. If anything, it's chiseling my psychotic thinking right into stone.

I run both hands through my hair, stroll over to the window, and look out and up. Basking in the light of her glow. Seeking all my warmth from her.

She's laughing and happy. A welcome change that could easily brighten every corner of the world.

What's making her so happy? I can't see what she's looking at. Maybe Trinity is in the room. Or maybe she's on her phone.

I grab my binoculars, the sick fuck that I am, and focus the lenses. *Hmmm.* With her phone held high, she snaps a shot. Not a selfie. Of someone else.

She takes a few steps backward, gesturing and directing whoever she's with. When a man steps into view, my arteries go numb.

"Hunter," I growl.

Hunter is laughing along, posing with muscled arms in a wide array of stances while Ivy snaps shot after shot. When they pose for a selfie, I can't breathe.

And when Hunter removes his shirt, I lose my shit entirely. *What. The. FUCK?*

I can't account for how, but in seconds, I am up the hill, in the mansion, and seconds from breaking down Ivy's door.

I struggle on my next move. Do I knock? Kick it in?

I suck in a breath of oxygen and, with it, rational thought. *Stay calm.*

Voices bleed through the door. "Nice tattoos. What else are you taking off, Hunter?" Ivy says, giggling.

I barge through the door. "Get your fucking hands off her!"

Hunter's hands fly high and surrender. "Easy, boss. It's not what you think."

I glare at Hunter murderously. "Out. *Now.*"

He grabs his shirt and rushes past me out the door. I slam it shut. "What the hell are you doing?"

Ivy crosses her arms. "That's none of your business, Leo."

We stare at each other, our gazes locked like horns in the stalemate of the century. It's clear she wants a fight. Funny enough, so do I.

I warn her with a glare. "Starting tomorrow, you work for me again."

Her smile is smooth. "That could be a problem." She leans closer, and that swirl of citrus and vanilla wraps around me like a spell. Her body closes in, and her lips are a whisper away. "What if I don't want to work for you?"

This is the moment a smart man would step away. Instead, I step into her space, pressing the full length of my erection against her soft, small body until her back is against the wall. "It's not your choice."

Her breaths align with mine, and the fire in her eyes is desperate and hungry. The air crackles around us. When she licks her lips, I nearly blow. "What do you want, Leo? Investigating and spying on me... You made it very clear you don't want me, so why bother?"

Why bother? Fantastic fucking question. If I had even one active brain cell I could switch on right now, maybe I'd have an answer. But I don't.

There's nothing I can say to explain. Arousal pumps hard through my body. My fingers strike a match down the bare skin of her arms, and goose bumps pebble in their wake. My large hands wrap around her delicate wrists, moving them behind her back.

I tighten my grip, and she gasps.

My words deliver heat to her ear. "You're playing with fire."

Her body shivers in my hold. "What do you mean?"

"You set this up. Paraded Hunter in front of the window around like a shirtless fucking show dog when you knew I was watching."

Torment flames behind the gaze in her eyes. "If you don't want me, then what does it matter?"

Another question I can't answer. Another slice across my heart that my body begs me not to feel. She's right. It shouldn't matter. But it does.

My forehead rests on hers. Our eyes shut. But my hands don't unlock from around her wrists. "I can't give you what you want, Ivy."

Her words are venom, compelling my body like a curse. "Then give me what I need," she whispers.

My mouth descends on hers, softly at first. Controlled. Our tongues dance in long laps of want and desire. My teeth graze down her neck, nipping her shoulder as my free hand cradles her breast.

"Leo, wait."

I freeze. "Wait? Or stop? There is no waiting, Ivy. Tell me to stop, and I'll leave. Tell me to wait..." I fist her hair and nip the sensitive spot on her neck, causing her to tremble. "And you'll learn that I don't wait."

Her eyes search mine. My little doe in headlights turns speechless. The air crackles, and something shifts between us because now, I know.

I own her.

In a trance, I release her and head to the door. But as soon as my hand touches the handle, instinct takes charge. I don't open the door. I lock it.

"Remove your clothes," I growl. I don't face her. I'm too busy on my phone.

There's surveillance up and down the halls—audio feeds that will pick up every sound from this room. I kill them all.

By the time I turn around, Ivy is stripped down to her bare skin, and the confidence she wears day in and day out is suddenly shrouded in doubt.

I step closer, tilting her chin so her eyes meet mine. My thumb swipes the fullest part of her lower lip. The raw emotions she stirs in me should have died long ago. I should be gentle with her, and treat her with kid gloves. Put her on a pedestal as high as the moon.

But the sooner Ivy gets it through her head that I'm far from her knight in shining armor, the better for both of us. "Where's your phone?"

She glances to the bed.

"I want you on all fours. Place the phone next to you."

She takes timid steps and centers herself on the bed as instructed.

"Unlock it."

"Why?" she asks.

My finger trails the length of her back. Her shiver pleases me, and I rest my palm on her ass. "Because I said to."

She opens the screen.

"How many pictures of Hunter are there?"

"Seven."

"Open the first one." As soon her finger swipes and the image appears, my hand cracks her flesh. "Count."

"One," she murmurs back.

I slice my tongue across her center. Her body shudders, and judging from the moans she releases, her first orgasm should be at around three. Maybe four.

"Next photo," I command, stern as I shed my clothes.

I force two fingers in her center and pump hard. Then, I drag my fingers out and spank her again.

"Two," she sighs without prompting.

By three, I've burrowed three fingers so deep, Ivy shudders, losing control as a freight train of an orgasm takes hold. "Leo," she whimpers.

My dick is angry and hard and has had just about enough. But we're not finished. This time, I give her butt two hard smacks, then rest my thumb at the tight hole of her butt.

Her body tenses. I can tell she's never done this before. Let a depraved man work her body for his sick pleasure. My tongue takes a greedy lick of her soaked pussy as her body rocks against me. And I know with every fiber of my being that there isn't a chance in hell my cock will make it to seven.

Condom on, I lift the head of my shaft to her entrance. I'm an inch into heaven, ready to kick down the gates and fuck my way to oblivion.

With the next inch, her walls grip so hard, I see stars. But it's the next inch that stops me. All I see is Ivy. My girl is in tears.

I kiss her back and drag myself out.

"Don't stop."

"I have to." I flip her around and hold myself above her so she and I are face-to-face. Teary, she turns away. "Look at me," I demand.

Her eyes are slow to reach mine, and I search hers for a long breath. When I see all the broken pieces behind her iron walls and she sees all of mine, she asks, "What are you doing?"

"I'm giving you what you need." A million years ago, I cast my heart away and got used to the emptiness it left behind.

Over and over again, Ivy brings it back to me. Intact and complete.

I kiss her. A long, slow burn of a kiss that tells her all the words I'll never say. Promises and dreams. Hidden secrets and cherished vows. My tongue dances with hers as my body rests between her parted legs. I reposition her calf to my shoulder, kissing her leg as we once again connect. In a single, sweeping move, I thrust. Pull out. Slide in.

Our rhythm is a heartbeat, waves crashing one after the next. There's no her or me.

Nothing exists but *us*.

Another climax takes hold of her, and I wait until she settles before I start again.

Her legs wrap around my back, and my body drives in again.

Hard. Deep. Possessive thrusts that feel so...

Right.

The sounds of wet arousal echoes with our moans. Her eyes roll back, and her body arches. "Leo."

"I'm here, angel." My body is desperate as it pounds in rhythmic time to hers. "I'm right here."

The riptide of orgasms takes us both under, and I pump hard, emptying all that I am deep into her core.

Our breathing evens as our eyes lock.

And without knowing how or why, there's nothing I can do to stop our collision course from happening.

Ivy is mine. And I am hers.

For a long while, we spoon in the dark, our fingers laced. My lips move from her back to her neck to her cheek as I'm soothed to sleep like a drug.

"Leo?"

"Hmm?"

"How did you know what I needed?"

I kiss her shoulder. "Because I needed it, too."

Ivy rolls in my arms so we're face to face. "I need to be more than a one-night-stand."

"I'm definitely counting more than one."

She smacks my chest. "You know what I mean. I need you to open up. Let me in."

"I think you have it backward." I press my erection against her soft body. "You're the one who needs to open up, and let *me* in. You've done it before. I have faith that you can do it again."

The cutest growl emerges from her throat. She frowns. "I need more, Leo."

Even in the darkness, I feel it. Her eyes searching for answers.

Part of me is fucked up and broken beyond repair. The dark, angry, unforgivable part that should've been discarded like litter at the city dump.

I release a heavy sigh and speak a vow I'm not sure I can keep. "I'll give you more."

CHAPTER 17

Ivy

I stretch on the bed as my body begins to wake. Every part of my body is sore and throbbing, and all I want is more. I smile as thoughts of my night with Leo returns. Leo demolished every part of me. But it's a wrecking ball to the gut to find him missing from my bed.

"Leo?"

"Hey," he replies as I turn on the light. His lips twist with barely a smile. His tall frame fills the corner of the room, and I'm irritated that he's already dressed. Pants, shirt, blazer—but not his shoes. Those would be in his hand.

My gut tells me he was hoping to slip out. My head tells me I'm an idiot. And my heart constricts with every beat as if caged in by barbed wire.

Casually, he checks his phone. "I need to get going."

I check the clock. "It's three-thirty."

He slips on one shoe and then the other, busying himself with tying the laces as he speaks. "The brothers are coming today. I need to prepare."

The brothers. How could I forget? I should be worried about meeting the most important men in my life. But in this moment, I'm too upset.

"How convenient," I huff under my breath.

He straightens his jacket. "What's that supposed to mean?"

"Oh, I don't know. A few hours ago, you said I was more than a one-night stand."

He takes a seat on the bed beside me. Arms crossed, I turn away. He pulls me into an unstoppable kiss. "You *are* more than a one-night stand, Ivy."

I roll my eyes.

"Do not roll your eyes at me. The D'Angelo brothers are coming today, and despite the fact that my first duty is to protect them, all I want is to keep them from killing each other. I'm not even kidding. I give it twenty-four hours before all hell breaks loose." He kisses my frown.

I call bullshit and square my shoulders.

He kisses the palm of my hand, and we sit there and stare.

"I don't need a fuck buddy, Leo."

"And I don't need a fight."

"Then go already."

In a huff of frustration, his body overtakes mine as he hops on the bed. Amused, he pins me in place. "Not without another kiss."

"Get off of me."

"Kiss me."

I wriggle, breathless. "Stop steamrolling me, and find a brother to kiss. You'll have plenty to choose from."

Leo eases his weight off by a fraction, holding himself in a pushup so our bodies barely touch. "Better?"

I don't answer.

"Kiss me."

I shove him. Hard.

It's no use. The man is a mountain. He doesn't budge.

"No," I snap. I'm a child having a tantrum, whipping my head to one side, then the other. Desperate, I wriggle hopelessly and try not to giggle. "You were about to leave without saying goodbye. You don't deserve a kiss."

"After wrecking your body with my dick, I wasn't abandoning you. I wanted to let you sleep." Which was actually thoughtful and sweet.

He pecks my neck. Then my chin. Then...my forehead. Anywhere but my lips. "What are you doing?" I ask.

"You had your chance."

"What?"

He nibbles my neck. "Oh, now you want a kiss?"

Leo holds himself up effortlessly as he smirks.

I brush my mouth to his. "Now I want a kiss."

His teeth tug my lower lip. "Then don't make me beg."

We kiss. Soft and slow. His tongue is a tease, coaxing mine to play.

Our kiss deepens, and all my defenses float away like fog under the sun.

"Fuck," he groans. "If I don't head out now, I'm not leaving. And if I don't leave, it'll be World War fucking III. We have preparations to finish, and the logistics are a nightmare."

Abruptly, I release him. "Then, go."

He sits up. "Fine."

"Okay."

"I will."

His smile is devilish as he inches the sheet from the bed. "But I can't leave before breakfast."

Impatient, he snaps back the covers. I giggle as his firm grip spreads my knees. His stubble burns as he nibbles his way up my thigh.

I inhale sharply as I clutch his hair "What happened to World War fucking III?"

His tongue flicks my clit. "It can wait."

CHAPTER 18

Leo

The weeks of prep work should have prepared us for anything. Apparently, anything didn't include me.

Six of my men ribbed me on my tardiness, and Smoke commented on my goofy grin. And you know what? I don't care. Every muscle in my body is sore and strained and aching for more of the Ivy Palmer triathlon.

I head to the kitchen, eager for a shot of caffeine and a snack. Despite the satisfaction of breakfast between Ivy's legs, I'm famished.

With coffee poured and bagel in hand, I know my minute's worth of peace won't last. The phone tickles the pocket of my blazer, and I look at the screen. It's the counterfeiter. I mean, photo restorationist.

I've had them checking out that image to see if there's anything we can salvage before I share it with Smoke. Every photo of his father is priceless. And I want to know what I'm dealing with before I reach for a grenade and pull out the pin.

"Hello."

"Hey, Z. We're almost done with the photo you sent us."

"Great. How does it look?"

"Not bad, considering someone ran it over with an ATV."

I wince at the comment. As luck would have it, it was *my* ATV that ran over it the night Trinity disappeared. "And after your restoration?"

"Like it was just printed yesterday."

I sigh in relief. "I thought it might be gone forever."

"Not forever, but we'll need it a little longer."

"Why?"

"There's some writing on the back we're trying to rescue."

"Is that hard?"

"Pen ink and photo printing are totally different. The work is a lot more delicate. It might take another day or two, but you'll have it soon. I can text you the image now if you'd like. We'll keep working on the back."

"Sounds great."

The call is ended as the text comes through. The image is unfamiliar. Funny, I thought I'd seen every image of Antonio there ever was. Committed them to memory. The man was like a father to me. Or as close as anyone has ever come to taking on that title.

He's in his usual suit and tie. A woman standing next to him is well dressed and at a professional distance. Perhaps she was from one of the committees. Antonio was a workaholic, but his wife loved the arts.

I study the woman closer. Her cherub cheeks and bright red lips are the perfect complement to her ebony skin. I know I've never seen this woman before, though something about her seems familiar. Probably some socialite that, at one point or another, ran with the D'Angelos.

I expand the shot and take a closer look. The glint in Antonio's eyes radiates even back then. His trademark silver patch is less prominent than I recall, and something about it calls to me. For a moment, I succumb to my memories, lost deep in thought.

"Coffee smells good," Hunter says, breezing through the door and fixing a cup. The dead man walking elevates my pulse to pounding. I tear another bite from my bagel. Eyes narrowed, I chew.

He fixes a cup and takes a seat beside me. "So?" he asks with keen interest.

"So...?" I ask back, imagining him in a chokehold.

"How'd she like it?"

I drop the bagel with a thud, then clasp my hands. "How'd she like...what?"

He scoots closer, checking the door so no one hears. Fear not, Hunter. The only one who'll hear your screams will be me.

"The pictures?" he asks low. "How did she like the pictures?"

I stare hard, dumbfounded at the death wish in his eyes. Hunter is a lethal mercenary. A former SEAL. Easily one of the sharpest tools in the shed. Today, the man beside me is straight-up suicidal.

I take a long, slow sip of my coffee, surprised he isn't as attached to his fingernails as I thought he'd be. A deadly smile lifts my face. As if he can read my thoughts, he backs away.

"Something wrong?" he asks, clueless.

"So, you want to know what she thinks of your photos?"

My cell dances on the table. "Hello," I snap. Hunter rushes from the room before I can gauge the size of his noose.

"It's starting," Smoke says, ominous and perturbed.

I dump the coffee down the drain and head out. "Let me guess. Enzo."

"The one and only." Even without seeing Smoke, I know that big, ugly vein in his forehead is about to blow.

I launch a preemptive strike. "I've got it." The call disconnects.

No one manages to get under Smoke's skin the way Enzo does. Smoke is the oldest. That comes with certain privileges, like being next in line—a royal Italian family passing down the crown. He could've also taken D'Angelo Holdings, but he didn't. Instead, he tied it in a bow and handed it to Enzo.

You'd think Enzo would be grateful. Instead, everyone knows Enzo will challenge Smoke for the coveted *Erede al Trono*. There's an old saying that power corrupts, and absolute power corrupts absolutely. With Enzo, absolute power corrupts absolutely everything. So, unless we want the D'Angelo estate to become a drug-peddling whore house with a private entry for Beelzebub himself, it's best for all that Smoke keeps his controlling interests and Enzo stays far, far away.

When I step into the foyer, Enzo is already there. All six-foot-three of him is dressed in Armani with a stance so rigid, the stick up his ass must be made of rebar. As usual, he scans the property, eager to mark his territory and piss on all he surveys.

"Z.," he says with enthusiasm. "Take my bags, will you? I'll be staying in the east wing." And just like that, Enzo's balls grow bigger than his ego.

I grab the nearest two suitcases. They're weighty, and I

wouldn't put it past Enzo for these to be stuffed with body parts from his victims. Smiling, I carry them out the front door. "Bad news. One, the east wing is occupied. By Smoke. A fact I'm sure you're aware of. And two, for safety's sake, you'll be bunking with me in the little cottage on the north side of the estate."

"You can't seriously expect me to stay in that hovel."

I shrug with a wide, obnoxious grin.

"That's absurd. The mansion has plenty of space."

"Oh, it's not a math problem. It's a safety problem. It's sort of like when the president and the vice president never fly on the same aircraft. We need to keep you and Smoke as separated as possible." I drop the suitcases in the back of the waiting van and graciously open the passenger door. "It's for your own protection."

"Careful, Z. Bunking with me can be detrimental to your health. Try sleeping with one eye open. I tend to sleep stab. It's a medical condition."

"I'm not worried at all. And word to the wise. Never bring a knife to a gunfight." Once he's seated, I shut the door and remind myself the entire arrangement is temporary.

Enzo lights a cigar, determined to fuck up the new leather interior with the strong scent of Cohibas. I rub the migraine from the bridge of my nose.

It's going to be a long fucking week.

CHAPTER 19
Leo

It's late. I should be focused on about a million other things, but Ivy curls around my mind like a vine. I now understand the reason for Grace's nickname.

The woman has me by the balls and doesn't even know it. That little stunt with Hunter earned her a punishment. A punishment I knew she'd enjoy. One *I* enjoyed.

That's the thing with her and I. The very fiber of my being always knows exactly what she needs. Our connection shouldn't make sense, but it does.

I'm always ready for combat. Quick to react. Suspicious of everyone. Ready for the kill.

And then, there's Ivy. Too trusting for her own good. Kind and generous, even when it's to her own detriment. Checking in on my humanity isn't exactly on my bucket list. Ivy, on the other hand, cares so much for others, I imagine she's a hop, skip, and jump from selling her own blood to get the necessary meds for Grace.

Ivy is the embodiment of good, and I am the antithesis. If opposites attract, we must be a super magnet.

For hours, I've stared at the computer screen and accomplished nothing. I'd rather be watching over my girl.

From my office, I can see Ivy curled up in the window seat, reading. The book is big and thick and looks like a textbook. Didn't she pawn all her books?

It's late, and she's probably winding down. I don't know what comes over me, but before I know it, my cell is in my hand, thumb on her number. I watch from my window, interest piqued as she stares at her phone, motionless. Answer it already. Is she seriously thinking about it?

After the third ring, and seconds from going to voicemail, she gives in, smiles, and picks up. "Hello?" she answers as if she has no idea who I am.

"You took your time answering the phone."

"You took your time calling me." She's got me there. "A little past your bedtime, isn't it?" Her voice is angelic as she yawns through a stretch.

My cock throbs to attention. "I had a hunch you might be up."

Ivy wiggles her fingers out the window, waving hello. She knows full well I can see everything she's doing. "I couldn't sleep, either."

"I guess it's a shame neither of us drinks."

"Yes. A shame." She makes herself comfortable, settling back on the window seat and picking up her book. "Reading helps," she offers.

"You don't say. What are you reading?" She holds the book up to the window. "My vision isn't bionic."

"Don't pretend you don't have binoculars at the ready."

Binoculars in hand, I focus and read the title aloud. "*Trust after Trauma: Breaking Down Barriers and Building Relationships*. So, you enjoy a little light reading on a Saturday night." I guess she got her books back.

I turn the knob and amplify the magnification. What's that little tag at the bottom of the spine? I magnify it more. What are those? Numbers? *616.852.*

A library book.

I watch as she shrugs. "Did you know distrust is a self-defense mechanism?"

"Why do I feel like you're about to shrink my brain?"

She giggles. "Like with a ray gun?"

"Something like that."

"Wrong, Mr. Zamparelli." She rolls her Rs. God, that's a turn on. "I'm going to dissect your beautiful mind, one invasive question at a time. Bwahahahaha." Her laugh is diabolical. And fun. And after the day I had, I'm up for a little fun.

But not for free. "Well, Ms. Palmer, if I'm about to become your guinea pig, I'm going to need something in return."

"Mm-hmm," she replies, scandal lacing her tone.

"Not sex."

"Boo," she scoffs with a frown.

"Here's how this works, Dr. Palmer. Ask me anything. I'll respond. Truthfully. Honestly."

"Completely?" she asks with a tone of skepticism.

I don't answer. And not because I don't want to answer period, but because I don't want to lie to Ivy. Not now. Still, I push back. "Completely could take weeks. Maybe months."

"Maybe years," she replies, holding up a pen and a fresh notebook. "Fine. We'll stick with truthfully and honestly."

"And once I've answered your questions, you'll answer mine. Do we have a deal?"

"Deal," she says with enough enthusiasm, my heart flips in my chest. It's been years since I've been nervous. A wave of flutters run through my gut. Ivy does this to me, and I kind of like it.

She begins. Her first question blindsides me so hard, I choke. "What was your wife like?"

I take a deep breath in, releasing it in a slow stagger of thought. I don't discuss Lori. But with the length of two football fields between us and the genuine curiosity in her voice, the cinder blocks of my defenses fade away.

"What was Lori like?" I start the way all snowballs start. Slow and steady. "Where do I begin? Lori was fun. Full of life. She never took anything too seriously. Never needed much. Life with her was as carefree as it was calm." I pause for a long stretch. Ivy gives me all the time I need. "I loved her with all my heart."

I'm sure Ivy can hear the sadness in my voice. "Leo, I'm sorry. We don't have to—"

"It's okay." And surprisingly, it is. Somehow, I always thought speaking her name would feel like my soul would turn to ash from the pain of a white-hot flame.

I'm still here.

I do something stupid and brave and something I haven't done in years. I pull up pictures of Lori. Happy ones. The ones that hurt the most.

If Ivy would just say one word, it would be enough of a speedbump for me to stop talking. And part of me thinks I should stop talking. But with Ivy quiet and patient, my thoughts have nowhere to hide. Ivy is a great listener. And I'm a shredded human being trying to shoulder a lot of messed up shit.

I keep going. "The worst part about losing someone you love is that most people don't understand. It's not something you get over or move on from. It's a hole. A big, gaping hole in your life that you can work around or try to hide, but it never goes away."

I pause. She says what they all say. "Go on."

The momentum releases with a force I can't stop. "Every once in a while, you trip and fall through it, and for a second, all the pain, all the sorrow, all the fucked up thoughts are gone because for one fleeting moment, you forget. You forget they're gone. And when you realize it again, it's like filling the hole with kerosene and lighting a match. The pain never goes away. It's just not burning me every second of every day." When the splash hits the face of my phone, I wipe it off, only then realizing I'm crying. I kill the photos and the torturous stroll down memory lane. The phone feels like a rock in my hand, and I nearly hurl it against the wall. But then, I hear it.

Traces of a sound through the phone. I raise my binoculars until Ivy is in view. She's covering her face. She's crying, too.

I clear my throat and move us along. "All right, Ms. Palmer. Your turn."

She sniffs and grabs a tissue. "Yes. My turn." Her voice chippers up. "Ask me anything."

There are so many questions I could ask in this moment.

But there's one I need the answer to, and only she can give it to me. "Why are you paying for Aunt Grace's prescriptions? Your payment plan in insane. There's no way you can keep up."

"How do you know about that?"

"It's my job," I say flatly. I know that won't fly. "I know a lot about you, Ivy. Some from investigating. Some from your Aunt Grace. Some from just paying attention to all the things that lift you up and drag you down. I know that you do the things you do. But all the investigating in the world will never tell me why."

"Because I love her."

"You love her enough to give up your entire paycheck."

"She loved me enough to give up hers." Ivy is quiet. I give her all the time she needs to open up. And I sit there and listen. "She and Uncle Jerry gave up their life's savings for me."

I say nothing. I know exactly what she's talking about but pretend I don't. "Oh?"

"Aunt Grace tried to adopt me years ago. My mother strung her along forever. It was the entire reason she and Uncle Jerry moved to Chicago. Found a great job where they could rebuild their nest egg. And they needed the benefits."

"Her health insurance." I take another breath. "That wasn't your fault."

"And I don't feel indebted, Leo. I feel...loved. There's no other way to say it. Why do you do what you do? Give up your nights and weekends...your life for the D'Angelos? Isn't it for love?"

"Ivy, I—" It's then that I look up and realize I'm not alone. I catch the long tail of Enzo's shadow lurking from the hall.

"I'm here for you, Leo. You can talk to me about anything. Even about your wife."

Ivy's paddling out to me in a life raft at the worst possible time. I have no options. There's only one thing to say. "I have to go." I don't let her get another word in. I disconnect before Enzo gathers any more ammunition. "You need something?" I ask.

Enzo leans on the door, studying me. I shut the drapes. Who knows how long the nosy fuck has been listening? "Just getting a nightcap." He swirls a glass of whiskey in the air.

His stare is unnerving. "What?" I snap.

"You were...smiling." He makes a sour face.

"So?"

"You never smile."

"Maybe it's just you. You tend to bring out the worst in people."

He makes himself comfortable, sitting at the desk and rummaging through the contents. None of what's in there is mine, so I shouldn't care. Still, I make a mental note to wipe his pillowcase with my ass later. Just because. "Looking for anything in particular?"

"Who's Ivy?" I hate the way he says her name. As if she's a long trail of honey he's dying to lick. It makes me want to take a nail gun to his tongue.

"She's Trinity's caretaker," I reply, apathetic and unconcerned.

He cocks his head. "Since when did Trinity get a caretaker?"

I shake my head, staring him down like the idiot he is. "Weeks ago. If you'd bother checking in on her more than once every millennium, you'd know more about the life of your little sister."

He waves his hand, bored. "That's Smoke's job." The table at the end of the room holding a chessboard grabs his attention. With a single finger, he summons me, inviting me to play as he slides a pawn to the next square. "I hear you'll be at Smoke's side at *Erede al Trono*."

I move my own pawn. "And?"

"That's quite the honor—for one who isn't family." I say nothing, and he makes another move. With free access, I scoot a bishop across the board. The pieces flow quickly. Enzo is skilled at chess. Bummer for him, I'm better.

Locking his queen in under eight moves, I let him stew over the board while I talk. "I know this will come as a shock to you, Enzo, but Smoke genuinely likes me. We're friends. This isn't just a role for his chief of security. Being by his side is an honor."

"So, you're not here to block my takeover of the estate?"

I clasp my hands. "Smoke's my best friend. I'll be there to support him as he accepts the honor of a dozen generations of D'Angelos." I lean in. "Cock blocking you is just icing on the cake."

Enzo snags my bishop, pointing it at me. "Careful, Z. I own half of Chicago and have a massive stake in the free world. From toy shops to tank manufacturers and all the little commodities in between." He knocks over my pawn, giving his bishop room for the space. "Bad things happen to men who stand in my way."

I stand with a finger on my queen. I warn him with a glare. "Is that supposed to scare me? Here's something for you to remember. When all hell breaks loose, I'm the son of a bitch who reassembles it. You don't have to threaten me. I'm here to cover the asses of all the D'Angelos. Even yours."

I flick my queen over, sacrificing her to make a point. Enzo stands her back up. "We're not finished." His grin is convincing. The fucker thrives on this shit.

"I am." I say nothing else and simply walk away.

CHAPTER 20

Ivy

Before the crack of dawn, I'm in the kitchen, deflated to see Leo's mug emptied and sitting in the sink. It's four-thirty in the morning, and I somehow managed to miss him.

Last night, I pushed too hard. Pried my way into his own private pandora's box—a part of his life he wasn't ready to put on display. I want to make it right. Prove to Leo I won't push my way into his life ... by pushing my way into his life at four-thirty in the morning.

Solid plan.

"Hello." The voice is deep and low and catches me off guard. When I turn, his face is unmistakable. He looks so much like Antonio, I nearly choke up. The only thing missing is the streak of silver across his hair.

"You must be Dante," I say and extend my hand. My decision to wear a plain blouse and flowy skirt pay off. I can meet with each and every one of them confidently. I try being graceful as I meet a man who might be my brother. "I'm Ivy."

"Ivy. Right." He rubs his chin. "Trinity's miracle worker."

The reference stuns me. Is that what they're calling me? "I really didn't do anything at all. Just tried to be there for her. Though I did help her rescue a baby swan."

Dante offers me my choice of pastry first. I grab my usual bagel. He opts for a blueberry bran muffin, popping it in the microwave. I slide him the butter, which he readily accepts.

He smiles that dazzling smile, and asks, "Did Trinity really name the swan Fluffer?"

My eyes widen in shock. "Oh, my God. No. Fluff. Not fluffer. Fluff is an adorable swan that still follows Trini around the lake like she's on a leash."

"And a fluffer is an occupation in the porn industry," he says with a beam. I get why his nickname is the Devil.

I smack him playfully on the shoulder, and instantly regret it. Dante's not my friend. He's a D'Angelo. Who has no idea I might be his sister, and is probably unaccustomed to being smacked around by the hired help.

He arches a brow. I shrink and apologize profusely. "I am so sorry. I didn't mean to—"

He tops off my coffee before pouring one for himself, and laughs. "It's okay. Don't worry, you didn't hit my bad arm."

"Your bad arm?"

"Yup. Trini socked me so hard this morning, it's definitely leaving a mark."

I smile into my mug. "If Trini socked you in the arm, you must have done something to deserve it."

"I might have made fun of her for her latest romance novel. Seriously, who reads that stuff? And why can't the men afford any shirts? Aren't they supposed to be billionaires?" He laughs a wicked laugh, and I have to compare it to Smoke's. Their laughs are joyous, but different. Which one of them laughs like our father?

Dante slathers butter over half of the steamy muffin, biting in as it melts. He stares as he chews. So much so, I'm uncomfortable.

"You're staring," I point out.

"Sorry." He glances away, then slowly circles back to stare at me again. "Do I know you?" he asks.

I study him back. He's a little too Henry Cavill for me not to remember. I shake my head. "I don't think so. I moved here from North Carolina a few weeks back."

"Oh," he says as he takes another bite.

I know time with the brothers—*my* brothers—will be fleeting, so I make the most of it. "What was it like? Growing up here?"

He thinks over my question as a warm, reflective smile reaches his eyes. "Loud. Competitive. The type of home where everybody knows everyone's shit, and the only reasonable privacy was taking your time in the bathroom."

"It sounds like heaven."

"Spoken like an only child."

"Guilty," I reply, slipping my hair behind an ear as my southern accent tries to make its way out. Dante finishes off his coffee and stares. "What?"

Whatever he was thinking, he shakes from his mind. "Just something about you is familiar." He studies my features for way too long. "I'm sure I've seen you somewhere."

I shrug. Maybe our paths have crossed. "I go into Chicago twice a week. Where do you work?"

"Here and there." His evasiveness isn't exactly helpful. Two buzzes light up his phone. He stands. "Enzo's on the rampage."

Worried, I ask, "What does he want?"

"Other than to make all our lives a living hell, who knows? Could be anything from fancy mineral water flown in fresh from the Alps to a string of sushi girls and hookers." He faces me, flashing what I've come to know as the D'Angelo smile. "It was very nice to meet you. And never change that."

"Change what?"

He points to the silver strands I've been subconsciously twirling around my finger. "Your Mallen streak. Our father had one, too."

He leaves the room, and the nerves I swallow land heavy in my gut. I can't keep hiding who I am, and not telling them who I might be is feeling more and more like a lie.

There's one person—the only person—who would believe I'm not some random gold digger after the D'Angelo fortune. I was only trying to find my father.

Trinity would believe that.

Trinity has come so far, so fast. Dressing in gowns. Chatting up a storm. Kickboxing her brothers. The fragile girl I was afraid to disturb isn't frail like she was. There's nothing stopping me from unloading this secret on the one person I'm closest to.

I round the corner, ready to climb the stairs when a small sound stops me. *What is that?*

The muffled whimpers grow louder as I check under the stairs. Is someone crying?

The winding staircase is grand, and I tiptoe around to check the alcove beneath it. Trinity has her knees against her chest, clinging to them as she weeps.

I kneel beside her, resting a gentle hand on hers. "Trini?"

She doesn't look up, but her hand latches on to mine. "Something's wrong with me," she says, staggering her words through a sea of tears.

My arms wrap tight around her. "I'm here. You're safe." I kiss her head and chase away every demon determined to steal her back to hell. Cold sweat drips from her neck, and the long scar along her wrist reminds me why I hadn't told her yet. I steel my voice. "There is nothing wrong with you," I insist. My words are strong and determined even as I fight back my own flood of tears.

Maybe I'll never know my father, but as far as the world is concerned, Antonio is gone. I'll be damned if I'm losing Trinity, too. Trinity is my sister. Case closed. God put me on this path for a reason. It wasn't to right the wrongs of my life. It was to right the wrongs of hers.

Her sobs settle into short pulses of breath. "I can't remember everything..."

I don't speak or ask any questions. Compassionately, attentively, I listen.

"But I remember little things. Smells. Cologne—or aftershave—a horrible...musk." Her breath fragments into hard, choppy pants as if she's about to throw up. Anger drives her words. "Why the hell can't I get over it?"

"You're safe," I assure her. "I'm here. I'll always be here for you."

Her trembles subside, and we sit for a long stretch, waiting

169

out the storm. Timid words break through her torment. "Have you ever held on to something, where the harder you squeeze, the faster it slips away? Like a cloud. One minute, it feels so close. But the next minute, it's suffocating me, and I can't see how to get out." Her eyes slam shut. "I can't see. I can't breathe."

"*Shhh*. You can breathe, Trinity." I suck in a deep breath, encouraging her to do the same. She does. "Now, let it out." We both blow it out.

We breathe as she wades through the darkness of her thoughts. My hand clasps hers like a tether. A lifeline.

A shadow moves along the floor. Leo. How long has he been silently keeping watch?

Trinity sits up, wiping her sad face as she gains her composure. "My brothers can't see me like this."

I reassure her. "They won't. Leo can help. His security team will check the halls and get you back to your room without them seeing." She understands and nods.

From where Leo stands, he must have heard me. Still, he waits until I wave him over, careful in his approach. Leo lifts her like cradling a wounded bird, carrying her through the halls and settling her in her room.

He sets her on the bed and moves past me. Then, with phantom steps, he's gone.

Is this the real Leo? Caring and loving one minute, detached and isolated the next.

It's mid-morning when Trinity falls asleep. I hope she can rest. In a few hours, I'll check in on her and bring her some lunch.

I slip out the door and into the hall. Leo is there. His strong arms wrap around me as he lays a kiss on my head. "How is she?"

"Resting. I'll check on her in a little while." He turns to face away. He's worried. "You could visit her later," I offer, hoping it will lift his spirits.

He shakes his head with regret. "I can't."

"Why?" He's been waiting outside her door for nearly two hours. He must want to see her.

"Because I'm here to protect her. When I see her like this —" He cuts himself off. With a long exhale, all his emotions are erased. "My feelings do me no good, Ivy. And I can't see her right now without feeling them. I can't keep her close and keep her safe at the same time."

What does he mean? "Aren't those one and the same?"

"No." His tone sharpens. "You don't get it. Either I'm a man who feels, or I'm a man who fights, but I can't be both. The D'Angelos need my protection. You're here to hold her hand. I'm here to hunt down anyone with a clue about what happened to her and drive shards of bamboo under their fingernails until they crack. And I can't do that unless I'm numb."

His hard expression melts to regret. He drags a hand down his face, and stares at his hand.

"Leo?"

Nothing.

He moves to leave. I block his path. He stares past me, rage building behind his eyes. "I need to leave. Now."

"Not until you talk to me." I wrap a hand around his.

He knocks it away so hard, I fall against a small table. A tall crystal vase topples with an ear-splitting crash as it shatters. "Don't move," Leo demands, his tone dark and hard.

I do as he says, keeping my body perfectly still as my head drops. A million tiny chips of light have splintered at my bare feet. There's blood. Hardly any, really, but enough to make a mess. "I can clean this up."

"Get Morris and Greer," he barks down the hall. "And get Smoke."

"Smoke? Why?" Jesus, does he have to make this a federal case? "It's fine. I saw a broom downstairs." Leo ignores me. In seconds, he hoists me high to his chest and cradles me tight.

Morris and Greer rush past us and tend to the mess. Leo charges in the direction of my room.

"Leo, stop."

His steps hasten.

"Your men aren't janitors. I can clean it."

More angry steps. I try to wriggle from his hold. It does no good. King Kong has a stronghold on me, whether I like it or not. My tone softens. "We're clear of the glass, Leo. I can walk."

Annoyed, he keeps going. "It isn't glass. It's vintage Baccarat."

"*Bah-cah-rah*," I repeat the pricey sounding word. "Sounds French. Is it expensive?"

"It's 33-percent fucking lead, that's what it is." He kicks in my door and enters my room. A new wave of anger crashes down harder than before. "Is this what you want, Ivy? A man who's cursed?" I'm set down on the side of the bed. "You need to move on."

Leo isn't pushing me aside for his job. He's shutting me out. Again. It's clear as *bah-cah-rah* that whatever we have between us isn't going anywhere. Or it should be.

I should back off and give him his space. But I am so over this. Outraged, I poke him in the chest. "Stop being a martyr."

His eyes bulge. That sets him off. "Stop acting as if we're more than a few one-night fucks, because we're not."

We stare for a long, breathless beat. A rap sounds at the door, and I bite back the tears. Smoke enters carrying a first aid kit and glances at the shattered door frame. He quickly scans me on the bed. Did he hear us? Does he know I'm half a second from disintegrating? The crease in his brow tells me just how unsettled he is. He smoothes it out, and addresses Leo. "You called for a doctor?"

"I broke Aunt Angelica's vase," he lies. Another martyr move that pisses me off.

"The door looks like your handiwork, too," Smoke says, patronizing him.

Leo yanks Smoke into the hall. I strain to listen. "There are crystal daggers lodged up and down Ivy's legs." Leo's voice is tense. It's only then that I notice the red specks up and down my legs. I usually wear jeans, but I wanted something nicer. Something to impress the brothers—possibly my brothers. *The one day a month I choose to wear a skirt ...*

With a few tissues from the nightstand, I blot them up.

"Do we need poison control?" Leo hushes.

Smoke tells him what I already knew. "She doesn't have lead poisoning, Leo."

"How do you know?"

"Because unless you crushed up the entire vase and fed it to her, lead poisoning is out."

Leo peers around the door to look at my legs. I dart him a *go-fuck-yourself* glare. And since his voice carries, the panic in his voice carries with it. "She's lost some blood."

I dab a few more spots—the dumbass has no idea I'd need to lose about a hundred times more to rival the first day of my period. "I'm fine, Leo," I shout.

Smoke enters and observes me, underwhelmed. "She looks fine."

I rub the tissue against a spot that's starting to pool. "Shit," I hiss, wincing. *That one stings.* Blotting it harder just makes it worse. I snag a few more tissues and hold them in place.

Leo looks at me, then my legs, and then at Smoke. When I think his simmer is about to cool, his head explodes. "She's injured. You're a doctor. Fix her!" he shouts before storming off.

"Fix her," Smoke repeats under his breath before striding over to me. "I love how that fucker thinks I work for him." He inhales, exhales, and pastes on a smile. "Hey, Ivy. How about I fix you?" He kneels before me and assesses my injuries—as microscopic as they are.

Mortified, I wave him back. "You don't have to—"

He sorts through his first aid kit, too busy to look up. "Yes, I do. Otherwise, I've got apeshit Leo to deal with the rest of the day." He zeroes in on the tissue I've glued to my shin. "Move that for a second." Carefully, I do. The bleeding is slight, but steady. He grabs tweezers from the kit. "Hold still."

My nerves get the better of me, and I ask a question I feel foolish asking. "Are you really a doctor?"

His smile lifts wryly. "I am."

He is? Why isn't he practicing? Did something happen? He steadies the tweezers, clamping on an invisible particle only he can see. It doesn't hurt at all until he dabs it with an alcohol wipe. "Ow." I hiss in pain. In an odd big-brotherly sort of way, he blows. The cool air soothes the cut instantly. "Better?" he asks.

I nod and smile, suddenly shy. What would it have been like having a brother? Someone like Smoke to share birthdays and holidays with. Talk about nothing for hours and glean nuggets of wisdom from his brotherly advice. Someone to lean on when life bears all its weight on you, and the bridge you've become threatens to snap.

I shake away the fantasy as my senses kick in. I have to tell him the truth. "I'm really sorry about the vase. Leo didn't break it. I did." He says nothing and sticks a small bandage to the cut. He gathers the first aid kit together, tosses a few items along with my tissue into the trash, and stands.

He studies me with tempered amusement. "Interesting."

"What is?"

"Leo says he broke the vase. Then, you do." He leans in. "Who should I believe?"

What do I say? His chief of security is a logical choice. Trustworthy, too. Smoke's Catch-22 doesn't escape me. It pins all the blame on Leo, and that's not exactly fair. Or true. At least, not entirely true.

And if I say me, well, I'm stuck paying for a demolished vase that would eat up my paychecks for months. Maybe longer. And what happens to Aunt Grace?

I have to do the right thing. My wallet cringes. I look up,

hoping he'll take pity on me for my good deed. "I wouldn't let him through." I leave out the part about me pushing him—again—because I'm determined to crack open my nutty guy with a sledgehammer.

"Maybe I could work out a payment plan?" I add. A really long payment plan with zero interest and lots of leniency for late payments. Not exactly what the mob is known for, but a girl can dream.

He pinches the bridge of his nose. "How about we make a deal?"

"Deal?" I ask, my throat suddenly dry. How very mafioso. I sport a clipped smile. He's giving me an offer I can't refuse. Literally.

"Come to *Erede al Trono*. Trini said you wanted to back out. If you come, we'll call it even." He isn't waiting for my reply—it's not a choice.

I nod meekly. I haven't told him the truth. Never mind that the gown I arrive in might be a flowy result of six rolls of toilet paper held together by dental floss and super glue. At least Aunt Grace's meds are intact.

"Deal?" he asks, his hand extended.

I clasp his, grateful we're not doing a blood oath. "Deal."

His chin points to the door. "I haven't seen Leo this unhinged in a long time. You seem to stir up a lot in him, Ivy."

I fiddle with my fingers. "My aunt always says, 'Kick up enough dust, you get a tornado.'"

He cracks a grin. "I like that. We Italians have a saying too. *Niente che valga la pena di avere è facile*." I tilt my head inquisitively. "Translation: nothing worth having comes easy." His hand lands soft on my shoulder. "He cares about you, Ivy. He just has a piss poor way of showing it." He taps my nose. I can't help but smile.

He walks away, and I'm left with a heart full of hope and the first brotherly advice of my life.

CHAPTER 21
Leo

Dear Diary,

I am an asshole.
The end.

I thump the pen against the page, disgusted with myself. I was brutal to her. Deliberately brutal. Ivy deserves to be swept off her feet. Arm in arm with a man who makes her feel fulfilled, content, and breathtakingly—

Happy.

I want her to be happy. Her life should be romantic dinners and roses, with a man who will cherish her to the ends of eternity. Ivy deserves to be loved.

And I don't.

"Goddammit!" I scream, slamming the worthless journal against the wall, knocking over a small Van Gogh, or Monet, or, whoever the fuck artist it is. Because today is the day I break all Smoke's shit. A knock sounds at the door. "Fuck off, Enzo."

A tiny voice calls out. "It's not Enzo." I whip around. It's Trinity. I run a hand through my hair, straightening it. She inches her way into the room, carrying a container in her hands. What's she doing here? "Enzo's out."

"I know. They're all having dinner." She hands me a heavy dish. "I thought you might be hungry."

Tuscan chicken. My favorite. I force a grateful smile and accept it, but I'm too forlorn to eat. "It looks wonderful."

"Ivy made it. She wanted to try her hand at making a big meal for everyone." Trini makes herself comfortable. "She didn't eat much."

I frown. I know I could make this right. Beg for her forgiveness. Be there for her. Cherish her. Worship her.

Then...what?

It'll only prolong the inevitable. I can't—*won't*—chain her to me. It doesn't matter how I feel about her. The thought of losing her wipes the fucking air from my lungs. But Ivy needs a man who...who isn't cursed. Bad things happen to the people I love. End of story.

"I wanted to thank you," Trinity continues. "For today. And every day, Leo. I hate being a burden."

"Whoa—" I set down the food and take both her hands in mine. Like I've done since she was a foot shorter and still in braces. "Listen to me, Trinity D'Angelo. Not now nor ever have you been a burden." She rolls her eyes. "Did you just roll your eyes at me?"

"I heard what you said."

"When?"

"When you thought I was sleeping. All that stuff you said in the hall. To Ivy."

Shit. I stand there and think hard. What did she hear? Fuck, I wasn't exactly whispering. She could've heard anything. Emotional vomiting at its finest. "I don't care what you heard, you're my responsibility to protect. Not a burden." I look her in the eyes to make sure she hears every word of this. "Protecting you and the rest of the family is a privilege. An honor. A promise that I'll continue to keep until my dying day."

"Ugh," she growls, flustered. "Stop giving up your life for us, Leo."

I laugh it off. "I'm not."

"Do you love her?" Trinity asks, her big blue eyes full of pink hearts and cupid arrows.

I start to say no, but the two-letter word dries up in my throat. I'm not even sure why except that it feels like...a lie.

The thing is, I can't lie to Trini. This, coming from me—the king of bullshit. Trini could always read me. She's got some Wonder Woman superpower over me. She always has since she was a girl.

I think over the question again. Do I love her?

Fuck, do I?

Nerve-struck, I rub my neck. *Is that sweat?* And they say *I'm* an interrogator. Microseconds tick by. The less I say, the more I'm fucked.

Trinity's smile widens. I half-expect her to tell me she's picked out a church and has a caterer for the cake. "Can't answer?" she taunts. "How about this? You're fired."

"What?" I scoff, laughing. "Did you just fire me?" My

laughter cuts short. Wait. Did she *really* fire me? Every one of these D'Angelo kids is technically my boss—even Trinity.

"Yup," she says, giggling. She grabs a pen and waves it about like a magic wand. "You're free of this life, this house, this world. Free of the D'Angelos. You're no longer Z., our brave enforcer. You're just Leo—an average guy on the street."

"Average?" Really?

"Fine. You're the above-average gem of a guy on the street."

Nodding, I approve. "I'm with you so far."

"You can do anything you want, Leo. So, now what?" she asks.

I shrug. "This is your fairy tale, you tell me."

Her smile is devilish. "That's the point, Leo. It's not my fairy tale. It's yours. As our father always said, *finché c'è vita c'è speranza*," she pronounces beautifully.

I dust off my Italian and give it a shot. "Where there is life, there is..." *What is that last word?* "Sparrows? Sparkles?"

She smacks my arm. "Hope," she says, with a lift in her voice. "Where there is life, there is hope."

I stare blankly. *What the hell does that even mean?*

"There's another way of saying it. Where there's a will—"

"There's a way." Geez, this kid's really got me. I could almost believe it. Ditch the family I vowed to protect, run off with the girl...whisk Ivy away to Paris or Fiji, or even the pristine beaches of North Carolina. Not a care in the world. Just her and me and our toes wiggling in the sand.

For about thirty seconds, it's a nice dream. Then reality hits me like a Muay Thai kick in the gut. I move to the window and glance up. Ivy's curtain is drawn closed. To my soul, she may as well have cut off the sun. I sigh. "It doesn't matter how I feel, Trinity. It's too late."

Trinity's palms caress my cheeks. "You and I both know when it's too late."

Between the loss of her father and the loss of my wife, she's right. She raises onto her tiptoes and plants a small peck on my cheek. "It's not too late."

"She probably hates me."

Trini nods. "Definitely."

I arch a brow. "Not helpful." She curls her feet beneath her as she takes a seat, attentive to my every word. "This may come as a shock to you, Trini, but some people consider me an ass."

"Everyone's an ass sometimes."

I mess up her naturally perfect hair as I take a seat on the plush couch opposite her. "You're not." I groan and wipe my face with my hands. "No matter what I do, I fuck up over and over again with Ivy. What do I do?"

"How about you try not fucking up?"

I deadpan. *Smartass.* "I'm sorry as fuck, Trinity. I'd do anything to reverse time and take it back."

"Why don't you say this to Ivy? Tell her how you feel."

"Because I'm an ex-SEAL who works for the mob. Open communication isn't exactly my strong suit." I lean into her, elbows on my knees. "Can you keep a secret?"

She nods enthusiastically. "Is my last name D'Angelo?"

Good point. "The truth is, I think I'm in love with her. And I'm terrified I've lost her for good."

A pillow flies in my face. I take the hit and Trinity squeals. "I knew it. You're in love." She bops the pillow square in my goofy grin again. "Now, what are you going to do about it?"

I shrug. "Flowers?"

She shrugs back. "Meh."

"Candy?"

"Seriously? Our pantry rivals Dylan's Candy Bar."

I puff air into my cheeks. She's got a point.

"Sounds like what you need is a grand gesture."

I twist my face, confused. "A what?"

CHAPTER 22
Ivy

I've lost half the morning on Enzo's latest insane demand: rearranging his collection of rare cigars in order of country, then price, then name. I finally finish when Hunter corners me in the hall. "Well?" he asks, all smiles and charm.

I don't have time for this. It's time for my confession with Father Smoke. "Well, what?" I pretend I haven't a clue what he's talking about. Did he want a reconnection with his heroic dog? Yes. Is he tripping all over himself because Brooke's that kind of gorgeous?

Duh. Of course, he is.

The behemoth towers over me, his big, brown puppy dog eyes tugging at my heart. "Fine. Brooke said if you're ever in town—"

"I'll be in town," he assures me. "In two weeks."

"Don't you have to work?"

He pulls out his phone. "Give me her contact information. I'll take it from there."

I enter her number and warn him sharply, "You better not get hitched without inviting me. I will take it personally."

I hand him back the phone. He takes it with a grin. "Ditto." He winks.

Before he can slip away, I ask, "Have you seen Smoke?"

He thinks for a minute. "Last I saw, he was in his office. I actually need to head there myself."

"Oh, then I'll wait."

"Nonsense. I'll only be a minute."

Butterflies swarm in my stomach. I've stalled long enough. It's time to tell him who I am. Or, at least, who I think I am. And while I'm at it, I'll mention that I have to decline his generous party invite because I'm funneling all my money to Aunt Grace's meds, and a gown for the ball didn't make my *can't live without* list.

This is way too much baggage to unpack at once. I'll start with the picture. The one of Antonio with my mother. The one I'll have to describe from memory because I no longer have it. It disappeared somewhere between interviewing for this job and being carted off to jail, courtesy of Uncle Andre.

God, what if they don't believe me? Or what if they do, and they reject me? If Smoke or Trinity rejects me, my heart would shatter. Just thinking about it, my chest writhes in pain.

With every step, my pulse kicks up a notch-and-a-half until I'm on the verge of hyperventilating. By the time we reach the large, framed door, I'm lightheaded. What if I pass out? I don't know if I can do this.

I'm about to turn and run when Hunter and his monstrous fist knocks. The door flies open, and Smoke looks down on me, surprised.

He hands the box off to Hunter. "You know where you're going?"

"Yes, sir."

I notice the flask with all the D'Angelo children's names on it in the box, along with small, framed photos and other memorabilia. "What's going on?"

"Don't ask," Smoke snaps back, and then apologizes. "Sorry, Ivy. Today's a bad day. I don't mean to take it out on you."

Hunter rushes away, and I stare after him. "Did you need me?" Smoke asks.

Do I? During his bad day? "No," I say, forcing a smile. "I don't mean to interrupt you. It can wait."

"As it would happen, I'm free now." Opening the door wide, he gestures for me to enter. "Come in."

I take baby steps, seeing he's still on edge. His neck is tense, his jaw is tight, and it's a good thing he can't shoot lasers from his eyes. I suck in a breath. This could make his bad day so much worse.

"Fuck!" he shouts before slumping in his chair.

I shut the door behind me and cautiously move in beside him. My timing couldn't be worse, and I pocket my big reveal.

But maybe my timing couldn't be better. It's obvious Smoke's upset, and he's trying to hold it all in. "I'm a terrific listener," I offer, certain that what this oversized giant needs is a safe place to get all that pent-up anger off his chest.

"Uncle Andre, the anti-Christ, somehow managed to get a judge to agree to let him keep a few items while we hash out the rest in court. I'll be lucky to ever see those again." He snatches several papers from his desk, waving them furiously.

"But that flask belongs to you and Trini and all your brothers. Each of you signed it."

It's obvious by the look on his face that I'm preaching to the pissed-off choir.

My hands fly through the air. Outraged, I shout hysterically. "He can't do that!" Smoke's eyes widen, surprised by my reaction. I need to reel it in—take it down a notch. "Can he?"

He nods once, defeated. "He can for the moment. It'll be months of court proceedings and negotiations. I'm pretty sure in the meantime, the son of a bitch will..." he uses his fingers to air quote, "...*'misplace'* it all." He tosses the documents across the room. "Goddamned motherfucking lowlife."

"Shitfaced, cock-sucking bastard," I add.

Smoke's huff breaks into a laugh. Amused, he stares at me. "Wow. You're really starting to sound like one of us."

One of us. I let his words swim around me, warm and free. Maybe I am one of them. My dark eyes meet his. Am I seeing things, or are they the exact same shade as mine?

His smile widens, welcoming me to tell him all the secrets I so desperately want to share. All I have to do is say it. Tell him. Right now.

A buzz sounds from his cell. He holds up one finger, indicating he'll just be a minute, and answers. "Hey, Leo."

Pause.

"Ivy's here. I've been in a deep counseling session with her, sharing my feelings."

Another pause.

"Fuck off," he smirks. "I do too have feelings. Just ask Ivy. Come on by."

My heartbeat thuds loudly in my chest. All I want to do is

confess a few sins and never see Leo again. Is that too much to ask?

I stand, and head for the door. "I'm sure you and Leo have things you need to do. I'll get going."

But the door opens swiftly, and there he is. The heartbeat that was beating as wild as a drum suddenly stops, and so does my breath.

His dark hair is mussed about—a sign he's been running his hands through it, thinking through his day. The navy shirt is painted-on perfection and wraps around the thick muscles of his arms, chest, and abs. His jeans are snug in all the worst places, and I can't help staring. I swear to God, the man is blessed with a porn-level endowment. Too bad for both of us my foot is itching to kick the living shit out of him right in his money maker.

"Hello, Ivy," he says, his smile boyish and genuine.

"Leo," I respond flatly.

After several rounds of awkward staring and nothing to say, Smoke clears his throat. "So, Ivy? Was there something you wanted to tell me?"

"*Mm-hmm*," I manage to choke out. This is ridiculous. I'm tongue-tied and flustered, and it's all because of Leo and his goddamned *fuck me* cologne. "I—"

"Ivy needs a day off," Leo says.

I whip him a glare, mouthing, "*What?*"

He hands me my purse and continues with what he was saying. "Ivy wasn't exactly prepared to move in here when she was hired, and she needs a day to buy a few things. She also needs a gown."

"A gown?" Smoke asks. I stare at Leo, confused.

Leo's mischievous eyes lock on mine. "For the ceremony."

Leo knows?

He might know that I don't have a dress. What he doesn't know is I have no way of paying for one. And I can't tell him.

Smoke nods. "Of course. If you need more than a day—"

"I won't," I cut in, a little embarrassed. "A day should be fine." Now, I can't back out. I'm forced to find a dress and go to the ceremony. Don't get me wrong. I want to go. I just don't want to show up looking like a long-lost foundling who was blessed with tickets to a 1980s prom.

And so far, that's what I'm faced with.

"How about today?" Leo offers, and I swear to God, I will smother him in his sleep if he keeps helping. "Trinity will be wrapped up in preparing for the festivities. Ivy can take off today."

"Sure," Smoke says before I can edge away from this mess.

"Perfect," Leo says with a shit-eating grin.

I can't complicate Smoke's catastrophe of a day. I force a smile. "Great."

CHAPTER 23

Ivy

From the street, I worry my lip between my teeth. It isn't until I get out of the car that I realize I crushed my front wheel against the curb. In all fairness, I've never really needed to parallel park until now. I resist the urge to fix it. Time is already ticking on the meter, and this spares me the agony of hunting for a parking garage. I tuck Mr. Whiskers in my purse and head inside.

The clothes are sorted in tidy little rows. As thrift shops go, this one is well organized and clean. The purple one in the window is what I really wanted to get a look at. The color is sweet and pretty, and in a size that might be roomy enough for my hips. With some doing, I could cinch her in at the waist.

From the window, I hoped I had a good sporting shot. Up close, it's clear there isn't enough Vaseline in all the world to squeeze my ass inside this dress.

"Looking for something?" a deep voice grumbles.

I jump. It's Leo. "Don't you have anything better to do than scare the bejesus out of me?" Breathing hard, I clutch my chest.

"What's a bejesus? Is that slang for Baby Jesus?" Confused, he tilts his head. "Why would anyone be scared of Baby Jesus?"

I look at him sideways. "Bejesus is not Baby Jesus. It's how we avoid swearing."

He nods. "So, instead of saying *scared the fuck* or *shit* out of me, you thought up a word that sounds an awful lot like an infant savior."

I browse through a nearby rack. "Just to set the record straight, I did not come up with this word." I turn, fully facing him. "What are you doing here?"

"Perhaps I'm here to annoy the bejesus out of you."

"You're doing a bang-up job."

"A bejesusing awesome job, I know."

I give him the hairiest eyeball in history, which is totally wasted on him. He's too busy studying the dress I was eyeing. "It won't fit," he says, matter-of-factly.

"I know," I say through gritted teeth. He's carrying a package roughly the size of a shoebox. The return address is front and center on the label: D'Angelo Holdings. "What's that?"

"Guy stuff. You wouldn't understand."

"Is that code for porn?"

"Maybe." He peruses a few dresses, holding up a dark green satin one to me. The puff sleeves and high collar neck make it a great contender for a Christmas tree. I deadpan his annoyingly gorgeous face. He returns it to the rack. "Nope."

The nerve of this ass. This isn't some hand-me-down dress he's dismissing. It's me. I come unglued and bolt out the door.

Heavy footsteps follow me. "I need to talk to you," he blares.

I pick up my pace.

"Stop running away."

"Stop stalking me!" I shout. Pedestrians move at a snail's pace when I'm trying to get to my car. It takes me another minute to fish my keys out of my purse. Poor Mr. Whiskers falls out. Before his beautiful nose dives face-first onto the pavement, Leo grabs him, an inch from the ground.

I hold out a hand expectantly.

Leo takes Mr. Whiskers hostage, lifting him high in the air and out of reach. "You're not leaving," he says like a jerk. "Not until we talk."

My sanity snaps, and I let him have it. I shove him. Hard. Again. And *again*. Like an ant moving a mountain, his body goes nowhere. "Did you ever think that maybe, just maybe, I don't want to talk to you?"

"Why? Because you ghosted five voicemails, twelve text messages, and didn't bother to say *thank you* for the three dozen roses? No, the thought never crossed my mind." His words drip sarcasm, but there's something pained behind his eyes. He's hurt. He lowers Mr. Whiskers and slips him into his pocket. His furry little face peeks out. "Five minutes. I know I don't deserve it, but there's something I have to tell you, then I'll go."

He makes five minutes sound small and insignificant, so why does it feel so much bigger than that? "Five minutes," I repeat and take a seat on the hood of my car.

Leo slides in beside me. "I want to tell you a story about a wolf and a crane."

I huff out an agitated giggle. "I know Aesop's fables, Leo. They were always Aunt Grace's favorite stories."

He turns beside me so his eyes connect with mine. "I'd love to hear the Aunt Grace version," he says with sincere interest.

"Okay. A wolf had a bone stuck in his throat when a crane came along—"

"Probably a bird bone."

I hush him and nudge my elbow at his. "*Shh*—"

He locks his lips with an imaginary key, then flicks it over his shoulder.

I continue. "The wolf offered the crane a handsome reward of gold if he removed the bone. Of course, he does. He holds his feathers out, requesting the reward, and gets stiffed. When the crane protests, the wolf smiles hungrily and says he's been given his reward. He didn't get eaten."

I'm not exactly sure when it happened, but Leo's hand has been holding mine. It's like his touch is an extension of my own. We look at each other, and I don't pull away. Between the heat of his body and the apology in his eyes, I know he's sorry. And every part of my body aches with missing him.

But we're more than a one-night stand. I need to know that he believes that.

His thumb rubs mine. "You forgot the moral," he says softly. "Don't expect a reward when you serve the wicked." His shoulders slump, and his grip tightens. "I'm sorry, Ivy. So fucking sorry. I wish I could take every word back..."

I hear the *but* coming and hold my breath.

"But I can't let anything happen to you. Like I've said, bad things happen to the people I care about." He releases his hand to show it to me. "Even your Aunt Grace saw it. She read my palm."

I shake my head. "Tell me she didn't."

He nods and balls his hand into a fist. "She said that I'd have to choose duty or love."

Is that why he said what he said? Telling me we weren't anything more than a few one-night stands. He wanted to push me away. "Hey..." I put my hand right back in his and tighten the grip. "I love my aunt, but you can't listen to her. This is the same woman that predicted that one day, I'd be royalty." I motion to my hair. "See a crown?"

Horns blare down the street as a small commotion erupts. We both look over. A car has stopped short of hitting a small girl. Her father scoops her up protectively and whisks her to safety. A minute later, the traffic resumes, and pedestrians move on as if nothing has happened.

Leo turns to me. "Trinity doesn't have a father to whisk her to safety. I can't leave her. Antonio's gone—"

"And I'd never ask you to. Trini means more to me than you could ever understand, and you should be the one protecting her. You'd do anything to keep her safe, and not because she's your job. Because she's your family. As much as—" I stop myself from saying *as much as they are my family.*

"As much as what?"

"As much as Aunt Grace is mine. Would you ask me to abandon Aunt Grace?"

"Not in a million years." He takes my hand in his and kisses it. "Not with how she bakes." His smile is heavy.

I want to erase his worry, his heartache...every damn thing that ever caused him all this pain and doubt. "How about we take it slow? There are things about me you don't know, and things I don't know about you. I know you're scared—"

"Scared?" He blows out a breath. "At the thought of losing

you, I'm scared fucking shitless. Pardon me, I mean bejesus bejesusless." He hops off the car and places both hands on either side of me. His blue eyes darken. "No matter what, I'll always protect you."

I nod, believing him.

"And since you said slow, Ms. Palmer," he says with a Rhett Butler southern drawl, "I will not kiss you."

I said slow, not parked with the emergency brake on. But maybe this is better. It lets me work out everything I need to tell the D'Angelos before I'm too far gone over Leo.

"Come on. Let's get out of here," he says and helps me off the car.

"But I have to find a dress."

"Lucky for you, I know every store in the city." He opens the passenger door to my car. "Keys," he demands.

"I can drive, Leo."

"Obviously." His cheeky grin assures me he's assessed my horrendous parking job. He takes the keys from my hand, not that I put up much of a fight. "But if I drive, you can tell me what you imagine in a dress, and I can take you to the exact spot you'll find it."

"What if I want easy? Off the shelf and..." *What's another word for inexpensive?* "Understated."

"By understated, you mean—"

"Dirt cheap," I say without an ounce of shame. "It's a one-night event. I don't need fancy. I just need passable."

"Passable and dirt cheap, huh? I've got just the spot." He fires up the engine. "Oh,"—with a quick tug, he frees Mr. Whiskers of his captivity and lays him in my hands—"don't forget this little guy."

Embarrassed, I slip him into my purse. "You aren't going to ask what a grown woman is doing toting around a toy?"

"Not unless you want to tell me," he says as we pull into traffic. "There are so many things I want to know about you, Ivy. The reason Mr. Whiskers is so important to you is just the start."

He does? "Like what?"

"Like why are you always reading textbooks? Why is it you smell like seductive vanilla and citrus, but almost every product you own is unscented? Do you want children, and if so, how many? How many of your aunt's recipes can you make? Why it is that you love tomatoes and spaghetti sauce, but hate ketchup?"

"*Bleh*. Because ketchup is disgusting." *Obviously.*

The light turns red, and we roll to a stop. He pulls me in for a kiss. A soft, tender kiss that deepens as he takes my face in his hands and, *damn*, can he kiss. He tears away and we're both left gasping for air.

"The point is, Ivy Palmer, I want to learn everything about you. Things beyond how many times a night I can make you come." I giggle softly as he kisses me again. "I'm dying to know everything there is to know about you the second you're willing to share them."

And just like that, I know...when it comes to Leo, I can't be worried about getting so wrapped around this man that I'm too far gone.

I'm already there.

CHAPTER 24
Ivy

At a posh Miracle Mile store, it's clear that I'm stuck on the shopping trip from hell. Dresses that cost more than major appliances do not meet the definitions of *passable* or *cheap*.

Why couldn't he leave me at the thrift shop? I could've made one of those dresses work. Maybe. I'm exhausted, my feet are about to fall off, and I'm so hangry, I could gnaw off Leo's right arm, eat it, and bitch about it missing barbeque sauce. I take a sweet red cocktail dress off the rack, hold it against me, then put it back. Defeated, I beg for mercy. "Why don't we call it a day?"

Leo looks down at me, analyzing my mood. "What's with the frown? I thought girls liked shopping."

"Not this girl."

He picks up the cocktail dress. "Why did you wrinkle your nose at this?"

"It's stupid expensive."

He narrows his eyes and magically taps into my mind. "No. That's not it. The truth," he demands.

I shrug. "It's just...not me."

"Ivy, you're looking at a man who's about to buy the whole damn store just to get out of here. I'm ready to eat a small child, and I'm exhausted just watching you stand here cherry-picking one hanger after another. This is worse than torture. And I know torture." He wipes a hand down his face. "Don't look at price tags. It's on me."

"I can't let you do that."

"Yes, you can. Just pick what you like, and let's go."

He's serious. I grab the nearest thing in arm's reach. "I'll take this."

He looks at me like I'm an alien. "You'll take what?"

I dangled the thin fabric from my hand. "It's a scarf."

"And probably the ugliest one on the planet."

He isn't wrong there. It's an over-the-top floral print straight from a rose garden, and shades of orange and purple aren't my favorite color combinations, but it's small, it's cheap, and it's my ticket out of this overpriced tourist trap. "I can make it work. With Brooke's dress and this, it'll be fancy enough for this super froufrou party. It's perfect."

"Because you've turned eighty?"

"Look," I slip it around my neck, forming some semblance of a loose bow. "It's versatile. I can add it to my clothes. Any outfit. Day or night, and *voila!* All dressed up."

"*Voila!*" he says with an exaggerated wave of his hands. "You're searching for your dentures on the way to the senior center to troll for dates." Slowly, he exhales through his nose, the faint whine of aggravation coming from somewhere deep in his chest. "Not. Happening."

He snatches it from my hand, hard, and notices the sale tag I've been hiding. "It's been marked down three times. Let me phone the bank. See if we can get the credit limit raised." He assaults a mannequin, wrapping the scarf around her breasts in a hideous bow. The inanimate woman seems to frown from the act. And I don't blame her. "See? Even as swimwear, it's atrocious."

I lower my voice, ready to level with him. "Are you blind, or has it totally escaped your eagle eyes that nothing in these stores will fit my,"—I motion to my derriere,—"ample assets? Unless, of course, I buy things three sizes too big and take absolutely everything else in. Now, I'm sure someone as polished and refined as you hasn't an inkling what a nightmare shopping is for me, so let me enlighten you. *It is.* Those three pairs of jeans I own took years to find and months to break in, but they fit like a goddamned glove. They've become a second skin. When I wear them, I'm comfortable. I'm me."

Leo takes it all in, and a glint emerges in his eye.

I think he gets it. Gets me. *Sees* me. "Now, if you're done torturing me, I'd like to go home."

He steps into my space, his smile devilish. "Oh, the torture has just begun."

<hr/>

Leo drags me up another block as if he's towing a toddler. "How about this place?" We peer into a window that's three stories tall. *ROBERTO'S* is splashed across it in gold letters taller than me. Beautiful dresses on pencil-thin mannequins wait behind it. And there's not a price tag in sight.

I'm ready with an excuse to move along when Leo's arm wraps around my back. Before I can speak, he ushers me in.

I step inside and—*What the hell?* Marble floors. Several large, plush, pink ottomans. A woman with a tray handing out champagne. *Champagne!* Nothing about this place is *cheap* or *passable.* It's opulent. Exquisite. The Milan runway version of couture.

This. Isn't. Me.

I'm used to shopping in big box stores, where I can grab some chips and a Coke on my way to the underwear section. *Nooo.* This is not happening.

I spin around, ready to bolt for the door.

Leo spins me back. "Pick something."

"Have you lost the last pinball marble in your head? I can't afford this."

"The D'Angelos have an account here. Grab whatever you like. I'll be waiting here." And oh, my God, he sits down on a chair and attends to his cell. As if he's my babysitter.

"I don't need a chaperone."

"And yet, here I am."

My scowl is wasted. He's ignoring me. After unleashing a few choice profanities—all in my head, of course—I let out a huff and walk away.

Through a sea of fine clothes, I browse. There are a few names I recognize like Gucci and Versace, but most of the designs are by Roberto. Brooke would die if she knew I was here. I'm pretty sure she'd give her left kidney for one of his designs.

Like a ten-year-old, I'm careful not to touch any of it. A single outfit is probably worth more than a year's worth of rent at my North Carolina apartment, and the last thing I need is a bill for something that won't even fit.

"Can I help you?" an elegant brunette says, scanning me from the tip of my head all the way to my toes. Her nametag says Amanda, and she greets me with a pageant smile.

I shrink. In my frayed jean shorts and favorite Outer Banks T-shirt, I look like I'm here to deliver DoorDash. "Looking for an evening dress," I say shyly.

"You came to the right place. We have several beautiful ones I'm happy to pull for you." Her kindness relaxes me a little. "Do you have a budget in mind?"

My smile vanishes.

"Unlimited," Leo says, stepping by my side.

My eyes pop. I'm about to protest when the woman squeals like a dolphin and claps her hands. "I love unlimited. Champagne? Pellegrino?" She waves over the attendant. "I'll be right back."

I fume as Leo grabs two small bottles and hands one to me. He thanks the attendant and sips. I glare. "What?" he asks.

"Unlimited budget?" I snap, whispering.

He clinks my sparkling water with his. "Just go with it."

Before I can ditch him and run for the hills, the woman has brought a rack—an actual wheeled rack—over to me. "I've got our premier dressing room ready for you."

Premier dressing room? Sounds like an upcharge. "Thank you, but I can't possibly—"

Leo cuts me off. "She can't possibly try these on without undergarments. Do you carry La Perla?"

What?

"Of course," the woman says. I watch as she mentally captures my bra size. "I'll take care of everything."

My eyes slam shut. *Kill me now.*

After forty-five minutes, I return to Leo. He's on the phone in the middle of some important call, making himself way too comfortable here. He sees me and stands. "Hang on one second," he says to someone on the phone. As soon as he realizes I'm in my old, comfy clothes, he frowns. "You didn't find anything?"

"I don't want to be here. I'd like to leave."

He rolls his eyes. "I don't want to be here, either, because I have chest hair and testicles. So, the sooner you pick out an outfit, the sooner we'll leave." He actually shoos me away with a few finger flicks.

I cross my arms.

He rolls his eyes and unmutes his phone. "I'll call you back," he says as he disconnects. Standing tall, he pockets his hands. "What?"

This time, I change tactics. "I couldn't find anything," I say with equal parts sweetness and *shucks, I gave it my best.*

He peers around me into the hellmouth of couture. "That's impossible."

You're impossible, I say with my inside voice. To hangry Leo, I smile hopefully. "I can make do with what I have."

"You could if you had a fairy godmother and a pumpkin. Don't be ridiculous." He wraps both hands on my shoulders. "This is a very important event."

"I know," I say guiltily. I can tell by the look on his face that he's worried. "I won't embarrass anyone." *Except maybe myself.* "I'll figure something out."

"I said no."

"No?" His alpha male dominance is usually attractive on him. But right here, right now, it's oh, so annoying. "Leo, just because the gowns cost the gross national product of an island doesn't mean they fit any better." People begin staring. "I don't want to cause a scene," I whisper.

Leo's nerves fry to a sizzle. "You have to buy something. Anything," he pleads.

"Please," I beg, prayer hands and all. "I'd like to go."

His voice ratchets up a hair above mine. "And I'd like to be fucking you against the premier dressing room's five-way mirror until we're all shouting hallelujah like a fucking choir, but *you* have a dress to find, and *I* said I'd take things slow."

"Z.?" a flamboyant man announces from across the room.

"About fucking time," Leo huffs under his breath. He eyes the man heading toward us and pulls me close. The act isn't intimate. He's using me as a shield.

The truly beautiful man with curly dark hair and bright hazel eyes extends a hand for Leo to shake. Or kiss.

Leo simply nods. "Hello, Roberto."

CHAPTER 25

Ivy

R oberto Ricci is a six-foot-four bronze god who looks exactly how he does on television. In a tight, button-down black shirt that clings to his solid biceps and ripped abs, the man is gorgeous. And I am gawking.

When he takes my hand and presses a kiss to it, I giggle. "I am Roberto," he says in a thick, foreign accent. Obviously Italian. "Welcome to my little shop."

"For fuck's sake," Leo sneers, rolling his eyes.

"It's a pleasure to meet such a stunning woman. I'll take extra good care of you," he says, casting his eyes up and down my body as he gives me a twirl. "Darling, you are perfect."

Irritated, Leo's hands land on his hips. "I thought you were gay."

Roberto wraps an arm around both of us. "My dear Z., just because I'm not a sculptor doesn't mean I don't appreciate art."

"As long as you don't appreciate it with your tongue." Leo glances at his watch. "How fast can you work?"

"*Tsk-tsk-tsk.*" Roberto waves a finger at him. "Perfection takes time."

"You have two hours. I'm ordering food." His eyes turn tenderly to mine. "What do you want?"

"Cobb salad," Roberto butts in.

Leo's blue eyes stay planted on me. "French fries," I answer hopefully. He kisses me.

"Garlic salt. No ketchup. You got it." Leo is a mind reader. We kiss again.

Roberto clears his throat and taps Leo's shoulder. "The usual arrangement?"

Leo rubs his chin and mutters something in Italian. I didn't even know Leo spoke Italian. Whatever he said makes Roberto clap both hands together and rub them excitedly. "Come, *Bellissima*. I'm going to make you look like a million bucks," he says before whisking me away.

"She needs to be in something off the shoulder. And do it without all the touching," Leo shouts.

Roberto whispers in my ear. "Someone's protective of his stuff."

<hr/>

Between bites of food, Roberto takes several measurements. He produces a color wheel and holds it against me. "With your skin tone, just about anything will look amazing."

I drop my head, taking a bitter glance at my jeans and T-shirt. "It really doesn't need to be too fancy," I say modestly.

"Nonsense. Z. ordered me here. He expects results. Besides, I only do exquisite."

"What do you mean he ordered you here? We dropped by."

Roberto smirks with a half smile. "Anything you say."

With half an hour to spare, I get a look at the nearly finished product. The gown flows off my shoulders like water, though the color is a rich cream. It hugs my curves in all the right places, but I can breathe. I turned sideways and glance in the mirror. Somehow, Roberto has managed to make my ass look well-proportioned and not nearly as big as the sun.

Breathless, I gasp. "It's...beautiful."

"You're beautiful," he gushes back. "All the right curves in all the right places."

"I can't believe you made me look like this."

"Like what?" he asks, fussing with my hair and deciding if it should be swept up or left down.

"Like I'm magically wearing Spanx but still feel comfortable like I'm in my favorite sweats."

He looks down at my feet. "Don't get too comfortable." He reaches into his bag and pulls out several pairs of stilettos, checking each for their size. "You're an eight?" He asks.

"Eight-and-a-half," I mutter with disdain.

Roberto uses his cell to call an attendant. "The Sophia collection. All eight-and-a-half." He moves his focus to the hem, adjusting it ever so slightly.

"You seem to know Leo—I mean Z. Have you known each other long?"

"Feels like eons," he says, feigning exhaustion.

"What did you mean earlier?" I ask as we wait. He quirks his head. "That he ordered you here. You're a world-renowned designer. How can you be ordered here?"

He plays it off. "Ordered is probably too strong a word." He refastens a pin to the hem and thinks for a moment. "The correct word is *enticed*."

"What does that mean?"

He blinks several times, tight-lipped and uncertain. A small smile emerges. "You really don't know?"

"Know what?"

Roberto stands and lifts my chin with his finger. "Once you're owned by the D'Angelos, they never let you go." His smile widens. "Or so I thought. Dressing you for this event pays my debt in full. Courtesy of Z."

Leo?

He kisses my cheek. "You must be incredibly valuable to him."

I have a million questions, but Roberto opens the door. "You can come in, Z." Leo enters, along with Roberto's assistant. The young man wheels in a cart with about a dozen pairs of dazzling shoes.

His assistant yanks one of my feet from under me, nearly toppling me in the process. He secures the heel and pats my other foot.

"She's not a horse," Leo reminds him as I raise my leg on cue.

"Not in these heels, she's not," Roberto says, scrutinizing the look. He stands, taking several steps back as his finger taps on his chin. Concerned, he wrinkles his face. "The entire gown is lopsided. Why are you standing like that?"

"Like what?" It feels like my feet are about to tumble from beneath me.

"Can you walk?" Leo asks.

Considering I've never really walked in heels, and these are about five inches higher than I'm used to, I'm not sure. "How far?" I reply.

"Oh, this is going to be fun." Roberto takes both my hands and leads me around, parading me like a prized pony. I concentrate, trying to look more regal and less like a fumbling newborn giraffe. To the surprise of everyone, me included, I do quite well. That is, until he lets go.

"*Argh...*" I fall backward, swallowed up by the strong arms of Leo.

Electricity swirls around us, and for a moment, I can't breathe.

"Should we leave you two alone?" Roberto asks suggestively.

Annoyed, Leo huffs and whirls me to my feet. His hand slides the gown strap off my shoulder. Considering that Roberto and his assistant are standing three feet from us, my eyes unhinge from their sockets. *What's he doing?*

Leo pinches the fabric just off the shoulder. "Here."

Roberto steps forward, nodding in agreement. "Yes, I believe you're right."

"I know I am," Leo says, and makes a small circle around me. "Where's the zipper?"

Roberto points to the back. "I am adding a small row of loop buttons, which will look absolutely incredible."

"What if I have to pee?" I ask, predicting the future.

"Hold it," Roberto answers directly.

My phone rings out Donna Summer's *Hot Stuff*, and Leo hands it to me without looking. "Aunt Grace," he says, all knowing.

I answer. The voice on the other end is loud and hysterical. "Ivy, honey, I need help."

"Aunt Grace, what is it?"

"Just hurry."

I'm already tearing at the gown. "I'll call 9-1-1," I insist, panicked as Roberto and his assistant rush to get it off.

"No!" she shrieks, ear-piercingly loud. "Just you."

Leo has my street clothes ready. "Send the gown to the house," Leo demands.

Roberto nods. "Will do."

In a whirlwind, I'm dressed and out the door. Leo has us back in his car and speeds off in her direction.

I blurt out, "Aunt Grace lives at—"

"12 Alexander Road, I know." His cell is ready. "I can get an ambulance. Or a medical chopper."

I get that I'm nerve-wracked, but why is he? "No," I say, clutching his hand. "If she needed one, she would have said so."

I hope.

CHAPTER 26

Ivy

Twenty minutes later, we arrive at Aunt Grace's. I unlock the door and swing it wide. "Aunt Grace?" I shout.

When I look over at Leo, he's posed like a member of the SWAT team, wielding his gun. Panicked, I pushed a hand hard against his chest. "Are you crazy? This isn't a D'Angelo emergency. It's a regular person emergency."

He scans the room suspiciously. "You don't know that for sure."

I dart him a glare. "You shouldn't even be here. She said just me." As usual, he ignores me. "At least put your gun away."

"In a minute." He moves in front of me as he makes his way through the room. I follow, shouting louder. "Aunt Grace?"

"Over here," Aunt Grace responds from the kitchen.

I rush for the kitchen, but Leo holds me back. "Stay here. I'll call you when it's clear."

"But—"

"I mean it, Ivy. Stay. Here." My stern protector gives me no choice. I nod in agreement. He heads in first.

"*Argh*," Leo hollers. "What the—"

That's close enough to an all-clear for me. I race into the room. My feet slosh, wet and cold. I nearly fall into Leo.

Water is everywhere. Aunt Grace is tucked under the sink, squished into the small space. She looks up at us, a wrench in one hand and a hammer in the other. Beneath a steady drip of water, Aunt Grace frowns. "I told you to come alone," she scolds.

"As if you could keep me from this." Leo smirks. In an inch of water, he takes a knee beside her and shuts off the valve. Amused, he smiles and assesses the situation. "Let me guess. You're stuck."

"Is a frog's ass watertight?" Aunt Grace snaps bristly. "I'm not laying here for my health. Of course, I'm stuck."

Her cell is lying on her belly. Leo picks it up and hands it to me. "Thank God you had your phone."

"I needed it for the flashlight."

Leo promptly removes the tools from her hands, eying the hammer. "How about I make you a deal. You stick to baking, and I do the repairs."

"With pleasure," she says.

I try helping, but Clark Kent has it covered. Leo eases Grace out of the cramped space gently before lifting her up. It's as if he's carrying a fawn. By the smile on my aunt's face, she's loving it.

"So, you and Ivy just happened to be together?" my dripping wet Aunt Grace asks as Leo sets her on her feet.

"Yes," he says, his smile curling up. "We keep bumping into each other."

"It's called stalking," I remind him under my breath.

He leans to my ear. "Guilty," he whispers.

He removes his blazer and rolls up his sleeves. It takes all of three seconds before he's in full military mode. "You," he points to my soaking wet aunt, "get into some dry clothes."

"Sir, yes, sir." My aunt salutes smartly and does a cute about-face.

"You," he points to me, "get some hot tea started. Just, *um*, be careful filling the pot." He winks before sliding beneath the sink to repair the lines. "Why the hell did she have a hammer?" he mumbles under his breath.

Aunt Grace returns in her trademark tracksuit. This one is a deep shade of royal blue that seems remarkably sedate for her inner J-Lo. Her hair is dried and freshly curled, and her coral lipstick is in full swing.

"So, Leo..." Aunt Grace moves to preheat the oven. "Are you seeing anyone special?" Her eyes light up. I roll mine and laugh.

"Off and on," he says without missing a beat. His smile is positively devilish.

Aunt Grace pulls out her cookbook, closes her eyes, and thumbs to a page. She opens her eyes and announces, "Double chocolate-chip oatmeal cookies."

"My favorite," Leo agrees from under the sink.

There's a bright orange bottle on the table that looks empty. I pick it up and give it a shake. Damnit. I forgot the doctor upped her dose. I should've been here yesterday.

"I need to grab something at the store," I say, making an excuse to head out.

Leo slides out from beneath the sink and pops a suspicious brow. "What are you getting?"

"Girl stuff," I lie.

⁂

The Lyft lets me out in front of the pharmacy. Heavy drops of rain have me rushing in, and the dark clouds make me wish I'd brought my own car—the one my umbrella is in.

But what if something happened to Aunt Grace while I was out? Leo would need it in case of an emergency. True, he could always use her Cadillac, but she can never find the keys when she needs them, and I swear the battery is sketchy at best.

Three people wait in the pharmacy line, which means the chances of me slipping out before the torrential downpour are slim to none.

The line is processed quicker than I expect, and I step up to the counter. "I'm here to pick up meds for—"

"Grace Everly," the pharmacist says, remembering me from last time. I smile graciously as he hands me the little white bag. "There you go."

"How much?" I ask with my wallet in hand.

"Nothing. It's all prepaid."

I double-check the name on the bag. Name and address are correct, but I don't want them calling Aunt Grace later. "I think there's been a mistake."

"There's no mistake," Leo says, suddenly beside me. He takes the bag from my hand and pockets it. "Thanks, Phil."

"Anytime, Z.," the pharmacist replies. *The pharmacist knows his name?*

"Leo, uh—"

Before I can ask my question, he motions me to look behind us. The small line for the pharmacy has grown. We step aside to let the next customer move up.

Leo has an umbrella ready as we make our way to the street. "How do you know the pharmacist? And why are Aunt Grace's meds suddenly free?"

"I'll explain later."

"I need to know now. Are they trying to own me?"

"Who?" he asks.

"The D'Angelos." He says nothing, so I spell it out. "All of a sudden, you know my aunt's address by heart, you and Phil, the pharmacist, are on a first-name basis, and her ultra-expensive meds are suddenly on the house. Everyone knows that once you're owned by the D'Angelos, they never let go."

"Lower your voice," he warns.

Lightning and a clap of thunder brings on heavier rain. I raise my voice above more rumbles of thunder. "You don't understand. The D'Angelos don't need to buy my allegiance—"

He sweeps me into the alleyway and up against the wall. "For fuck's sake, Ivy. You want to skywrite it?"

"I need to talk to Smoke."

I try to move, but he doesn't let me. "No, you don't. Smoke knows nothing about this."

His body is too hot, his stare too intense. "What are you saying?"

"I'm saying that I paid for the meds. And everything else."

"But what about the dress? And the shoes? And a custom fitting by an internationally renowned designer?"

"I paid for all of it. Every last cent including all the money Roberto owed."

I press a hand to his chest. His heart pounds hard against my palm. "I don't know what to say. You didn't have to do that."

"Well, I had to do something. You were about to show up at *Erede al Trono* in a burlap sack and pay for Grace's meds by selling fetish pictures and blood."

My heart swells. "Why would you do this for me?"

He leans down and kisses me deep and hard and freer than he ever has, and God, I swear I feel it all the way to my toes. "I've tried fighting this, Ivy. I can't. I have to be the man in your life."

"You do?" I sigh into his mouth.

"Trust me to take care of you."

His command spears straight to my heart. I trust him. I do. I trust that he won't hurt me, toy with me, tear me apart, or abandon me. My feelings for him are stronger than I've ever felt for anyone, but it's more than trust.

I love him.

The drizzle transforms, hammering down as I shiver into him. He fists my hair and runs tender kisses along my neck and face. "Trust that I'm the only man who knows how to give you what you need."

He keeps the umbrella trained over our heads as his lips graze my temple. His finger finds its way beneath my dress and between my legs, drifting across my panties. We're in an alley. Anyone can see. "Leo?" My eyes question his. "This isn't slow."

His erection is pressed hard against me. "You're about to get slow."

I suck in a breath as his fingertips brush my thigh. I look around nervously.

"Trust me." He kisses me. "When the weather's bad, people scatter. There are no windows on either building in this alley." His thumb dusts my sex.

I should stop this. Stop him.

His teeth drag along my ear. "This is me giving you slow."

God, is he ever. I moan as his thumb rubs tantalizing circles along my clit.

His growl is low and enticing. "Spread your legs."

I do.

He tugs my panties to the side, giving himself full access. His finger traces a line between my ass cheeks, across my folds, and up to my clit.

My head falls back. I shut my eyes, trembling as I say the only thing I can. "Yes."

His finger slides in as the rain pounds around us. I let every gasp, every moan, every loud, raw, erotic sound free. He pumps me deep and hard, and, true to his word, agonizingly slow.

He forces a second finger in, each thrust shattering my inhibitions. My doubts.

"Look at me." My eyes flutter open and lock with his. "Is this slow enough for you?"

His kiss crashes on my lips, and I whimper into his mouth.

"Come for me," he demands. I grip his shoulders and hold on for dear life as I ride his hand—torturously slow—to oblivion.

CHAPTER 27

Leo

By the time we return to the little white house Aunt Grace lives in, the rain has let up. We're both soaking wet. Ivy is warmed by the pure heat of afterglow, and I'm warmed by her. I roll to a stop at the curb as Ivy searches the car.

"Where's the umbrella?" she asks.

God, she's adorable. "A willing sacrifice to the gods of lust. What time do you want me to pick you up in the morning?"

Her kiss-swollen lips turn down. "You're not coming in?"

I hate tearing myself away from her, but I should get back. I kiss her fingertips and urge her to leave. "You and your aunt should have some time together."

She removes her seatbelt with an exaggerated sigh. "So be it. But my death will be on your hands."

I chuckle. "What?"

She points to the house. "That woman will dredge me through batter and deep fry me if I return without you. You rescued her sink. She's indebted. And when a southern woman is indebted, her kitchen overfloweth."

I stare at the front door. This deal is too good to pass up. The truth is, I want more time with Ivy. This gives me an excuse to stay close. "Fine," I say as if settling. "With the way your aunt cooks, I'll be big as a house in no time. I'm guessing the two of you are fattening me up to eat me."

"Just me." She giggles with a wink.

An entire fried chicken later, we enjoy cookies and several rounds of Jenga. There's one thing I've learned about Ivy that I never would've guessed. This girl cheats.

I point a wooden block straight at her nose. "Don't."

She bats her eyes, innocent and sweet.

"I'm warning you," I say firmly.

As soon as I attempt the pièce de résistance, sliding the block into a hole that's nearly two and a half feet high, the vixen goes right for my side rib. She knows I'm ticklish. How? I have no idea.

The tower collapses, and I lunge for her, chasing her playfully around the couch. Hearing Ivy and her aunt in stitches makes me laugh louder. I can't remember the last time I laughed so loud.

Or laughed at all.

"Well, I'm pooped," Aunt Grace announces.

I check my watch. Midnight. Where did the time go?

Grace pulls me into a hug. "Goodnight, Leo. If you're here in the morning, peach muffins are on the menu."

"You're quite the temptress," I tease.

"And you're quite the knight in shining armor," she insists as I let her kiss my cheek. Before I can argue with her, she moves to Ivy, whisking her into a hearty, swaying hug. Their love is apparent. Beautiful. No matter what, they have each other. I don't know why that thought fills me with relief, but it does.

"Come with me, Ivy Vine." They lock arms and disappear into a room, which gives me time to look around. There are two more rooms down the opposite end of the hall. I wonder which one is Ivy's.

She moves in beside me with a small pile of clothes in her hands. "What's this?" I ask.

"Fresh towel. T-shirt. Sweats. Aunt Grace kept all my uncle's favorite things. You're welcome to these if you'd like." The T-shirt says U.S.M.C.

Knowing she lost her uncle two years ago, I take the pile in reverence.

Ivy offers to let me relax as she attempts to do the dishes without me. Fat chance. I change and return to the kitchen. We glide into a natural rhythm of washing and drying, tidying, and turning out the lights. The simple dance normal couples do— the steps I'd almost forgotten.

Her hand tangles with mine, her dark skin radiant against my lighter, Italian tones.

I lead her to a little room at the far end of the house. "This is your room."

She looks surprised. "How did you know that?"

I peel away her shirt, dusting kisses along her neck and shoulders as I breathe her in. "I know your scent. Vanilla. Citrus. I'd know it anywhere." I nip at her neck. "You could say I'm addicted."

"I see." Her hands smooth down my shirt. I remove the rest of her clothes, and she works to take off mine.

The modest twin bed we land on struggles to hold our weight. "There's a good chance we're breaking this tonight, angel."

I tug a nipple into my mouth, and she moans. "I dare you," she sighs.

I slide between her legs, gliding the tip of my cock across her entrance. "Fuck, you're wet."

This woman is gorgeous, sexy, came for me in the middle of an alley, and just dared me to fuck her hard enough to break her bed.

"Challenge accepted." I take a breath and thrust in to the hilt, my head falling back in pleasure.

Her legs wrap around me, and her moans are a drug. Ivy Palmer is an addiction I can't go without. Our rhythm is hard. Fast. Instinctual. Two people whose only thoughts revolve around pure, primal need.

Every cell in my body is alive, fired up, and electric. I move her legs to my shoulders, kissing her tenderly as I fuck her so deep that nothing else exists. Nothing but her.

I watch her, back arched, every movement in ecstasy. I've never seen anything so beautiful. Her body begs to be taken hard, and mine aches to give her more.

When she quivers beneath me, I know she's close. "Open your eyes," I command, our glistening bodies lit by pale streaks of moonlight.

She flutters them open. And it's all there. Want. Need. Lust. Love.

I didn't want to see it before. Now, I can't not see it. See her. See us. Together.

She looks up at me, and I know she sees it, too.

I give her more, my thrusts rising. Our bodies slapping loud —skin against skin—sweat-drenched sounds echoing in the dark.

I empty everything inside her. All I have. All I am.

We crash into each other, wave upon wave, until there's nothing but the loudness of our breaths and the beating of our hearts and her beautiful, tender words.

"I love you," she says as she drifts to sleep.

With Ivy, I'm freefalling from one life into another—from the life I have to the one I want. And for the first time in as long as I can remember, I feel it. My heart. It pounds a drumbeat of elated happiness one minute, followed by an unnerving S.O.S. signal the next.

Her body rests peacefully on mine. Her breaths are heavy. Peaceful. With my heart in her hands, she sleeps. I kiss her head and hold her close.

She loves me.

I'm not exactly sure what I feel in this moment. But one thing is for damn well sure.

Everything is about to change.

CHAPTER 28

Leo

"Let me guess…it's a vagina," I say, studying the art from the greenery of the east lawns. The midday sun picks up every fleck of pink.

Smoke scans the oil painting. "Enzo had it delivered?"

Both men holding the flesh-toned painting nod. The piece is big and garish and made even tackier by a gold-plated frame.

Smoke tilts his head. "Is it upside down?"

"Does it matter?" I ask, shaking my head. "A vagina's a vagina no matter which way you position it."

The men holding the art nod again.

Smoke's chin tilts to the sky. "Why is it in my face?"

"Because it's a gift. From Enzo. A special touch for your ceremony." I check the paperwork from the Juliet Griffin Fine Art Gallery. "Yup. He blew three hundred thousand dollars on this baby."

Smoke lets out a distressed sigh. "Get it out of here," he says to my men.

They look back at the house, and then at each other, perplexed. "Where should we put it?"

I know what Smoke is thinking. "Say the North Cottage, and I'm sending it to a landfill."

"Sounds like a win-win," Smoke smirks with a dumb-ass grin. "Fine. I'll call Juliet and see if the gallery might be up for an exchange. Just put it in the basement for now."

The men take off, and Smoke and I scan the grounds one last time. "The new surveillance is all online, and twelve additional personnel from the towers will be on security detail."

"Mm-hmm," he says, rubbing his chin as he studies me. "Something you want to discuss, Leo?"

I'm quieter than normal. Pensive. I'm thinking. Dangerous, I know. I'm about to do something. Something rash and impulsive. Something I should be worried about, but I'm not.

I play it off. "Like what?"

"Like why you and Ivy were gone all day yesterday. Last night, too. And why Roberto is suddenly off our books. His entire debt paid."

My feet shuffle along a tree-lined area of the gravel path. I don't know why I blurt it out, but I do. "Ivy's moving in with me. After Enzo leaves."

There. I said it. I haven't told Ivy yet—small technicality.

Smoke stops mid-step and presses a hand to my forehead. "Are you delirious?"

"No more so than usual."

"Is she pregnant?"

I beam with an elated laugh that comes out of nowhere. "I'd love that, but not that I know of."

"Are you sure about this?"

I nod and don't bother trying to stifle my goofy grin. "I know it's fast—"

"From shouting that the two of you are nothing more than a few *one-night-fucks*—"

"Not my proudest moment."

"To wanting her to move in." He nods, deep in thought. "This could go a lot of different ways. What if it doesn't work out?"

"Been there. Done that. Got the T-shirt, the bumper sticker, and the seventy-two-ounce mug."

He shakes his head. "There's no harm in taking it slow."

"I've tried. Even told Ivy I would, but slow is a tough speed for me. In the beginning, I broke it off and cut all ties with her. I even put Hunter between us."

"We all saw how that went."

I shrug. "I've never been more fucked-up with jealousy in my life."

We chuckle and stop at a small clearing, marveling at the childhood treehouse that towers over our heads. "You sure about this?" he asks.

"I know you have reservations, but you were the one who said to go after what I wanted, and I want her. It's like shoving all my feelings into grenades. As soon as I cast them aside, they explode."

"And her security check?"

"Clean and *nearly* complete." He gives me that look. The *wrong fucking answer* look.

I hate that look.

My voice sobers. "The only loose thread is a father she's

never met. Fucker abandoned her and her mother from the moment of birth."

"I see," is all he says, his tone apparent.

"Children aren't responsible for the sins of their parents."

"I wasn't judging Ivy."

"Then you're judging me."

He takes a breath. "There's a reason I wasn't allowed to treat Trinity after her attack. Emotions always cloud judgment. Maybe you're too close to Ivy to complete the investigation."

I'm ready to bark *go fuck yourself* at him, but then I'll end up proving his point, so I tamp down my feelings, and keep my voice dull and monotone. "My investigation hasn't stopped. If anything, my investigation of her is more comprehensive than my own team."

"Spare me the details of your deep probe into Ivy."

It was definitely deep. I clear my throat. "As I was saying, her investigation was thorough. As far as I can tell, neither Ivy nor anyone in her inner circle has a clue who her father is, and they've tried finding him for years. I doubt he poses a threat to anyone except perhaps himself if he ever materialized. As far as everyone in North Carolina is concerned, the asshole might as well be dead."

We approach the mansion and see Ivy and Trini in the distance. They're in the garden, followed by their faithful swan. Trini looks happier than I've seen in years, and Ivy is beauty personified.

"Does this make her your date?" Smoke asks.

"Date?"

"Tomorrow night. She's in a gown. You're in a tux. Sounds like a date."

Warmth fills my chest. It certainly does.

～～～

Smoke and Trinity make their way to the house as I steal Ivy away for a walk. When we near the cottage, I pull the slip of fabric from my pocket. "Still trust me?"

Amused, she giggles. "Do you always carry a blindfold?"

"Don't ask questions you don't want the answers to."

I slip it over her eyes and wave a hand in front of her face. Nothing. Confident she can't see a thing, I ease her hand around my arm and nudge her to walk with me. I watch Ivy twist her fingers, quietly settling her nerves. She's nervous, and I'll admit, for the first time in a long time, I'm nervous, too. This could go either way, and I don't want to scare her off.

We arrive at the cottage, and I stare at the steps. Hmm, how should I do this?

"Hang on," I say and scoop her up against my chest. Her arms wrap naturally around my neck. "Leo?"

"Almost there." I climb the steps with ease, then set her down on the landing. Instinctively, her arms fly out, mummy-like, as she feels around. It only takes a second before she's fidgeting with the blindfold.

I give her hand a playful smack. "No peeking." My voice is stern and gruff as I enter the code for the lock.

"You can remove the blindfold."

She does, and it takes a second for her eyes to adjust. Her smile grows as she peers inside the door. "Where are we?"

"My secret hideaway. The North Cottage. It's a guest house

on the estate." I take her hand. "I'd like you to move in with me."

"What?" she gasps.

I take her in my arms and kiss her, releasing a big sigh. "Not right away. We'll do it whenever you're comfortable. And after I evict my roommate."

She frowns, confused. "Roommate?"

"Enzo is bunking here."

"Enzo, the high-powered CEO of D'Angelo Holdings? You two must be close."

"As close as I am to a scorpion."

"Then why is he staying here instead of the lavish mansion on the hill? Somehow, I imagined a man like that would need... tending to."

"Let's just say I'm keeping him grounded." I close the door and explain. "It's just a precaution. Keeping Smoke and Enzo separate is a good safety measure. Plus, it keeps Smoke from murdering Enzo, which is certain to happen if those two end up living under the same roof." I slide my arms around her. "Enough about Enzo. Focus on us."

"Are you asking me because you know I have the recipes for all of Aunt Grace's muffins?"

I kiss her. "That and spying on you from here is murder on my neck." I rub my neck for effect. "Watching you this close will be easier."

Her gaze falls. She's right here in front of me, but I can feel her drift a million miles away. Maybe I'm pushing too hard. "You don't have to decide now. It's an open invitation. Whenever you're ready."

Her fingers circle my shoulder, and I can tell she wants to say yes. What's holding her back?

I cup her cheeks. "Enzo leaves after the *Erede al Trono*." I sweeten the deal. "I'll move everything in for you."

"Shirtless?" she teases.

"Man Candy Moving Company, at your service. You won't have to lift a finger." I kiss her fingertips, one by one.

A smile emerges, and her shoulders relax. "Even Mr. Whiskers?" she kids though I know she's serious. She does that thing where she worries her lip through her teeth.

Mr. Whiskers. Her small stuffed animal. The cuddly furball is in every photo I could find of her from childhood. She totes him around as a therapy technique, downplaying his importance. But I know his significance in her life. A small detail Aunt Grace let slip out. Ivy believes Mr. Whiskers was a gift from her father. At least she has that.

I sport a noncommittal shrug before pointing to the mantle. Next to a vase full of roses, he sits. Her smile is priceless. "Who else will keep me company when I'm home alone?"

She kisses me, letting the last of her defenses fall away. I love the way this woman kisses. Warm and tender. Hot and deep. I need her more than I'll admit, even to myself. But my kiss will never hold back. And this little white dress she's been teasing me with is about to be torn off.

We make our way through the house and arrive at my room. Soon to be *our* room. I rush to remove her clothes. She squeals as I toss her on the bed. "What about your roommate?"

What she doesn't know is that Enzo is a creature of habit. Leaves early. Comes home late. Sometimes, not at all. My men will alert me if he returns ahead of schedule. Rule number one in security: the boss is never surprised.

I tug off my shirt and remove my jeans. My mouth works up her body, nibbling along her breasts and neck until I find her ear. "Ah, this is another trust exercise."

Her eyes flutter open. She notices the door hasn't been shut. "What if he comes in?"

I lie back against the pillows and wrap her thick, beautiful curls around my fist. "The only man you should worry about coming is me."

"Yes, sir," she says, slicing her tongue down my abs as my legs widen around her. Her tongue flicks the tip of my hard cock before lazily circling the shaft.

"That's it. Take me in, angel." Ivy sucks my dick so hard I lose feeling in my toes. *Yes.* She hums around my length, and I inch closer to losing all control. When my tip hits the back of her throat, I'm done. "Get up here," I demand.

Ivy straddles me. My hand moves between her legs, ready to slip her panties aside, and *fuck.*

"Something wrong?" she asks innocently, nibbling my lips.

I growl with satisfaction. "No panties. You're about to get it." I smack her butt cheek and move her into position, the heat of her sex wet and ready. I remove her dress, grab her hips, and slam her body onto me in one unforgiving thrust. We stare at each other as electricity sparks all around us. Our bodies move, pounding out a sacred beat, propelling the earth around the sun.

I flip her to her back and drag my length from the heat of her. "What are you doing?"

"I want your first orgasm on my tongue," I demand and

spread her knees wide. I pump two fingers inside her as I lick, suck, feed, fuck—I devour her. When her body shudders, I thrust my thick length in. Again and again, I take her. Need her. Claim her. Climbing to a pace that's rough, igniting me until every cell in my body explodes.

Her back arches, and I feel her body shatter into a million more pieces beneath me. My climax crashes on me hard as the world falls away.

Ivy's hand caresses my chest as my cell pings.

I'm too busy catching my breath to care about who the fuck it is.

It pings a second time. "Maybe it's important," Ivy whispers, nuzzling into my neck and planting kisses there.

I squeeze her tightly. "Impossible. All important things aren't due until tomorrow."

She hands me my cell. Two texts from Wilson, the man who owns the photo restoration company. I didn't expect to hear from him until next week. I read the messages.

Almost done: Call when you can.

"I need to take this."

I kiss her forehead as she curls into the blanket. I close the doors and move down the hall as I call Wilson.

"Z., glad I caught you. I'm going out of town this weekend and wanted to get this to you before I leave."

"So, you're done?"

"Almost. I can give it to you now if you're in a rush, but it's not perfect."

"How long for perfection?"

"Tomorrow evening at the latest. But I can text it to you ahead of time."

"No, don't." I'm looking forward to being surprised. To seeing an image of Antonio I've never seen before. I intend to give it to Smoke, but still, it feels like a small gift for me.

"If you're in the city, I can drop it off when I'm done."

"Do me a favor. Drop it off at D'Angelo Towers. Leave it with security. I'll have someone deliver it here."

"You've got it."

I hang up and hear water running. Ivy's making herself comfortable and taking a shower. I join her, eager to lather up every breathtakingly gorgeous inch. Between all the differences in her features and mine, I wonder what our kids will look like. With her hair and mine both dark with wavy curls, I feel like that's a given.

But what about that beautiful strand of silver? Is that something she would pass down?

"Who was it?" she asks as I lather soap along her back.

"Wilson."

"Is he new? I don't think I've met him."

"He's a photo restoration guy. He's been working on a project for me."

"You're having a photo restored?"

"One of Antonio. It was found on the property, demolished by the rain. Every image of him is precious and rare, and—"

Ivy whips around. "Can I see it?" Her eyes are full of emotion and hope. I love how she latches on to every aspect of the D'Angelo world, always interested in learning more about the family that means the world to me.

"Sure. But I won't have it until tomorrow night." I take my time, toweling her off. She falls into a million-mile stare. "What's that look?"

She snaps back and meets my gaze. "Tomorrow is *Erede al Trono*."

I nod. "I'm hoping the photo comes before that. Depending on how it turns out, I might give it to Smoke as a gift. A piece of D'Angelo history he's never seen."

CHAPTER 29

Ivy

The photograph.

All night, I tossed and turned with restless dreams about Antonio and his silver streak and my mother smiling beside him. The photo that Leo is having restored...is it mine?

I have to tell Smoke. Or Trinity. Someone who will believe that I don't want the fame or fortune associated with the D'Angelo name. I just want to tell them...*what?*

I suck in a breath. That I think I'm family?

Not the best conversation starter, but it is a start.

After spending the better part of the day chasing them down, I quickly realize today is not the day. With five times the security and staff, bodies huddle around every D'Angelo like ants around a Christmas feast. It's like a kingdom before a coronation day. I've got better odds finding a real live leprechaun with a pot of gold than stealing a D'Angelo away for a second.

Smoke distinctly said it would be a small ceremony with

family and friends. Maybe in their world, a hundred people is small.

I finally catch a break. Trinity is alone, taking a walk around the small pond. I walk up to her. It's the perfect time to set five little words free. *I might be your sister.*

"Ivy." Trinity wraps me in a big hug. "You're back." Her smile is bigger than usual, reaching all the way to her inquisitive eyes.

"Yes, I wanted to talk to you. Tell you something important."

"Is it about you and Leo?"

Heat rises up my neck and cheeks. I shrug, suddenly embarrassed that I must be basking in the afterglow of Leo. "Is it obvious?"

"You were both gone. I was hoping, I guess."

"Hoping?"

Trinity links arms with me as we amble around the lake. Fluff the swan has become quite domestic, hugging the pebble coast as she swims alongside beside us. "It's so rare that anyone around here finds love."

"Love," I say, letting the romantic word swirl around and sink in. "Can you keep a secret?"

"I'm a vault," she assures me.

I let out a long, slow breath. "Leo asked me to move in with him."

"And?"

"And I'm nervous. My relationship with Leo feels like a game of *Red Light, Green Light*, where I'm never in control. I'm head over heels in love with the man, and with my track record, I'm terrified he's going to break my heart."

Her mouth twists in a tender smile. She plucks two pale gardenias from a shrub. She fixes one behind my ear, or as close as she can get with the unruly bed of curls that's gone extra haywire with the humidity. "It's okay to be cautious. Look at my brothers.

All of them are rich, powerful, attractive men. Yet none of them are involved. Early on, our family learned the hard way to guard our hearts, our name, and our money because, to some degree, our power draws the worst sorts of attention. Being a D'Angelo and having trust issues goes hand in hand."

I squeeze her arm. "I didn't realize that."

"When you're born into it, you have no choice. I love my heritage and who I am. But more often than not, being a D'Angelo feels like a curse."

We slowly start to stroll, quietly along the path as I take in the consequences of what it would be like to carry the name D'Angelo. I never considered how my being a D'Angelo could become a double-edged sword.

Why am I only now considering that?

Antonio has been missing and presumed dead. Trinity was brutally attacked—raped, beaten, and left for dead. All I have to do is look around. At any given time, a dozen guards are on constant patrol, canvassing the estate. There's a reason they've gone to extremes to protect their well-being.

God, what about Aunt Grace? What about Leo? What would it mean for us? For him? If Leo had an inkling I was a D'Angelo, there's no way he'd ask me to move in. Knowing him, he'd bypass the bubble wrap and roll me in six layers of Kevlar.

"Trust yourself," Trinity says as she wraps me in one of her super tight hugs. "Trust your heart."

Mateo hollers across the lawn. "Trinity. Five minutes."

"Okay," she shouts back with a wave and returns her attention to me. "Was that what you wanted to talk about?"

Is it? If I say even one word, it changes everything. Transforms the world for all the people I love.

I swallow hard and nod.

Trinity sighs, dreamy-eyed. "I never imagined Leo would ever let himself fall in love again."

Again. Emotions overwhelm me. I could almost forget that Leo had a wife. "I can't imagine how hard it was for Leo...to lose the woman he loved."

Trinity studies me, her bright blue eyes steady on mine. "He hasn't told you, has he?"

"Told me what?"

"Any day now!" Mateo shouts playfully.

"You should go," I say, nudging her away.

"Do I look okay?" she asks, combing her fingers through her long, blonde hair. "The photographer is here."

For a beat, my heart stops. The photographer. Of course. Family photos. The D'Angelo family.

I straighten the gardenia in her hair as I fight back an unruly tear. I've always wanted a family—*my* family—but I know that if I come out as a D'Angelo, I lose Leo. And all of a sudden, the choice is easy.

"You look beautiful," I say to Trini, and send her off. She's swept into a hug as Mateo ushers her away.

My cell rings, and Leo's name lights up the screen. I swipe the tears from my cheeks and answer. "Hi."

"I need you at our house. Now." *Our house* grabs my attention over Leo barking *now*. My beautiful Alpha male wants me home.

"What's in it for me?" I tease.

"My magical dick," he replies with zero modesty.

"That is tempting. I'm thinking it over."

"You should be sprinting. Do not make me track you down and fling you over my shoulder, caveman-style."

"Is that a promise?"

"*Now*, woman!" he barks.

This man makes me laugh. "Yes, sir."

I rush back to the North Cottage—*our* house—shedding any and every desire to ever admit who I am. Not that I ever knew for sure. It was all speculation. A wildly concocted dream that is no longer my confession to make. And the family I've always wanted, I have. Aunt Grace and the whole Everly tribe. And the D'Angelos will always be in my life, even if they never know the connection we share.

I skip up the steps and arrive at the door. Giddy and filled with a flutter of excitement, I knock. It opens. Leo is disheveled and too hot for words. In a white button-down shirt and jeans, his hair still has that *just fucked* look that raises his heat factor to volcanic. He bears down on me, unsettled. "What are you doing?"

"Huh?"

"This is your home. Why are you knocking?"

"I don't know." I shrug, cluelessly holding up my hands. "It's literally been hours, and I haven't said I was moving in."

"Oh, you're moving in. It's just a question of when." He whisks me in, laying a smoldering kiss on me until my legs are about to give. I'm seconds from dry humping him when I hear a throat being cleared. My eyes pop open.

Oh, shit. My hand is on Leo's massive length when I realize we have an audience. A small crew of people are standing behind him, along with Roberto.

My head sinks into Leo's shoulder, mortified.

"Don't worry, angel," Leo whispers. "Everyone knows you're swayed to its magnetic pull."

Roberto locks his arms in mine, dragging me to another room. "We'll let you know when she's ready."

"You have two hours," Leo says firmly.

My jaw falls slack. "Two hours? I don't need two hours to slip into a dress."

Roberto stares me down like I'm simple. "Darling, you'll be lucky if we're done by then. Final fit on the dress. Makeup. Hair." He fluffs my mop of humidity-wild curls. "How do you feel about a trim?"

Leo's voice booms from out of sight. "Touch her hair and you die."

Roberto shouts over his shoulder. "No one needs to die, Z." He smiles down at me and leans closer to my ear. "So possessive."

For the next two hours, I'm primped and prodded to within an inch of my life. I'm learning a lot about Roberto. He was born in Florence. He's a Pisces. And he apparently has no idea that women have lungs to breathe with. The *breathing-optional* Spanx are out. If I want a breath, I have to fight for it.

As soon as Roberto and his staff make triple checks of everything from my hemline to my pulse, I'm rushed to the great room. Roberto insists that I wait for my cue. It feels a little silly, but he's worked so hard. I'm far from a runway model, but the least I can do is oblige him with a show.

Roberto's voice bellows from the other room. "May I present to you Ms. Ivy Palmer."

I gather my nerves and step out. The gown is silk cream, and in it, I feel like I'm floating on a cloud. My hair was left down, and there was no way I was going anywhere without the gardenia from Trini.

I take three steps into the room, and my breath hitches. Leo is dressed to the nines in a drool-worthy blend of handsome and sexy. His black suit is fitted to perfection with the top two buttons left open because, for whatever reason, the man hates ties. His dark blue eyes lock onto mine as he steals my breath.

"Leave us," he orders sharply. Everyone files out, and Roberto blows me a kiss as he exits the room. Leo moves closer until his tall body towers over mine. "You're breathtaking," he says, his voice dark.

Instead of looking at me sex-crazed or adoringly, his face is full of regret. Before I can ask, he presses an envelope into my hand. I open it and pull out the photograph. "You must get your beauty from your mother, Ivy. Or do you prefer Olivia?"

CHAPTER 30
Ivy

I look up at Leo—nostrils flared as he grapples for control. "I can explain," I say calmly.

"Can you? Explain how there's a photo of Antonio D'Angelo with your mother? With your name penned on the back, and a date that would put you, oh, I don't know, three months along in your mother's stomach. How you weaseled your way onto this property and into the lives of everyone here. Including me. How everything you've told us—*told me*—has been one big lie? Then do it, Ms. Palmer. Explain."

His deep voice is cold and distant. I shiver, scrambling for just the right words.

"Explain!" he shouts.

Startled, I jump. "I didn't lie."

"Trust me, Ivy, this is not the time to test the limits of my patience."

"Just because I didn't tell you doesn't mean I lied. You haven't told me everything about your late wife—it doesn't make you a liar."

Leo loses control, grabbing a half-filled decanter and hurling it across the room. It shatters. Frightened, I run for the door, but Leo is too fast. As soon as it opens, he slams it shut. His body is all around mine—a dark cage closing me in. "You have sixty seconds to tell me who you are and what you want."

Tears threaten as the truth spills out. "I don't know who I am. But I think—"

"What?" he snaps impatiently.

"I think Antonio D'Angelo might have been my father."

Leo takes half a breath before completely losing his shit. "Antonio D'Angelo abandoned a child? Not a fucking chance." He paces back and forth, looking at me as though I've lost my mind. "How did you get the photo?"

The name Sin is on the tip of my tongue. But I can't say it. Leo isn't asking for himself or for us. Everything I tell him, he'll tell Smoke. And I have no idea who Sin is in this dynamic. A friend of the family? Or what if he's working for Uncle Andre? Instead, I stick with the only real truth I know. "It was given to me. On my twenty-fourth birthday."

"You're...twenty-four?" He looks away, losing himself in thought.

"I don't want anything, Leo. I just wanted to get to know my family."

"If that were true, you would've said so the first day."

"I tried. Everyone assumed I was here for the interview. And then the timing wasn't right—"

"The timing wasn't right for a month? Bullshit!" He takes a breath. "Last chance, Ivy. Tell me the truth. You won't like what happens if you don't."

Leo is cold and distant, and all I want to do is get away. But

I can't. My stomach is knotted so hard, I might be sick. My heart tightens in my chest; I should have told him. I know I should have told him.

But that doesn't matter now. I need to explain. Make him understand why I did what I did.

"When I first got here, all I wanted to do was find my father. I didn't even know that the man in the photo was Antonio D'Angelo. Once I found out, I figured I'd meet him. Tell him who I was. After that, I was prepared to walk away. But it was too late. He was gone." Tears blur my vision. "Then I discovered Smoke and Trini and I couldn't leave. They were right here —an entire family I knew nothing about. I didn't come out and tell them who I was because…"

"Because what?"

I don't know how to explain. How rejection cuts your heart in two. How you never recover. "I was afraid they'd reject me."

He closes his eyes. "Reject you?"

"I wanted them to at least get to know me. And I wanted the chance to get to know each of them."

"Right. You didn't say a word because you wanted to know each other like the fucking Brady Bunch." His eyes pin mine. "Well, there's no time like the present."

He yanks my wrist and moves to the door. I struggle to break free.

"Leo, wait. You can't tell them."

His grip on my wrist tightens as he ignores me.

My gown snags on the corner of the end table, ripping as I land on the floor. As soon as Leo reaches for me, he stops. "Get up."

I do as he says. Desperate, I rush to him and cup his face.

"You told me you'd wait for me to share everything about myself. I wanted to tell them first. Leo, please, you have to believe me."

"Believe you?" He laughs sardonically. "And why would I do that?"

"Because no D'Angelo has held their name without suffering the consequences. I don't want that. If I say nothing, everything stays the same. They're in my life. Aunt Grace is in my life. And you...you're in my life." Tears hit me hard and fast, and I tell Leo the biggest truth I know. "I love you, Leo."

For a second, his forehead rests on mine.

"You love me?" he asks, angered. "But in all this time, you couldn't trust me enough to tell me any of this?" There are tears in his eyes. "You see, you did lie, Ivy. When you told me you trusted me, *that* was a lie."

Leo isn't hateful. He's hurt. And he's right. My heart drops to the floor. "I didn't want to lose you."

Tight-jawed, he shouts, enraged, "You already have!"

I try to hold him and wrap my arms around him tight until he listens. "Please—" I sob, unable to breathe.

But he tears away, unable to look at me. "Remember what your aunt saw on my palm? My loyalty is to them, Ivy. Not you. *Never* you."

This isn't the Leo I fell in love with. The man who asked me to move in with him. He can't mean that.

He straightens his suit and looks down on me. "It's time."

My voice, small, trembles. "Time for what?"

Leo's voice calms as he moves to the door. His hand touches the knob. "Time to end this once and for all." He takes one final, haunting look at me before opening it.

Two men stand there. The one on the left with the pitch-black eyes and deadly glare terrifies me. It's Enzo, holding several papers in his hand. But it's the one on the right I can't look away from. It's the emotionless look in his eyes that slices my heart in two. "Smoke."

CHAPTER 31

Leo

Enzo pats my shoulder. "Stay," he says like a cantankerous prick.

Goddamnit, Smoke. We agreed. I hand over Ivy and leave. Enzo wasn't part of the deal.

I watch as Enzo strolls in with a cocksucker's grin, fanning himself with several pages of paper. He and Smoke circle Ivy before they each take a seat. They're both dressed in black suits, their faces hard and serious. Smoke alone would've been enough. Enzo's too hotheaded and bloodthirsty to be rational.

My position was clear. Scare her, fine—but leave me out of it. Harm her, and—*fuck*. My wrath wouldn't end until either they were destroyed, or I was.

I glare at Smoke, but he ignores me. "Take a seat, Ivy," he says and motions for the couch. Trembling, she doesn't move.

Smoke sees my frustration. "You made a vow to my father, Leo. To protect the D'Angelos. At all costs. Sit her down. Now."

I don't even have to look at Ivy to know that I have to

comply. Get her off her goddamned feet before Enzo mistakes her fear for defiance. I drag Ivy to the sofa and stand by her side—a silent reminder of our arrangement, in case Smoke forgets.

I see so many memories in the sadness on her face. Me, being an ass. Me, using her like a drug before throwing her away.

And her, the very first time we met. I didn't devastate her to tears that night, but her sadness was unmistakable. She was seated across the way from D'Angelo Towers. What was it she said?

I think my future might be in that building.

Could she have meant Antonio? I thumb through my brain for snippets of our conversation. *Fuck*, did I convince her to stay? To take this job? To do this?

Her gown is torn, and her eyes are burned red with tears. My heart squeezes, but I do what I always do. I shut it down.

Smoke takes the pages from Enzo's hands. "It appears you've filed a lawsuit, Ms. Palmer."

"Lawsuit?" I seethe, tight-jawed. I grab her shoulder and force her to face me.

Ivy winces. "No," she sobs, pleading. "Leo, you have to believe me. I don't know about a lawsuit."

"Of course, you don't," Enzo says, laughing. "It's a lawsuit miracle. An immaculate conception of greed." Enzo slithers up to her and pets her hair.

My fists ball up, white-knuckled with restraint. I know he sees them secured at my sides. This isn't just about Ivy. He wants to take his shot at me.

"I must admit," Enzo says. "You're very convincing. You

even managed to seduce our chief of security." With one hand, he lifts her face. "I would've paid good money just for that."

Blood thumps hard in my ears. But no matter what Enzo's agenda is, I hold my post. I have to.

I can tell he isn't hurting her, but what does it matter if he is? She lied to me. Maybe she deserves what she gets.

"Leave us," Enzo says. To my *what the fuck* surprise, Smoke motions for me to exit the room.

He walks out and I rush after him. The door barely has a chance to close before I lose my shit. "You want to tell me what the hell you're doing?"

Smoke glares in warning. "You want to watch your tone?"

"You're leaving Ivy alone in a room with Enzo. The man is psychotic."

"Did you know?" Smoke's patience is razor thin. "Answer me," he snaps. "Did. You. Know?"

I'm seconds from going thermonuclear on both my boss and best friend. "I told you everything I knew the second I knew it."

"You didn't say anything about the lawsuit."

"I'm security, not a goddamned psychic."

Smoke pinches the bridge of his nose. "Leo, that girl has lived with us. She's probably sitting on enough ammunition to decimate our entire family, and you rolled out your dick like a red fucking carpet."

He tosses me a small stack of paperwork that I try to decipher. The name Olivia Ann Palmer is listed amongst the plaintiffs. The rest of it may as well be written in Greek.

I hand it back. "Since when do the D'Angelos care about a lawsuit? Dante lives for that shit. Send him and his two dozen lawyers after it." Smoke gives me a look, and I can see it. I'm missing something. Something big. "What?"

Smoke folds the stack neatly into thirds before pocketing it. "If that girl is my sister, it means that our father cheated. My grandfather's will was explicit. Any discovery of infidelity at any time nullifies the original will. And the codicil stands. It all goes to Uncle Andre. The mansion. D'Angelo Holdings. Everything."

Fuck, now I remember. Twenty-four. She turned twenty-four. "There's more," I say, wiping my hand down my face. "Whoever gave her that photo was probably on Andre's team. They gave it to her on her twenty-fourth birthday."

For the first time in my life, the look behind Smoke's eyes isn't confident, methodical control. It's fear. Could Andre really take everything? What would that do to them? To Trini?

"No," I mutter, shaking my head.

Smoke narrows his gaze, confused.

Nothing makes sense. "No. Ivy would never do this to Trini."

Smoke puffs out an annoyed breath. "Is that your dick talking?"

I shake my head. "No. And it isn't my heart, either. I watched them—the connection they have. I'm not saying I believe everything that comes out of her mouth, but on this, I believe her."

Smoke blinks, underwhelmed.

"Think about it like she *is* one of you."

"I'm going to pretend you didn't say that."

"If Ivy is Antonio's daughter and she wins the lawsuit, guess what? She loses, too. It's not just your inheritance on the line.

It's hers." Smoke rubs his jaw. I say it again. "It's a catch-22. If Ivy sues you and wins, she still loses her inheritance like the rest of you. The only winner in this is Andre."

"Maybe she didn't know that," Smoke scoffs.

"Or maybe you're being played."

A blood-curdling scream howls from behind the door, and I bolt through it. Ivy is on the floor, wailing and clutching her hand. I grab Enzo by the shirt and shove him hard against the wall, ready to end him. "What did you do?"

He shoves me off. "Nothing to warrant this, Z. I assure you."

In an instant, my Glock is lodged at his throat. My voice lowers in warning. "I'm not asking again. Five seconds. What did you do?"

Smoke tries talking me off the ledge; the one I'm ready to freefall from. "Calm down."

"Four," I seethe.

Enzo begins to sweat.

"Three."

In surrender, Enzo raises his hands. "The toy. Her stupid, fucking toy. I only meant to scare her. When I tossed it into the fireplace, psycho bitch went after it with her bare goddamned hand!"

By the time I turn around, Smoke has Ivy on the sofa. Her face is buried against a big square pillow as he's busy assessing her hand. "What the hell were you thinking?" I hear him fume.

Shelled-shocked, I stare. Mr. Whisker is still clutched tight in her hand. "How is she?" I ask, my voice weak with worry.

Smoke lets out a long huff. "The burns are superficial. I can take care of it."

"She doesn't need you; she needs a hospital."

He looks at me, incredulous. "I am still a surgeon."

"This isn't a bullet wound or a goddamned mob hit. She needs a hospital," I repeat.

Smoke ignores me and turns to Enzo. "In my room, in the safe. Grab both bags on the floor."

"I'll do it," I insist.

"No," Smoke demands. "It has to be Enzo." Once Enzo leaves, he turns to me. "Get out, Leo."

I stare in disbelief. "I'm not leaving." Arms crossed, I cement my feet to the floor.

Smoke stares me down. "Well, I'm not starting until you leave."

Enzo returns and hands him the bags. They exchange a glance, and without a word, Enzo walks out. True to his word, Smoke sits down, hands clasped, silently refusing to do a thing. Fucker has me by the balls, and there's nothing I can do about it.

God knows I'd take a bullet for Smoke and any one of his family. Still, I glare at him in warning. "I'll be right outside." Slowly, helplessly, I make my way from the room as uneasiness sets in.

There's nothing I can do.

Ivy didn't trust me enough to tell me the truth. And I didn't trust Ivy enough to give her the benefit of the doubt.

There's pain in my chest—the torturous agony of my heart caving in.

We both fucked up.

And I'd sell my soul to the devil if we could just undo today and make it fucking right.

CHAPTER 32
Ivy

Terrified, I stare at the needle.

It's large and scary, not that I'm particularly afraid of needles. But Smoke has already bandaged my hand, so what's he doing with it?

Smoke looks at the massive needle and waves it in my face. "It's time you and I had a little talk."

Blood pounds loud in my ears, deafening me. I look around. Smoke took Mr. Whiskers when he bandaged my hand. Now, he's gone.

Lightheaded and dizzy, my palms begin to sweat. "What are you going to do to me?"

"Nothing you won't want."

"I don't want a lawn dart in the arm. Polite pass." I squirm as he stares at me. He's trying to intimidate me, and his *scare-the-hell-out-of-Ivy* tactic is working. With controlled breaths, I steady my nerves. I need to remain calm. "Just let me go."

Slowly, he shakes his head. "A lawsuit. Really? Even if you

left now, there's nowhere to run. You started this, Ivy. And I am going to finish it."

Smoke holds out his own arm and hands me a rubber tourniquet.

I swallow hard. "You want my help shooting up?"

Smoke deadpans. "You worked in assisted living. Can you tie a tourniquet?"

I have no choice. My fingers tremble at first, but Smoke waits it out as I secure it the way I was trained. When I'm done, I sit and wait, nervous to see what he does next.

Smoke takes the needle, and carefully inserts it into his arm. He's casual as he fills the small vial of blood. "You're not the first long-lost relative to come knocking. But I'll give you credit, you're the first to make it through the front door."

When he's done, he motions for me to complete the next steps as he keeps a tight hold on the blood. *Our* blood.

His tone is calm, but his eyes are filled with pain. "I've lived my whole life worshiping a man you've accused of being a liar and a cheat. A dead-beat dad with no sense of obligation. Since you've been here, you've asked a lot of questions about my father. So, Ivy, what have you learned?" he asks with contempt.

My throat is dry, but I push through it. "Antonio D'Angelo believed that family was more important than money or power. He cherished his family and adored his children. He sacrificed everything for the ones he loved."

Smoke nods. "Here's a question you haven't asked. Is there a chance in hell he'd ever abandon one of his children?" Smoke's eyes well up, grief-stricken. It's clear the old wound I just reopened had never really healed. I don't want to hurt him or Trini or any of them. But what he's asking isn't fair.

"Don't you get it?" I ask softly. "I want to believe in Antonio D'Angelo. Answer your question with a big, resounding *no*. But then I see this." My finger glides around my silver curl. "And it's my pain, too." Defeated, my eyes fill with fresh tears.

We sit there for a long moment in silence before he places the vial in my hand.

"What are you doing?" I ask.

"Proving a point. I have nothing to hide. None of us do. If you're a D'Angelo, no one will welcome you more than I will." He busies himself with another syringe. "But if you're not, and I highly suspect that to be the case, then your days in Chicago are numbered, and you better pray to God almighty that I never see you again."

"I don't want this. The anger. The hatred."

Smoke says nothing. I may as well plead to the wind.

I choke back the tears and stretch out my arm. The pinch is so slight, I'm not sure he's done anything at all. Then, it's over. I tell him what I should've said the first day we met. "Getting to know you, and letting you get to know me, is all I've ever wanted."

He doesn't bother looking at me. Once he pockets the vial, he heads to the door. "Your car is waiting, and your belongings will be delivered to you soon. It's in your own best interest that you don't make a scene. And stay away from Trinity."

"My pay," I holler before Smoke reaches the door.

He turns, heated. "What?"

I can't depend on Leo to pay for the meds. And I have to have that money. "I worked here—did everything I was contracted to do. You owe me two weeks' pay."

"You think I'm paying you after this?"

"I earned it." And a bottle of pills is almost a month's rent.

"Earned it? How? By fucking my chief of security. Pull out your contract and read the fine print." He shakes his head, disgusted. "You want your money? Sue me."

It's been an hour since I've been sitting in my car outside of Aunt Grace's house. I can't go in. Not yet. Sobbing, I stare off into nothing.

All I had to do was say, *"Hi, I'm Ivy. I might be your sister."*

I should've said it. Right upfront. Losing my father was one thing. But now, I've lost everything, and I'm petrified that if I don't find a way to pay for those meds, I'll lose Aunt Grace, too.

A fresh wave of tears washes down my face as I rest my head on the wheel. My cell dances on the seat beside me. It's Aunt Grace. I wipe my cheeks and answer cheerily. "Hey."

"Hey, Ivy Vine. Are you coming in? Or am I bunking in the car with you tonight? It seems a little squished, but by God, we'll make it work."

I love this woman more than sweet tea and muffins. I turn to find her standing in the open doorway, hair curlers and all, waving me in. I watch as she speaks into her cell. "Come on, baby girl. I've got a pint of mint chocolate chip calling our names."

Mint chocolate chip. How can ice cream always manage to make a horrendous situation a little bit better?

Aunt Grace waves two spoons at me and raises a canister of whipped cream. I walk over, unable to rein in the tidal wave of tears. Her hugs are a forklift whenever my soul collapses, and right now, I've hit rock bottom at her feet.

"You know the drill," she says softly.

The act is so juvenile, I instantly smile and open my mouth wide. The second I do, whipped cream fills my mouth.

"*Mmm*," I sigh through sobs—my mouth full of sweetness, my heart full of pain.

Aunt Grace soothes me with a kiss to the temple and hands me the can. I take it, determined to empty the whole damn thing.

"Come on," she says in her upbeat way. "I've got a tracksuit with your name on it."

My laugh is half-hearted. "Is *Ivy* bedazzled on the butt?"

With an arm wrapped around me, she squeezes. "Sequins, baby girl."

I hug her hard and remind myself that no matter what, she is my family. Aunt Grace has always been there for me, through happiness and heartbreak. I'm tethered to a woman who would never abandon me. She's more than my aunt.

She is my home.

CHAPTER 33

Leo

I pour a scotch so fast, it sloshes over the edge. I pound it back, and the amber fluid burns down my throat. With any luck, it'll demolish my heart, too.

To my disappointment, the fucker still beats.

"What are you doing?" Smoke moves to my side and attempts to swipe the lowball from my hand.

"Back off. And don't give me that disapproving look. You want to look down on someone, try that asshole." I point to Enzo.

The son of a bitch speaks. "How was I supposed to know the woman was stark-raving mad? Who grabs something in a fucking fire? Insane people, that's who."

"Hold this." I hand my glass to Smoke and lunge at Enzo, punching him hard in the gut. He clocks me in the jaw, and I really let him have it.

"Enough!" Smoke shouts, loud and god-like.

His command from Mt. Olympus does no good. By now, Enzo and I are rolling around on the rug, and I've got the bastard in a chokehold that satisfies a very dark and sadistic side of me.

"What's going on?" Trinity's soft voice pierces the air, and we both freeze.

We rise to our feet, straightening our suits as Trinity walks in, still dressed to the nines. Elegant in a way that makes me mournful and filled with regret.

Forecast for today? Joyous. A celebration that would've had Ivy and me eating our weight in Italian food, dancing till our feet fell off, and fucking until dawn.

All it took was one photograph to turn *Erede al Trono* into a gold-plated bucket of shit.

I retrieve my drink from Smoke's hands and toss back another mouthful.

Trinity's eyes widen with alarm. "What are you doing?"

"Having a drink," I reply, my words ripe with sarcasm. I mouth *sorry*. My *fuck off* attitude wasn't meant for Trinity.

Her glance flies across the three of us and lands on my lips. What's she looking at? I lick around and taste the blood. *Ooh, it's more swollen than I thought.*

"You don't drink," she reminds me sternly. Judgment weighs on me from every set of eyes in the room, and *fuck it*, I toss back a little more. "Stop," she begs.

"Relax, Trinity, I'm not an alcoholic. Just a man who prefers to keep his mind *sstharp*." *Am I slurring?* I hold my glass high and focus on both of her. "Tonight, I'd rather be drunk."

She wrestles the glass from me. "What happened?"

"Why don't you ask your douchebag brother?" I point an accusatory finger at Enzo.

Enzo takes a seat and straightens his tie. "There's no good

way to say this, Trini. Ivy Palmer isn't who she said she is. She's suing us. Claiming to be some long-lost relative."

Horrified, Trinity's face pales. "Did you do something to her?" Enzo doesn't speak. *Like the pussy he is.* Her gaze moves around the room, hitting each of us in rapid succession. "Answer me!" she snaps impatiently. Stunned, we're all a little taken aback.

Calmly, Smoke approaches her and wraps both hands around her shoulders. "I know this will be hard for you to take in since you and Ivy have become close, but—"

With both hands, Trinity shoves his chest. "Did you hurt her?"

Trinity is formidable. Daunting. Reclaiming that tough-as-nails badass we all used to know and love. Again, it's all because of Ivy, even if none of us want to admit it.

Smoke turns away. He can't even look at her. Even *Enzo the Toy Arsonist* avoids any and all eye contact with his baby sister. Then, her big blue eyes glare fiercely at me. I hold up my hands. "Don't look at me."

Trinity assesses each of us, one by one. And likewise, we're all assessing her. I know what they're all thinking. I'm thinking it, too. She's been through so much. Too much. Four years of barely talking, walking, *living*—and it was Ivy who ripped her from the bowels of hell and brought her back. And now, Ivy's gone.

Not one of them is stepping forward to say that.

As soon as Trinity steps to the fireplace, I know we're fucked. Mr. Whiskers stares up at her, fur freshly charred. She snaps him up, pointing his scorched little face straight at me. I deflect and point an angry finger at Enzo. "He's the pyro."

He points to Smoke. "He took her blood."

Smoke rolls his eyes and raises both hands in surrender. "We exchanged blood. I have a vial of hers. She has a vial of mine." Horrified, Trini widens her eyes. And just when I thought it couldn't get worse, it does.

Trini stomps over to me, shoving poor Mr. Whiskers right in my face. "You work for me. You said so yourself. As much as you work for either one of them. Now, I am ordering you. Tell me what happened."

Maybe it's all the wasp-like stings of emotions still fresh in my chest, or maybe it's the booze, but I can't hold it in. I jump to my feet, and God help me, I explode. "You want to know what happened? I'll tell you what happened. Ivy brought this on herself. She. Lied. Period. End of story."

Trinity is sedate and calm as she questions me. "How did she lie, Leo?"

"She said she trusted me," I snarl. When Trinity blinks back, confused, I realize that one sounded better in my head. I suck in a breath and rack my brain for an answer that sounds a little more legitimate and a little less drunk.

"Well?"

"This." I tear the photo from my pocket. I point to it. "Here is your father." I point again. "And here is her mother— Samara Palmer." I slap the picture in Trinity's hand, furious. "This whole time, she and her adorable silver curl have been lying. To everyone."

And Goddamnit, especially to me.

I decide to refill my drink. Trinity slips her delicate hand over the opening of the glass. I huff at her, irate.

Trini voices her next question tenderly. "Did you tell her about Lori?"

My lungs collapse, and my eyes slam shut. *Why is everything about Lori? Lori has nothing to do with this.*

I feel Trini's small hand squeeze mine. "It doesn't make you a liar," she whispers. "It just guards your heart."

"She's suing us," Smoke blurts out, snapping us back to reality as he delivers the small stack of legalese.

Trini flips through the pages. "Then we'll discuss it," she says like a boss, serious and businesslike.

"Unwise," Enzo decides to say. Trini smacks him on the head with the pages.

Trini looks up and turns to me. "I'll take the Maserati. Text me her address."

"I can't let you do that," Smoke interjects, blocking her path.

She arches her brow. "You can't stop me."

"It's not safe," he counters.

"Then I'll bring security." Her big, innocent eyes land squarely on me. "Let's go."

I should go with her. I swore I'd keep all the D'Angelos safe. *All the D'Angelos...*

Shit, what about Ivy? If she's a D'Angelo, shouldn't I be keeping her safe, too? This is what she meant. I can't be in a relationship with a D'Angelo and keep her safe, and she knows it. She was choosing me...while I was letting her slip through my fucking fingers.

I want to race to her. See if she's all right. Tell her I understand now. How, no matter what, I will always be the man by her side.

Except...I can't.

I can't keep Ivy close and keep her safe. Everything I've believed in has never been truer than right now. Aunt Grace was right. I have a choice to make. And I choose this. Duty. To keep Ivy safe. Because I love her.

Trini stands near the door and waits expectantly.

To make it clear I'm not going, I don't say a word. I stand there like an asshole and throw back another drink.

"Fine," she says, disapproval ripe in her tone. "I'll take Hunter," she sings with evil glee.

"No, you won't," I blurt out before I can help it. Fine. I'm jealous. But I'm still not going. Her brow lifts, and I know she's waiting for me to join her. Instead, I reach for my phone. "Daniels and Montgomery will escort you. Hunter is busy."

Her eyes take their time, studying mine—probably searching for the soul I recently bludgeoned. Still, her silent disappointment is as unnerving as barbed wire being dredged over my skull.

I take another swallow and turn away. *Jesus, Trinity, just fucking go already.*

Eventually, she does. And I get to work pouring lowball number three.

CHAPTER 34

Ivy

In an absent-minded haze, I stare as the credits roll across the screen. We've been watching a movie for the better part of two hours, and now, it's suddenly over. I have no idea what it was.

"You pick the next one," Aunt Grace says, tossing the remote in my lap. Wads of tissue are everywhere, along with the empty container of whipped cream. At any second, I feel as though another rush of tears might overtake me. How did a day that began so wonderfully end up like this?

"What's this in the fridge?" Aunt Grace hollers from the kitchen.

I bolt to my feet, rushing over. "Nothing." I try to sound normal and calm. *Please don't open it.* "Just ignore it—"

"*Ewww!*" She pinches the corner of the ziplock and lifts it out of the fridge. Inside is a small glass vial. Across her face is a look of morbid curiosity. "Is this...blood?"

I wrinkle my nose and nod. "Uh-huh."

"Honey, you aren't trying to sell it for money, are you?"

262

I giggle sadly. "No. Who would pay for two teaspoons of blood?"

She shakes her head. "Fetish freaks. I know the type."

"You do?" She's lifting my spirits, and I giggle some more. "T. M. I., Aunt Grace. T. M. I."

She gives my hand a gentle squeeze. "If you need cash, I've got a few hundred dollars saved up for a rainy day. It's all yours."

Before me stands a woman who can't even buy her own medicine, and she offers me every penny to her name. You know what? Fuck them. Her love is worth ten times what the D'Angelos have, and I wouldn't trade it for all the world.

Playfully, I give her a suspicious sneer. "And how exactly did you earn that money?"

She wiggles her hips. "Pole dancing. And there's more where that came from." She dangles the bag in front of my face. "Are you sure this should be in our fridge?"

"It definitely shouldn't." I take the ziplock from her hands and fling it into the trash. "That's where it belongs," I say and wrap myself around her as tight as a vine—forever her Ivy Vine.

She hugs me back, then snatches a container of raw cookie dough from the fridge. "Come on. We can talk while we Netflix and chill."

My eyes fly wide, and I snort with laughter. "That doesn't mean what you think it does."

She blinks adorably. "Then what does it mean?"

Several knocks sound at the door. Aunt Grace and I shoot each other telepathic thoughts. She fixes my hair as I wipe my face. On the offhand chance it's Leo, he needs to see me at my best when I tell him to go fuck himself.

By the second string of knocks, we're both at the door,

opening it. But it isn't Leo. "Trinity?" I notice her gown, realizing she didn't change. She just rushed right over. "What are you doing here? Is everything all right?"

"Nothing is all right. Can we come in?"

"We?" I look around. Forcefully, Trinity yanks a man's arm. He'd been standing out of sight and to the side. Shocked, my mouth drops.

The man is every bit as tall as the day I met him, with a sheepishness I would've never imagined. I blink several times, flabbergasted.

He extends a hand in introduction. "Bryce Jacob Sinclair," he says to my aunt.

"Sin," I state flatly, introducing him to my aunt as he introduced himself to me. She shakes his hand as I elaborate. "Sin is the mysterious stranger who slipped me the photo, then vanished."

"Oh," she says with a surprised grin. "Come in. Come in!" She opens the door wide and scuttles them into the room. "Got any pictures of Ivy as a baby? I don't have any of those."

While Aunt Grace prepares tea, I offer our guests her latest batch of cookies. "White-chocolate-rum-raisin-macadamia-nut," she says. "Or rum nutters as I call them."

Her eyes nudge mine as Trini fixes her tea. Cream. No sugar. Just like me. The Everlys always wondered how it was that I never took sugar in my tea. Now, we know.

"You're expected in court tomorrow. Ten o'clock sharp," Sin informs me with misguided authority.

I point my cookie at him in protest. "I did not file a lawsuit. And there's no way I'm taking the D'Angelos to court." I whisper to Trini. "He's crazy."

He leans across the table. "I heard that." He snatches the cookie from my hand licks it and tries to hand it back.

I stare at him, stunned. "See?" I point a fresh cookie at him. "Batshit crazy."

This Sin isn't nearly as shadowy and mysterious as the first time we met. He relaxes back in the chair, chomping with narrowed eyes and sadistic delight.

Trini's hand squeezes mine. "Sin is the good kind of crazy. Brilliant in court. We know you didn't file the paperwork. It was filed on your behalf."

Blankly, I stare. "That doesn't make any sense. Who would file a lawsuit on my behalf?"

We're all staring at Sin. After a moment of silence, Trini elbows him. "I was chewing," he says and continues. "Uncle Andre filed it."

Sin opens a handsome briefcase, removes a folder, and hands it to me. I skim the legal jargon, barely able to make sense of anything other than the date and my name.

"Tell me honestly. Do you have a relationship with Uncle Andre?" Trinity asks delicately.

"*Hmm.*" I pretend to ponder the question. "The son of a bitch had me thrown in jail, and I despise him. Does that constitute a relationship?" I finish thumbing through the documents and give up on getting the gist through osmosis. "What's this about? And why would he file a lawsuit on my behalf?"

The table bumps. By the pained look on Sin's face, I can only imagine Trini just kicked him. Hard. "Fine," he confesses. "Andre was the one who gave me the photo in the first place. We wanted to be sure he hadn't swayed you to help him. Offered you money in exchange for the lawsuit."

"He didn't," I say, perturbed.

"Who's Uncle Andre?" Aunt Grace asks.

"Andre D'Angelo," Sin begins. "Antonio's brother. Trini's father. Suspected spawn of Satan."

I shake my head, confused. "Why would Andre give you the picture?"

Sin clasps his hands. "Because every D'Angelo child is entitled to their share of the family wealth at age twenty-four with one stipulation: they have to actively petition for it."

"Well that sounds stupid," Aunt Grace says.

"Right?" Trinity agrees.

Sin settles the women down by knocking a cookie on his plate like it's a gavel. "The reason for this is because it establishes the legitimacy of heritage." His steepled fingers point at me. "The problem for you, my dear, is legitimacy becomes a double-edged sword."

"I don't understand."

He moves the cookies around the table like a family tree. "Here's Antonio and here's Andre. Antonio's heirs amount to half a football team. Andre has none. Their father, Vito D'Angelo, was of the old country and very set in his ways. A devout Catholic, he believed the sanctity of marriage was absolute. And his will stipulated as such. Because Antonio was married and the oldest, the lion's share of the D'Angelo fortune was passed to him. But there was a caveat. An infidelity clause."

"A what?" I ask.

Aunt Grace jumps in, laying it out in good old-fashioned English. "I get it. If Antonio was a cheater-cheater-pumpkin-eater, the brother gets it all." She elbows Sin. "How am I doin' keeping up?"

He smiles respectfully. "Quite well, actually." They exchange a glance. If I didn't know better, I'd swear the man was charmed.

"And the photo?" I ask.

He and Aunt Grace break their connection. "Andre demanded I submit the photo and file the lawsuit straight away." He sips his tea and continues. "Unfortunately for him, the last person I work for is Andre D'Angelo."

"Who do you work for?" I ask. "Smoke and Trini?"

"None of the above. I represent the interests of the estate. An impartial third party who oversees the execution of the will of Vito D'Angelo, emphasis on the word *impartial*. Rather than get in the midst of the whole D'ANGELO vs. D'ANGELO drama, I gave the photograph to the rightful owner. You. Unfortunately, that put Andre into a tailspin."

"What do you mean?" I question, worried for him. "Did he threaten you?"

"He always does. Andre throws one tantrum after another." Sin pulls out his phone to show us. "Twenty texts and voicemails a day. It got to the point that I blocked him. Repeatedly." The screen of his phone displays an endless list of numbers.

Recognition sparks. "Can I see that?"

Sin hands over his cell.

"Are you sure all of these are Andre?"

Warily, he nods and takes it back. "The bastard has more burner phones than the witness protection program."

I pull out my phone and compare it to the numbers I blocked. They all match. "He's been trying to contact me."

"Did you answer?" Trini asks, worry in her tone.

"No. I thought they were telemarketers. Like the one I showed you. After you blocked that one, I blocked the rest."

I pound my fist on the table, grabbing everyone's attention. "Andre can't get away with this. I won't let him. I could leave town. Then they'd dismiss the case."

"No," Trini says with strength of conviction. "You have to be in court. If anyone has a right to be there, you do. And if you aren't there, Uncle Andre will use your absence to twist the facts. Make it look as if we've intimidated or threatened you. Plus, with Smoke's blood, we could prove who you are."

I shake my head. "I'm not submitting it. I already threw it away."

Sin furrows his brow. "And you call me the crazy one."

"Trini, I never wanted the money. I just wanted to find my family. And I have. If I go through with this, you and your brothers stand to lose everything."

"Not everything," she assures me, patting my hand. "We still have you." Her big blue eyes are teary, and her words come out genuine and heartfelt. "I love my father with all my heart, but we're not hiding who you are."

"And who am I?" I try to reason with her. "All I have is a photo, a silver curl, and a hunch. No matter how this turns out, I'll still have nothing. Exactly what I came in with. But Trini, you and your brothers would be giving up millions."

"*Billions*," Sin says, correcting me. The table jumps higher than before. He winces from Trinity's second kick. "But none of that matters now. From a practical standpoint, Trinity is right. There's no hiding you now. Andre is already on the move. He's gearing up for battle, and we need to do the same. As for the DNA, he could compel the court for a DNA test."

"He can do that?"

"Well…" Sin shrugs. "He can do the petition. Only the court can compel you to do so."

A strange thought crosses my mind. Why hasn't Andre done that already?

Aunt Grace takes both my hands in hers. "If you're going to court, you can't just wing it on the fly. We need a plan."

"Not we," I insist. "Me." I don't want anything aggravating Aunt Grace's heart condition. But a plan? I stare at them all. "I don't have a plan. I don't even have an attorney."

Sin straightens his tie. "You do now."

CHAPTER 35

Leo

Two brisk pats on the arm jolt me from sleep. "What?" I snap angrily and roll over.

I'm nudged again.

"Fuck off," I growl. My body smells like ass, my mouth has the consistency of bark, and I think there might be superglue in my eyes. In my hand, I feel him. The soft, snuggly, matted fur of Mr. Whiskers. I take a deep breath and cuddle him up to my chin. *Ahh*. He smells like Ivy…if Ivy strolled through a campfire.

"Wake. Up." Smoke flips on the lamp.

Like a vampire burned by daylight, I cringe. "I will shoot you," I seethe through gritty, foul-tasting teeth.

Smoke sits on my bed and slaps my arm. I peel open an eye. He hands me a water. *Why won't the fucker just go away?*

Fine. I sit up, certain that any minute now I might puke all over him. Still, I drink, grateful to wash away the nasty flavor of butthole left behind by the scotch. "Are you waking me up because Enzo is wounded, maimed, or dead? I'll gladly get up to dance on his grave."

270

"I got the blood test back," he says, despondent. He tosses an envelope on the bed. I rub my eyes and blink until the blur of words come into focus.

"Inconclusive?" I shake my head. "What the hell does that mean? It's a paternity test." I poke the pages hard. "I've seen the talk shows. They fucking know."

Smoke frowns. "It's not a paternity test because we have no one paternal whose blood we can use. It's a sibling test to see if we share common traits. I thought mine would clearly establish that we're not related. But—" he shrugs—"we kind of are."

"Kind of?"

"We share common traits."

I mock him. "I didn't realize Ivy enjoyed coffee enemas, too?"

"Fuck off."

I reread the results, trying to make sense of the medical lingo and percentages. "With these scores, are you siblings?"

He puffs air into his cheeks. "Maybe. But maybe I wasn't careful with the sample. Maybe I contaminated her blood with mine."

"Is that possible?"

"Fuck, I don't know. But now, we have another issue." He rubs his neck. "Sin."

"Sin is back?"

Smoke nods. "I'm seeing him tomorrow."

"Why?"

"He sent an email to our side and Andre's. First thing tomorrow, he's petitioning the court on behalf of the estate. And brace yourself."

I hold up Mr. Whiskers. We both brace for impact.

"He's representing Ivy." Smoke gives Mr. Whiskers a sideways glance. "You and Enzo really have it bad for Ivy's little toy."

I look down at him. Ivy's toy. We all know why I'm clinging to him like he's my last shred of sanity. Because he is. A sweet, little Ivy memento that moves my obsession with her from sweet to stalkerish.

But what's with Enzo?

Sunlight breaks through the curtains. It's early, and Enzo will be up soon. I strategically pivot Mr. Whiskers to balance him, placing him dead center on the table. It'll be the first thing that asshole sees. And if he pisses me off, maybe the last.

From down the hall come the footsteps. I count them. From his bedroom to here, it's twenty-three steps. Plenty of time for me to twist on the silencer, take a seat, and wait.

Enzo walks into the room, the epitome of money and power in a ten-thousand-dollar suit. He smiles like the world is his diamond-studded oyster. It's funny how fast my Glock can wipe away that grin. "Good morning, shithead."

He raises his hands in surrender. "Put down the gun, Z."

I don't say a word, and my position stays steady.

It takes him a minute to see the toy. "I didn't know it meant that much to her," he says apologetically. I narrow my eyes and he begins to babble. "She's nobody. You said it yourself, she's a liar. A threat to our family. A—"

I shoot a piece off the chessboard without even looking.

He flinches. "For fuck's sake, Z. It's just a goddamned toy."

"Is that what it is? Just a toy?" That shuts him up. I pick up little Mr. Whiskers, lifting him high in the palm of my hand. "And yet, he was important enough to burn." His Adam's apple bobs as he swallows hard. I aim for that next. "You've got sixty seconds, Enzo. What is it?"

"A toy," he says, shrugging. "For God's sake, it's a toy," he says, drawing out every word as if I'm an idiot.

I lower my weapon to his crotch. "Fifty seconds."

Silence.

"Forty seconds."

He moves a nervous hand in front of his dick.

That makes me smile. "Your hand isn't bulletproof, dipshit. Thirty seconds."

"All right, all right. It was Trinity's!" he shouts, closing his eyes.

"Trinity made you do this?" That's an atrocious lie. I should put him out of his misery for that.

"No, not that it was *Trinity*," he explains with an eyeroll. "It. Was. Trinity's." He sucks in a breath and exhales loudly. "It's her toy."

I look at Mr. Whiskers. He simply stares back. "What do you mean this is Trinity's toy?"

He shrinks where he stands. "I recognized it." Cautiously, he snatches the little guy from my hand, flips him over, and unzips the small compartment. He holds Mr. Whiskers up so I can see.

Something is stitched under the label, but I can't make it out. "What is that?"

"The letter *T*. Trini stitched her initial into all of them. This toy was part of a set. There were a dozen, I think." Enzo curls his lip down the way he always does when he's got more to say and won't. I fire a round so close to his ear, he jumps. "Goddammit, Z.!" he shouts, clasping that side of his worthless fucking head.

My smile is sadistic. God, I love this. "It's confession time, Enzo. What else do you know?"

Enzo slumps into a chair. "We used to have a summer picnic every year. All family. Even Uncle Andre. And the occasional plus one. The whole place was a fucking carnival. Elephants and zebras and shit."

I circle my gun in the air. "Get to the point.".

"It was loud and noisy, and Trinity was being a pain." I narrow my eyes. "What? She was five. I was twelve. "

"And?"

"And I snatched her grubby little toy from her and escaped for a little quiet time."

I nod in understanding. "You slipped away to smoke a joint. Go on."

"I headed for the alcove under the stairs. Uncle Andre caught me. Took the toy. Took my weed. And left." He points to Mr. Whiskers with a scowl. "Trini had a million toys, which were damned near everywhere. You'd think she'd hardly miss one. Yet she did. No one believed me when I said Uncle Andre took it. And I was stuck reading bedtime stories to her for a month...all because of that stupid toy."

"So, Ivy...is a D'Angelo?"

Enzo pinches his brow. "You don't get it. No, Z., she's not. That's our story. Period. Because if she is, everything our family has built collapses, and I can't let that happen. How about we negotiate?"

"How about I blow off your fucking head? That's usually how I negotiate."

"That's enough," Smoke's voice booms as he enters the room.

"You heard?" I ask.

He nods. "You were right, Leo. Unfortunately, so is Enzo. Everything he said about what our family built is true." He pats Enzo's shoulder as they exchange a look. Without a word, Enzo leaves, and it's just me and Smoke. "There's more you need to know, Leo—about our grandfather's will."

As Smoke lays out the details of Vito's will, I already know where this is going. "You're going to screw your own flesh and blood?"

"I never said that."

"No, I did."

"If Ivy goes through with this, she gets nothing. All she's managed to do is wipe away our inheritance. D'Angelo Holdings. The estate. They all go to Andre."

"This is exactly what she was afraid of. Rejection. Abandonment." I stand and stare in disbelief. "Goddammit, Smoke, she's your sister." Smoke stares back, pensive and silent.

Smoke has been my best friend for the better half of ten years. We stood beside each other at Antonio's funeral. Swapped shifts when Trinity first returned from the hospital. I'd kill for him. Die for him. We're not as close as brothers. We're *closer*.

And still, he stands there, hands in his pockets with nothing to say.

I collect every raw, angry emotion and ball it up, then swing, hard, and send a punch straight to his jaw. He staggers back. "Fuck. You!" I spit.

When he doesn't move, I hit him harder. So hard, he plummets back to the floor.

"And what happens to Trinity?" he shouts back. His eyes lock hard with mine.

Neither of us have an answer.

It takes a minute for Smoke to get to his feet. I don't help the sack of shit, but I don't punch him again either, so maybe that's progress.

He spits some blood on the floor. I'm not sure who he's expecting to clean that up. "I need you to do something. No arguments. And if you want to hit me afterward, by all means."

I ball a fist. "Fine. I'm listening."

"Stay away from Ivy. Stay away from the court. At least for now."

"Why? Are you going to ambush her?"

"No. Because you're too goddamned close to her, that's why. I don't know what will set you off, and between Andre and the judge, you have to stay away."

He studies me because I want to tell him to go to hell and that there is nothing that would keep me from being there for her. Protecting her. Maybe even loving her.

But he knows what I know. Even Aunt Grace knew it, too. I'm chained to a vow I made to Antonio. And when there's a choice to make, I don't hesitate. He's asked me to protect the family—even if it is by my absence—and he knows I'll do it.

It was all Smoke had to say to earn one final, colossal punch.

CHAPTER 36

Ivy

We arrive at the courthouse by mid-morning, and I wish I'd taken Trinity up on her offer. I could be confidently heading into court in a Roberto Ricci custom-made suit. Instead, I went with unpretentious and practical. In Brooke's hand-me-down blazer and a pair of sensible flats, I take a deep breath, determined to be myself. Because I'm an idiot.

"Don't be nervous," she assures me as we climb the long length of steps. "Sin will do all the talking. You don't have to say a word."

"Don't be nervous. Don't say a word. Got it," I say to Trini as her hand squeezes mine.

Sin ran through the procedures with me, and I go through them again and again in my head. I nearly walked past Leo at the entrance. In a dark navy suit, he stands as a silent sentry, keeping watch. Scruffier than usual, his lip sports a swollen bruise. *Was he in a fight?*

"A word?" he asks low.

277

Trini releases my hand. "I'll get a seat." She kisses me on the cheek and heads inside.

Leo looks beat down and haggard with the eyes of a stranger. The regret that flashes across his face hardens, and that electric spark we used to share is gone.

"I'm not supposed to be here, Ivy."

"Why?"

"I can't explain. Just listen to me. You can't go through with this," he warns. "A lot of people will get hurt."

I know Leo's background. Ex-SEAL. Dangerous enforcer. But this can't be him. "Is that a threat?" I ask as tears prick my eyes.

"What?" He grabs my arms. "You don't understand. You're about to unlock Pandora's box on the people you care about—"

What's he saying? Does he mean Aunt Grace? The Everlys? I whip away. "Let go of me."

"Ivy, stop—"

"Something wrong?" Sin asks, stepping between us. "Anything you need to say to Ms. Palmer, you can say to me."

Leo frowns. "I only want to talk."

"Then talk to me," Sin insists, standing between us.

Leo hesitates like a storm struggling for direction. His parting words are low and haunting. "Goodbye, Ivy." He walks away as pieces of my heart join him. How could everything we had go so wrong?

An attendant approaches. "Five minutes," he says to Sin.

"Thank you." He takes a furtive glance at the courtroom, then at me. "Ready?"

I nod and take one last searching look for Leo. But he's gone.

There are three tables before the judge. Smoke and his attorney are seated on the left. Andre and his half-dozen attorneys swarm a table to the right because he can't stop overcompensating.

Sin and I take our seats at the table between them. "Good morning, Ivy," Smoke says, his expression as regretful and sad as Leo's was. I do a double-take. His perfectly square jaw is also bruised and swollen. Either he and Leo took on the cartel, or they pounded each other senseless in a fight.

I glance around the room. Between Smoke and his attorney, and Andre and his entourage, I'm glad I have Sin.

He sits tall and confident, seemingly unconcerned at being my only shield against the two teams and their over-the-top pissing contest. He whispers, "Trinity said to protect you at all costs."

"What does that mean?"

"It means I need to preserve the estate and protect you. I'm about to make an unorthodox request. Just go with it."

Before I can ask anything else, he discretely hushes me as the judge enters and we all stand. Her hair is in a professional bun and her long, black robe stately and official.

As she moves behind the bench, she announces, "Please, be seated." We all sit. Everyone but Sin.

Sin remains standing. "Apologies to the court, your honor. I've only just been brought in as council for Ms. Palmer and on behalf of my client, we have a request."

She nods. "A continuance?"

He shakes his head. "Your honor, in light of the case before us, we demand a paternity test."

Gasps flutter around the courtroom, and I'm pretty sure it was Smoke's voice that let out a *fuck*.

"What are you doing?" I insist, tugging as his sleeve. "This isn't what I wanted," I seethe under my breath.

"Trust me, I know what I'm doing. It'll tie up the case for years, and everything the D'Angelos have will stay safely out of reach until we come up with another strategy."

My gaze drifts to Trini, beautiful and angelic. Then at Smoke. He's liable to crack a molar if he keeps tensing his jaw.

Smoke's attorney leaps to his feet, frantic. "Your honor, you can't allow this request. Antonio D'Angelo has been missing—presumed dead—for over four years. Any DNA we have is insignificant at best."

Sin chimes in. "Perfectly understandable, your honor. We're in no hurry."

"Well, I am," Andre huffs.

Sin remains calm. "Are you anxious enough to provide your own DNA? Perhaps we could pursue this via a process of elimination."

Now it's my turn to kick Sin beneath the table. "Don't worry," Sin says, rubbing his chin. "Andre's always been paranoid about giving up anything remotely close to DNA. I just said it to irritate him."

Andre chuckles, and it's obnoxious. "Your mother must have been quite the prize. Two D'Angelo men. How flattering for her." The judge slams her gavel.

Heat boils below my skin as Sin simply repeats himself. "It's a process of elimination."

The judge bangs her gavel again and commands, "Order."

"You don't need that. There's a photo of them," Andre

counters, addressing the court. "Of Samara Palmer and Antonio D'Angelo together." He makes it sound suggestive and lewd.

Smoke's attorney objects. The rules of protocol go flying out the window as I pile on to his objection. "Unless they were in the process of making me when it was taken, photos aren't proof."

Sin clears his throat. "Begging the court's indulgence, your honor. But in full disclosure, we are aware of a photo. It was provided directly to me from Andre D'Angelo himself."

I blast off at Andre. "This isn't even my lawsuit. You're the one who filed on my behalf."

Andre laughs loud. "Right. You and I never discussed it. I just filed on your behalf out of the blue." He winks.

Outraged, I jump to my feet. Sin yanks me back in my chair. "He's lying!" I shout.

The judge turns to Sin. "Control your client."

"Yes, your honor."

Andre pipes up again. "Your honor, may I speak?"

The judge nods. I can't believe she's allowing this.

"Mr. Sinclair's client is obviously a delusional girl. It's a well-known fact she's been harassing me for weeks. And I don't even want to bring up her time in jail. The poor girl just needs a little psychiatric help."

Sin looks at me. Like a maniac, I explode. "Because of him!" It isn't until I hear the gavel bang repeatedly that I realizing Andre got exactly what he wanted. An out-of-control display from a delusional girl.

The judge narrows her eyes and points at Sin with her gavel. "Is that true? Does Ms. Palmer have a criminal record?"

This time, Sin locks a hand around my wrist like a cuff, chaining me in place. He frowns, confused, and responds to the judge. "I need time to confer with my client, your honor."

She strikes the gavel down again. "Ms. Palmer. False imprisonment is a serious accusation, and Mr. Andre D'Angelo is an upstanding member of the community. Unless you have some way to back it up, I'll cite you with contempt and throw you in jail myself. Understood?"

Adrenaline courses as my blood pumps cold. He did it. Andre D'Angelo spun the perfect web, and I did a spectacular swan dive into the heart of it. I suck in a breath, desperate to steady my nerves.

Before I can say a word and make it any worse, Sin speaks for me. "Yes, your honor. She understands."

The judge slams her gavel three times. "In light of this new evidence, we'll adjourn. You have twenty-four hours. I'll expect you and your evidence in front of me tomorrow."

"Thank you, your honor."

She slams her gavel again, and everyone leaves the room. Smoke is already gone, and Leo is nowhere in sight.

Sin ensures we're alone. "Why were you in jail?" he asks, direct and to the point.

I shrink. "I know how it looks. Andre had me thrown in jail. Shortly after meeting the D'Angelos."

His eyes narrow. "Why?"

"For no reason." He crosses his arms. I flail mine about. "I know how this sounds."

"Yes, insane. But I wouldn't put it past Andre. We just need proof." Sin rubs his chin and thinks. "Is there anyone who can back your claim?"

I close my eyes and nod. "Leo can."

***

"Hi. It's Ivy. Again. I really need to talk with you, Leo. Call me. Okay?" I disconnect. If this were anyone else in the world, I might understand. But this is Leo, and I'm devastated.

Voicemails. Text messages. No matter how I try to reach Leo, I get nothing. "Why won't you call me?" I whisper in frustration to the phone. From Sin's office, I can see the wonderland of Chicago. The restaurant Leo took me to. The Bean.

His image smiles from my home screen. A cruel reminder of Leo at his happiest. Of the Leo I thought I loved.

But for nine long hours now, not a single word.

"Stop ghosting us," Trini mutters to her phone as she dials his number again. I press the button and end her call. "What are you doing?" she asks.

"It's all right." I sigh. Trini is exhausted. So is Sin. So am I. This day is one crappy hour after the other, and I'm so over it right now. "Go home, Trini. I'll see you tomorrow."

She flashes me a look that tells me she's not having it.

I force a smile and pretend everything will be okay. "I promise, I'll be fine."

I ignore my own advice and in a last-ditch effort to get in contact with Leo, I send a text. Then, I pray. And I wait.

Leo, please. I need your help.

The text comes back undelivered. *Am I blocked?*

CHAPTER 37

Ivy

I t's morning, about an hour before we're due in court, and Sin's bloodshot eyes must rival mine. At one a.m., we sent for a driver to take Trini home, though not without a fight. We assured her that if anything, she could try to track down Leo. Between the security staff and Smoke insisting Leo hasn't been around, the only way we were tracking him down was if Trini snatched a bloodhound and did it herself.

I stare at the unforgiving clock. "Why can't I just drop the lawsuit?" I ask with a hopeful smile.

"Because you didn't file it," Sin explains for the umpteenth time and retaliates with his own question of the hour. "No word from Leo?"

I hang my head. "No." I don't elaborate about him blocking me. Some things hurt less when you don't say them out loud.

My phone buzzes, and I snap it up. "Leo?"

"Is this Olivia Palmer?" I check the caller ID. *Hospital?* I feel the blood drain from my face. I don't know how I do it, but I speak. "Yes."

"This is registration at Northwestern Memorial Hospital. We've just admitted Grace Everly. She's resting and stable, but we need to discuss treatment options. Can you come down?"

"I'll be right there." I race for the door, stopped by the massive tower of Sin. "I have to go."

"You can't leave now. You're due in court."

My body shoves his aside, hard. "Screw the court."

He doesn't budge. "You'll be in contempt." He's calm and logical. "You'll lose the case *and* go to jail. Doesn't she have other family?"

"They're out of state. It's an emergency!" *Why am I the only one who sees this?*

"I heard the call. She's resting. If you don't show up after the judge's request, she'll issue a bench warrant on the spot. And Andre will latch on to that. Don't you see? You're giving him the ammunition he needs to drag this on and on."

I can't lose her. "I don't care about the stupid case. I don't even care about jail. Aunt Grace needs me, and I'm going to be there for her." I race to the elevator. Sin shuffles behind.

"I'll call the hospital. Send staff to look in on her," Sin says, doing his best to reason with me.

He has no idea how little rational thought I have left. "There is something you can do," I tell him. "Call Andre. Tell him I'll give him everything he wants if he drops the case. But he has to take my call."

"Ivy, you're not thinking clearly. Trust me, he's got nothing to lose by going through with this. He'll never agree to speak with you."

The elevator arrives and I get in, jabbing the first-floor button with force. "Trust me, he will."

Sin's expression flashes with doubt and confusion. I meet his eyes as the doors begin to close. Sleep deprived and exhausted, I bark one last desperate command. "Do it!"

CHAPTER 38
Ivy

"Northwestern Memorial Hospital, and step on it."

"Right away." The cab driver understands my urgency and weaves into traffic. His speed aligns with my pulse.

He drops me off in front of the emergency room, and I die on the spot. I have no cash and no way to pay him.

"I don't have my purse," I say, apologizing. "I'm sorry. It's an emergency. I need to find my aunt."

"Something wrong?" a man asks, sounding out every vowel of his southern drawl. The sight of Officer Friendly gives me greater faith in God. He was at D'Angelo Towers the first day I arrived. "Yes," I say with hands begging. "Do you have any money?"

He rolls his eyes, charmed. "What is it about me that screams ATM?" He fishes out his wallet and ducks down to check the fare with the cabby. "Got change for a twenty?"

"Thank you. I'll pay you back."

"Yeah, yeah," he says and waves me along.

The receptionist is fast and efficient in processing my visitor request. "You must be Ivy."

"Yes," I reply, my voice trembling.

"Through those elevators. Fifth floor. Room 502."

My heart pounds with my feet as I race down each hall and corridor until I get to 502.

The room is dark with beeps coming from the other side of a curtain. I peel it back.

"Aunt Grace?"

She's lying in the bed, still.

"You must be Ivy," a man says quietly, and I'm starting to wonder why everyone keeps saying that to me. "I'm Dr. Locke. We've been expecting you."

"Is she going to be all right?"

He nods. "She's fine. She said she couldn't sleep with all the bells and whistles, so we gave her a mild sedative. It'll wear off soon."

I exhale, relieved. "Was it her blood pressure?"

He checks his chart and scribbles on it. "Yes. We may need to tinker with her medication. Perhaps even lower the dose." I shiver and wrap myself in a hug.

"We try to keep the rooms subzero," he complains.

He grabs the IV and fiddles with the lead. "Will you be available to discuss some treatment options?"

"She doesn't have much in the way of insurance," I say.

He nods with an understanding grin. "There's a man at the billing department sorting that now."

"Who?"

But without answering, Dr. Locke pats my hand and leaves, closing the door behind him. Aunt Grace is on her side, and with her soft, steady breaths and adorable snore, I tear up and smile, relieved. I squeeze her hand tight. "Ivy?" she says in her sleep.

"I'm here, Aunt Grace. I'll always be here." My cell chimes softly—a text from Sin.

Andre agreed.
I'm wrapping things up with the court.
Call me if you or your aunt need anything.

With Aunt Grace asleep again, I make my way to the lobby and steel my nerves. I find a quiet spot near a window and search through a dozen blocked numbers. I unblock the very first one, and click to dial.

It answers on the first ring. "Olivia?"

His voice alone makes me angered and outraged. Queasy and sick. I want to tell him to go to hell, suck a dick, and go royally fuck himself, but I can't. I have one card to play and too much to lose. I've lost Leo and the D'Angelos. I can't lose Aunt Grace too.

I choke down my frustration—my fear. I could be wrong. But it doesn't matter. It's my one shot, and I let the puzzle piece fall in place like a guillotine. "Hello, father."

***

With a heart full of lead, I return to the room. I open the door, and see him, standing there as if he belongs here. Belongs in my life. "Hi, Ivy," Leo says. He moves a hand through his hair. "Your aunt's one tough cookie."

I agree and squeeze her hand. "What do you want?"

Leo thinks for a minute and blows out a breath. "I'm sorry. I had to stay away. But when Sin and Trini tracked me down and told me about Aunt Grace—"

"You what, Leo? I've been calling and calling. You disappeared. Blocked my number."

"I know, angel. I know." He closes the distance, and maybe I'm too exhausted, but I don't pull away. I'm too numb.

He kisses me. His tongue makes its way between my lips, a slow, cautious build as he reminds me of his touch, his warmth, his need. He reminds me of what we had.

And what we lost.

I tear up and smile. He catches each tear with his thumbs. "Your aunt was right, Ivy. I have a choice to make, and I choose—"

"Don't, Leo." *Don't say it.* My heart is heavy, weighed down with regret. I'm in love with a man I shouldn't love. I shut my eyes, too overwhelmed to meet his gaze. What's done is done. It's too late. Leo will always have the D'Angelos to protect, and what about me?

I have my arrangement. Trinity will hate it, but I know she'll understand.

I step back and take a needed breath. "Aunt Grace and I are returning to North Carolina. As soon as she's well enough to travel. She needs to be surrounded by family, and I need her."

"I quit my job. I could go with you."

He quit his job? Smoke would never stand for that. I give a wry laugh. "No, Leo. You can't. It's too late."

Confusion and pain swirl behind his eyes. They search mine. "It's not too late. It can't be."

"You said it yourself: your loyalty would never be to me."

"And I've regretted it every goddamned day since. I'm so fucking sorry, Ivy. Smoke was listening right out side the door. He had to believe I would pick him over you. That my feelings were shut off."

My heart aches for him, but I know I have to do this. It's for the best. "You'll always have your walls up, and so will I. Our timing is never right." Hot tears well in my eyes. "We don't mean to hurt each other, but we always do. And we always will."

"That's not true," he says, pained.

My words are a whisper. "Your place is here. Protecting the D'Angelos. And mine isn't."

He pulls me into him. His chest. His heart. His love. "I'm not letting you go."

I kiss him goodbye. "You already did."

CHAPTER 39
Leo

"Name?"

I deadpan. *Is he fucking serious right now?* I've been chief of security for the D'Angelos for, I don't know, ever. And if he bothered to look at the image recognition screen, his homework would be done. Smoke summons me for a meeting, then puts the new guy at the gate. Hilarious.

"Leo Zamparelli," I announce.

He actually checks his list. I wipe a hand down my face. "I'm sorry, sir. I don't see you on the visitor roster."

I narrow my eyes and glare at the camera. "Let. Me. In."

The gate buzzes open. I salute sharply and drive through. It takes me twenty minutes to park and get to Smoke because, apparently, two blow-up dolls decided to take a golf cart for a spin and park in my spot.

Smoke relaxes back with his feet on his desk, smirking. "Problem with security?"

"Not at all. Sharp kid. Just doing his job."

Smoke chuckles. "Ready to take your job back?"

"No."

That wipes the grin from his arrogant face. "No?"

I take a seat and crack my knuckles. "I've saved up. I'm thinking about going to Mexico."

"Right," he says, fingers steepled to his chin. "The man who's allergic to cilantro is parking his ass in Mexico. Send me a postcard. Let me know how that goes."

"With pleasure." We glare at each other for a solid minute, and damn it to hell, I give in first. "You need to look out for Ivy."

"We are."

"In North Carolina?"

Smoke sits up. "It's probably part of her deal with Andre. I had nothing to do with that."

My jaw tightens. "Why would she make a deal with Andre? She's a D'Angelo."

"Not according to this." He waves a sheet of paper in the air and slides it over to me.

I, Olivia Ann Palmer, dismiss any and all claims against Antonio and Andre D'Angelo.

I give him a subatomic death glare. "What the fuck, Smoke? She's a D'Angelo. I saw the blood test. Case closed."

"I didn't ask her to do this. All I know is the case was dropped, and this was the result."

"How fucking convenient for you."

His brow knits, and the uneasiness that forms from it means the ultimate control freak really doesn't know. "Look over there," he says.

On the table in the corner, the little flask stands center stage. I can almost make out the names from here.

"Whatever deal with the devil Ivy cooked up, that was part of it. It's all been returned. That and a few other things Andre stole from us over the years."

I move to it and take the shiny silver flask in my hands. I cradle it and trace a finger against each of their names, and all of a sudden, I choke up, overwhelmed. Ivy did what no one else could do—she got a piece of Antonio back. I tear up, and it isn't even my fucking flask. "How did she do it?"

Smoke leans across his desk. "I'd give anything to know that...and to have you back." I smile but don't turn to face him. He flicks a paperclip at my head just to make sure I'm listening. "Don't quit."

I check my watch. "It's only been a day. What's wrong, Smoke? Can't live without me?"

His eyes roll in concession. "Something like that."

I stroll over opposite him, palm my hands to the desk and lean into his space. "Then how about you do something for me for once? And for Ivy."

CHAPTER 40
Ivy

hat should have been two days in the hospital turned into two weeks, thanks to an allergic reaction to the IV contrast. But thankfully, tomorrow, Aunt Grace will be released. And then, we go home.

The doctors have cleared her for the trip back to North Carolina, and all the Everlys have pitched in with a rock star party bus. As excited as we were for the queen bed to keep her comfy, she was over the moon with the traveling stripper pole.

It should be good news, right? So why does it feel like my chest is heavy and full of lead?

Aunt Grace sleeps peacefully, and I take a look around before I head home for the night. My last night in Chicago. The hospital room is fragrant with roses and crowded with teddy bears and gifts from every D'Angelo and Everly, and one from Leo.

A box of homemade cookies. Trini said he burned four batches to get to this one. I nibble a bite and laugh. Without sugar, they're awful.

Two soft knocks sound at the door. "How's she doing?" Smoke walks in shyly, and a lump forms in my throat.

"She's been resting off and on all day." I straighten, determined. "She'll be fine."

Smoke scans the monitors and checks her chart. It all seems second nature to him. He keeps his voice hushed though she hasn't stirred. "Does your aunt need anything? Do you?"

"Do you?" I ask, pointing out the lingering bruises around his face.

He cradles his jaw. "I'd like to say you should see the other guy, but I'm the other guy." Both our smiles are small as he makes his way around the room. He selects a get-well card from the sea of them, reads it, then returns it carefully back in place. "I was wrong, Ivy, and I'm sorry. You don't have to leave."

How do I explain that I do? This isn't even about my contract with Andre. It's about Leo. It's always about Leo. Loving Leo is like loving the pain of a trampled heart. Sooner or later, it breaks for good. "It's better for my aunt," I say softly.

Smoke pops the nose of a small, beige teddy bear. "We've set another date for *Erede al Trono*. Trini would love for you to come." When I say nothing, he clears his throat. "We'd all love it if you could come."

"Enzo, too?" I joke half-heartedly.

"Enzo the asshole, too." He laughs sadly. "He's actually the sorriest of all of us. His jet is at your disposal, for you and your aunt." The silence dredges on, becoming awkward and strained. "We could set up an account. Get you a car. A house. Find a nice place for you and your aunt—"

"You don't have to do that," I say, my smile a smidge wider.

He plucks a flower from the assortment—a bright yellow

rose—and hands it to me. "You and I both know I do." I take a small whiff of the sweet perfume. I can see he's trying, and it's a start. "Look, I don't know what deal you made with Uncle Andre, but I know he got the goldmine, and you got the shaft."

I let out a long, even breath. "I got what I needed."

"You deserve more than the shaft, Ivy."

"What can I say to that? I agree," I say, trying to laugh it off. "Besides, you paid for the hospital bill."

Smoke cocks a mild grin. "I could pretend I know nothing about that, but we're family now, so full disclosure. I would have, but I didn't. It was all Leo."

"Of course, it was," I sigh with regret. "How is he?"

Smoke blows out a breath. "I'm not sure. MIA most of the time."

I nod sadly.

"Here." He hands me a folded piece of paper and waits while I open it. "The blood test was inconclusive. But, for what it's worth, you're definitely a D'Angelo." He places a paternal hand on my shoulder, and I can see it in his eyes—a sense of connection. Somehow, I know that no matter what's happened between us, he wants to repair it. Smoke wants to make this right. "Can I at least offer you a ride?" he asks.

I grab my purse since my tab with Officer Friendly is beginning to pile up. "Yes."

We make our way to the parking garage. Leo leans against a car, waiting. I freeze in place, breathless.

"I can still give you a ride," Smoke explains. "But Leo was

hoping he could. It's your call."

What do I do? My heart wells up with love and pain, and I can't decide. Do I run into his arms?

Or run away?

I walk to him as he meets me halfway. "What do you want, Leo?" I ask the question, then hold my breath, anxious for his response.

Smoke's footsteps move quietly away, but my eyes stay on Leo. And his are on mine.

Leo takes my hand in both of his. "Forgiveness. A miracle." His eyes well up, and so do mine. "One night."

I lose myself in the skyline of the city. "I'll miss Chicago," I whisper. I press a palm to the glass, and I spot the locations of every beautiful memory Leo gave me. HAYDON'S ON THE SHORE. Dancing in front of The Bean. Even this hotel. Dread begins to fill my heart, weighing it down with sadness and grief.

"You don't have to leave," he whispers sadly in the dark.

I turn. I want him to see me when I say this. Hold him to our promise—the one I have to keep. I repeat his words back as a reminder—to Leo as much as to me. "One night."

He nods. We kiss, and I breathe him in, memorizing this. Us. Soft kisses trail along my neck and chin as he slowly peels away my clothes and his. He holds me tenderly and in reverence. An intimate moment where his soul binds with mine, tangled in our breaths and our heartbeats.

And our...love.

He lifts me to the bed and climbs on top of me. My legs

spread, allowing him to settle between them. Our eyes lock. Our breathing stops. "Don't go," he whispers.

I glide my wetness along his length as my eyes flutter back. I won't stay. I can't.

In one swift, unforgiving move, he enters, filling me with more of him than I think I can take—a hard, punishing thrust. "More," I beg.

He moves slowly at first—careful, intentional strokes that are filled with pleasure, passion, sadness, and pain. An imprint of something beautiful and devastating that will forever be ours.

He tries to speak, and I kiss him soft and tender, raw and rough. I kiss him again and again because I can give him this. Not what he wants.

But what I can give.

He drives into me harder. Deep, desperate thrusts that threaten to tear me apart. He controls me—owns me—until I shudder hard. Then, he fucks me harder. "Stay," he demands, giving me no reprieve. No way to escape. No way not to answer.

He rips one climax from me and prepares my shattered body for another.

I try to kiss him, but he turns away. "Goddammit, Ivy, stay."

Tears break free. "I can't."

He forces a leg over his shoulder, pumping deep. The sweat of his body slaps the wetness of mine. His thick length grows. Widens. Deepens. Until there is nothing of me but him. His thrusts break through my every barrier and defense. His body slams harder. "Stay."

I can't. I won't. My back arches, and every piece of me shatters beneath him. With violent, uncontrolled jerks, he collapses, spent, on top of me.

His voice is tired, and I'm not sure if he's saying this to me or to himself. "I hate you, Ivy Palmer."

I laugh in the dark, shifting to spoon against his chest. "Is that so?"

His leg wraps around me. "I hate you for leaving me."

I tear up. This isn't him putting up walls. Leo is tearing them down. I line up a brick along the wall of my defenses and take a baseball bat to it. "I hate you, Leo, for breaking my heart."

He squeezes me tighter. "I hate that I can't get you out of my head."

"I hate that no one will ever give me the orgasms you do."

His laugh is hearty. He thinks for a minute and comes up with another one. "I hate that you put everyone's needs above your own. You never put yourself first."

I weave my hand into his. "You do that, too," I say sadly.

He kisses my shoulder. "Do you hate that about me?"

"I guess not," I say with a shrug.

"Then it doesn't count." He kisses my neck. "Still your turn."

This game is ridiculous. But it makes me feel better, so I play on. I secretly hate that there's something about his late wife that no one will tell me—some reason he has for guarding the delicate softness of his heart— but I can't say that. Instead, I wrap it into a bigger issue. "I hate that everyone knows more about you than I do."

He turns me so we're face to face. His eyes are raw and red.

"I hate that you're the only woman who will ever have my heart." We kiss a long, slow, meaningful kiss. We melt into each other, and he says the last thing he hates about me. "I hate how much I love you."

CHAPTER 41

Ivy

How's the house?

I greet the tiny text with a sad smile. It's Leo. Again. It's been weeks of him reaching out by flowers and candy and text. I'm grateful he hasn't called. The last thing I need is his growly voice melting my defenses again. I haven't replied, but he still manages to keep tabs on me. I smile at the text. *He knows about the house.*

He's also been holding onto Mr. Whiskers and texted me an image of the two of them titled, *My Hostage*. Trinity assured me she'd send it back, all while letting it slip that Mr. Whiskers miraculously turns up everywhere Leo is—like his office and his car, and even in front of that cross-stitched pillow of his childhood dog she made him. I secretly love that they're together.

Mr. Whiskers has returned to his original home—the D'Angelo estate—and Leo has a memento to remember me by.

"Last box," Aunt Grace announces triumphantly, meaning she's finally unpacked the last wardrobe box.

I look around the closet you could practically park a jet in. "Plenty of room for all the athleisure and tracksuits you could shake a stick at," I tease.

"Challenge accepted." Aunt Grace flaunts a gold tracksuit with dazzling stripes down each leg, and two daisies stitched on her butt. She plucks an extra bright, ombre pink-and-fuchsia one from her closet and holds it up to me. "I can't imagine how we managed to snag a rental like this."

I find creative ways to avoid answering her unspoken questions each time she doesn't ask. "Yes, amazing."

"Who did you say owns it again?"

"An acquaintance of Sin's." It's the truth. A mortal enemy acquaintance of Sin's, but she doesn't need to know that. The last thing we need is her blood pressure skyrocketing and this beautiful home burned to the ground.

I didn't tell her about my arrangement with my father, but I did tell her who he was. Which makes Andre D'Angelo the only member of her party-of-one shit list.

"Was it Leo?" she asks with a little too much hope in her tone.

"No," I say softly as my heart squeezes because, for some unshakeable reason, neither of us would put it past him. Except Leo would've bought it outright as a *Welcome Back to North Carolina* gift. This is from Andre, and it's no gift. My father is praying to God that I'll slip and break our contract.

He didn't gift the home to Aunt Grace. For all intents and purposes, it's a rental. A rental at exactly zero dollars a month for the fee so long as I hold up my part of the bargain and stay out of Chicago.

By the look on her face, she doesn't believe me. "No?"

I hang my head and reassure her. "It wasn't Leo."

A sad moment passes between us. "Good!" she says, spitting piss and vinegar. "The last thing I want is to owe a debt to that security guard." Her bright eyes meet mine. "Zumba?" she asks with a shake of her hips. Since moving back, Aunt Grace's energy could light a city.

I shake my head. "I am on a mission to relax."

"You're on a mission to scour the internet for a job." I help collect her gym bag, and we make our way to her car.

Embarrassed, I shrug. "I have an interview tomorrow. With Derrick."

With both hands, she pinches my cheeks. "How about I have Wade and his crew straighten that boy out?"

My hands wrap around hers. "As much as I'd like to get the line started for the Derrick ball-kicking booth, it's not a great impression on the man who might become my boss...again."

I follow her out to the porch because watching her take off is like watching the first firework on the Fourth of July. Sin gifted her a little cherry-red Mercedes convertible that she's damned near dangerous in. He called it a tax write-off. I call him smitten. "Don't speed," I warn her.

She slides her sunglasses down the tip of her nose. "If I don't, I'm breaking my word. With Sin." She pops open the glove compartment and hands me a card.

Dance like no one is watching,
Love like you've never been hurt,
Sing like no one is listening,
And gun it for all it's worth.

SINS & IVY

The car revs as I hand her back the card. "I double-dog dare you to show your brother this sound legal advice."

"*If* he pulls me over. He'll have to catch me first."

CHAPTER 42
Ivy

My phone pings again. This time, instead of sending a few dozen roses or a box of Vosges chocolate truffles, Leo has sent me an image. It's a hand-written page with the words *Dear Diary* at the top along with a date.

Dear Diary,

They say if you love something, set them free.

If they love you back, they'll return.

If not, then they were never yours to begin with.

The fact that there's no deadline makes this bullshit task impossible.

She loves me. And I love her.

So why is this taking so long?

I wish she would call me.

Somewhere between laughter and pain, I'm left staring at his words. The image is erased by an incoming alarm. A reminder.

Interview with Derrick
Noon

CHAPTER 43

Leo

S   moke sits back in his chair, having summoned me like
       he's the master, and I'm his Igor. Trinity sits across
       from him, looking up with innocent eyes. I release a
weight-of-the-world exhale. They're up to something.

"There's something I need you to do," Smoke says.

Furious, I explode. "Are you fucking kidding me? The last
time you said those words, you had me stay away from Ivy. No
calls. No contact."

He glares at me, heated and unamused, as his eyes roll over
to Trinity. Obviously, she didn't know. Well, the cat's out of the
bag now, dumbass.

Trinity smacks him hard upside the back of his head. I smile
with delight.

Smoke growls. "As I was saying, I have a job for you."

My ears perk up. Am I roughing up someone? Because all
my pent-up frustration could sure use an outlet. I say a silent
prayer. *Please let it be Enzo.*

"Andre is being nice. Too nice," he sneers. "Find out why."

Underwhelmed, I decline. "I'm chief of security, not the figure-out-Andre lackey. You need him shot? I'm your guy. You need him psychoanalyzed? Call Dr. Phil." I crack my knuckles. "Are we done?"

Trinity sits straighter. "Ivy isn't coming to *Erede al Trono*. Please find out why."

Fuck, I don't know how to say this, so I blurt it out. "She's not exactly baring her soul to me these days, Trinity."

She frowns. "Oh, I'm sorry, Leo. I didn't know. She said you sent her beautiful flowers, and I thought—"

"What else did she say?" I ask, needing reassurance...a sign... just one glimmer of hope.

Trini thinks about it for a moment, sifting through what she can tell me and what she can't. "She didn't know you wrote in a diary."

"You write in a diary?" Smoke asks, chuckling.

"Edison and Darwin both kept diaries," I fire back.

"So did Kahlo and Da Vinci," Trini adds because she's my favorite.

"You see?" I say to Smoke. "I'm right up there with Edison and Da Vinci, so fuck off." My phone rings. Fuckface Derrick. I cup a hand over the phone. "I really need to take this."

Smoke blinks. "Sure you do."

Smoke mumbles something about Andre and Ivy as I excuse myself and leave the room. *Do him a favor?* Sure. When Olympic figure skating is sponsored by hell.

"What?" I bark to the phone.

"Yes, Mr. Z. You said you wanted to be informed if she ever made contact. She's coming in."

"Today?" I pocket a hand. "Do you know why?"

"She wants a job." He stammers nervously. "What do I do?"

"What do you mean what do you do?" No response. "Give. Her. One." I demand. "At twice your salary."

"Twice *my* salary? But—"

"But what?" My patience is non-existent and my tone deadly.

He takes the hint. "Nothing, sir. I'll take care of it."

CHAPTER 44
Ivy

The gardens at Sparrow Assisted Living are in full bloom, and the air is fragrant and welcoming. It's only been a few months since I worked here, but so much has changed. Or maybe I'm the only one who's changed.

I walk into the admissions area and look around. "Hello?" It's quiet and empty. I peer into the grand parlor. My breath catches, and I stand frozen, staring at a painting.

"Oh, good afternoon, Ms. Palmer," Derrick shouts from a mile down the hall. Since when am I *Ms. Palmer?* He stampedes into the room, stops short of toppling over me, and struggles to catch his breath. *Huff-huff.* "I'm so sorry I wasn't here to greet you." *One last extra-long huff.* "But I made sure the entry was cleared."

"Why?"

He leans in and whispers, "To respect your privacy."

Huh? I pretend his sanity is intact and force a smile because I really need a job.

He motions to the painting with a showman's hand. "Is this to your liking?"

I glare at him sideways, and not because I don't like Angie's painting. I love it. But something is off.

The painting of me is flanked on both sides with fresh flowers. I stare, suddenly horrified. "Is this a. . .shrine?"

His eyes widen to a deer-in-the-headlights level. "No, but with a few candles and a plaque with your name on it, yeah. Sure. I can totally see it."

He wraps a hand around my shoulders and leans in. "Whatever job you want is yours. And if you need anything, and I mean *anything*, you let me know."

Eww. I peel his arm from my shoulder and take several steps back. I take in Derrick Landon. With his hair slicked back, his best cheeseball grin, and that disaster of a purplish-gray three-piece suit, I have no idea what I ever saw in him. Repulsed, I shudder. "I need to go."

"You can't." He falls to his knees. "I'll do anything." He begs with prayer hands. "Please."

Stunned, I stare. "Are you proposing?"

His throat bobs as he gulps. "Uh, okay. Sure. Yeah. Is that what you want?"

What the fuck?

"Ivy?" a meek voice calls from the entry. Angie waves, and it's just the excuse I need to ditch Derrick.

I feel Derrick pull at my skirt as soon as I try to step away. "You can't leave me," Derrick insists and scans the room in a paranoid fashion. "He won't like it."

"First, release my skirt if you want to avoid a thumb in the eye and a restraining order." He does. "Now, *who* won't like *what*?"

"The new owner. He said I had to offer you the job...at twice my salary." He rolls his eyes at me. At least now I know the old Derrick is somewhere in there, and still a dumbass.

"Who's the new owner?"

"You *m-m-m*ust mean Mr. Z.," Angie says as she squeezes my hand. "He b-b-bought the painting, too." She shows me her Venmo and beams with pride at the generous payment.

Dumbfounded, I stare at the payment note.

Brought to you by the letter Z.

CHAPTER 45

Ivy

For nearly an hour, I've plucked a dozen wild daisies in the hopes of answering the one question I wrestle with daily: call or don't call? So far, it's a tie.

When his usual text pops up, my heart tugs extra hard.

How was your day?

That's it. I can't keep hoping Leo will move along. He won't. I decide on the bravest course of action I can think of. I call.

"Hey, angel," he answers, his voice growly and tired because, *shit*, it's late. "Before you say anything, I want to show you something."

My cell pings, and Leo has sent a photo of a box. "What is this?"

"When we were in the thrift shop, you asked me about the box I was carrying."

I smile, remembering.

"Don't you want to know what's in it?"

"I don't want to see what's in your box of guy stuff porn if that's what you're asking."

"I know you're curious," Leo says with a confident sales pitch. "Inside this box is everything you ever wanted to know about me, and it can be yours for a price."

I listen, already knowing whatever he's about to ask, it'll be more than I can give.

"Come back to Chicago." *Pause.* "There are fourteen days before the *Erede al Trono* reboot. Smoke wants you there." *Pause.* "And so does Trinity." *Pause again.* "And so do I."

I want to be there with them—with him. But I can't, and I can't tell him why. Leo is a lightning strike. White-hot in the moment. Devastation in the aftermath. Even without Andre's contract keeping me from Chicago, I can't crawl back to Leo. I'll hand him my heart, and he'll demolish me again.

I swipe hot tears from my face, and whisper back, "I can't."

"Is this because of Andre?" he spews. "Tell me what it is, and I'll fix it."

"You can't fix this, Leo."

"At least let me try," he cries, unnerved. The strain in his voice settles. "I know I broke us," he whispers. "Let me make this right."

I want to say there's nothing to make right. Nothing to forgive. But I'd only be prolonging the inevitable. "Leo, your world is wrapped up with the D'Angelos, and I wouldn't have it any other way. It's over."

"What are you saying?" He unleashes his emotions. "You said you loved me."

"And you said one night," I cry and rip off the rest of the

bandage. "Trini needs you. And so does Smoke. You need to get over me. And I need to move on."

"Ivy, don't do this."

I smother a sob and force the weak breath from my throat. "Please don't call again."

"All right," he says, and I can tell he's hurt. "I'd better let you go."

"Goodbye, Leo."

CHAPTER 46
Leo

I ping-pong around Chicago and scout each of the five residences Andre owns. I know what's going on. The fucker is hiding out.

After checking out his three penthouse apartments and his house on the lake, I arrive at this one. A fortress. It's contemporary with thirteen foot walls, state-of-the-art technology, and a few armed guards. Bypassing all of that takes some doing, but for Ivy, I do it. The fucker better be home.

Familiar sounds echo from the hall. A football game is on in the den. As soon as he sees me, he shuts off the game. "Hello, Andre." His mouth falls slack. I love that look on his face. In seconds, I memorize my surroundings. Original Louis XV piano. Cheetah print rug. Solid-gold candle holder filled with candles that look like tiny penises. "Nice place," I smirk.

In under sixty seconds, I'm swarmed by a small team of security. "How did you get in here?" the big one blasts.

And that's why they don't work for me. If they did, they'd be fired. "I teleported," I say arrogantly. Andre gives them a nod, and the second one swings the butt of his rifle to the center of my abs.

I breathe through it and stand up straight. "I want to know about your arrangement with Ivy."

A droll expression passes his face. "Who?"

Wow, he really doesn't know her. "Olivia Ann Palmer," I say, enunciating every syllable.

That gets his attention. He waves his men away and pours himself a drink. *Hey, you just fucked up my insides, but no, I couldn't use a water or anything, thanks.*

He sips his drink, confused. "She's *your* girlfriend. What do you want to know?"

I glance at him sideways. He only saw us together once. Granted, at the time, I had a gun pointed at his head, but Ivy and I weren't in a relationship then. And I doubt they've had a heart-to-heart. My words come out casual and indifferent. "Why would you call her that?"

He raises his glass. "Lucky guess."

He waves for me to have a seat, and I do. Mostly to recover. "I want to know about your arrangement with Ivy. Olivia," I add, correcting myself.

"And what's in it for me, Z.?"

I sit down and wing an arm over the back of the chair. "Oh, I don't know. How about I not give a list of detailed instructions to every enemy you have on how I broke in here. Which, before you get any ideas, is already sitting in my outbox on auto-send." I glance at my watch. "Tick tock."

He says nothing.

"I already know your little secret," I bluff. It's a crapshoot, but I roll the dice.

"Did Olivia tell you?"

"No. If she did, I wouldn't be here. I want the details of whatever arrangement you made."

He thinks on it for a minute and stares. His huff is long and loud and whining. "Fine. She gave me four demands, and I gave her only two in return."

A meager victory, but good for her. "What were they?" I ask with piqued interest.

"For starters, Olivia wanted everything I legally sequestered from Antonio's kids returned."

I smirk. "You had to return the stuff you stole. Got it."

"She also wanted some woman named Grace taken care of. A house. Her bills. Chump change." I wait for him to continue. And ..." he grumbles, "I have to go to therapy. With her."

Therapy? For what? I sit back and look Andre up and down. If she thinks this fucker's redeemable, she's wrong. "And last?"

His smile dulls. "I couldn't touch you. Not now, not ever."

And she calls me the martyr. "You let your henchman clock me in the gut."

He shrugs. "I didn't recognize you." He sips with a grin. *Fucktard.*

"And what did Ivy agree to do?" Again with the blank stare. I'm dealing with an imbecile. "O-liv-i-a," I pronounce out.

"For starters, she had to dismiss her claim to any money or inheritance." I let that sink in for a moment. *Her* claim. What claim? He was the one who filed the lawsuit to begin with—suing the estate on her behalf. I'm missing something. He continues. "And she has to stay the hell out of Chicago."

"Why?"

"Because I don't want to see her!" he shouts, losing all control. His shoulders slump as he deflates. A sad whine releases from his body as he sinks back in his chair. "Not any more than I have to."

"Oh, my God. You're. . .Ivy's father," I say, the taste putrid and phlegmy in my mouth.

He doesn't bother looking up. "Still the sharpest tool in the shed, I see." His expression fades.

My smile lifts in delight. "And she's making you go to family fucking therapy. To get to know you."

His eyes slam shut. "Don't remind me."

There's a light that warms me from the inside out. A feeling that, for once, the stars have aligned, and all is right in the universe. Ivy never wanted the money, she said so herself. She wanted this. To find her father and get to know him. Andre is a ruthless, power-hungry bully, but today, he's hiding out in his mansion, depressed and defeated. Ivy finally gets everything she ever wanted, and Andre gets emotionally fucked over in the process. There is a God.

I stand and look around. His 20,000-square-foot mansion is filled to the rafters with exquisite paintings and rich, antique rugs. "She's your own flesh and blood. You're really not giving her what's rightfully hers? Her inheritance."

He beams and clings tight to his last shred of righteous dick-headedness. "Not one cent."

I debate killing him, but take a meditative breath and decide to walk away. And not because I wouldn't enjoy bashing his brains in with his tacky as fuck dick candelabra. That would be glorious. But because my girlfriend is batshit crazy, and she wants to get to know the son of a bitch, God help me, I want that for her.

"Oh, Z.," Andre sings, stopping me before I step out the door.

I turn.

"Don't hurt Olivia."

I raise a brow in surprise.

"It gives me the perfect excuse to kill you."

Smirking, I leave. Even the world's biggest asshole isn't immune to the *Ivy Effect*. If I know Ivy, she'll have him bitching about his mommy issues and balled up in the fetal position in no time.

Enjoy therapy, prick.

CHAPTER 47

Leo

N oon.

Hi, this is Ivy. I can't come to the phone right now, but if you leave your name, number, and a message, I'll call you back.
Beep.

"Ivy, I know why you can't come to Chicago. We can work it out. Call me."

Three p.m. and fourteen calls later.

Hi, this is Ivy. I can't come to the phone right now, but if you leave your name, number, and a message, I'll call you back.

Beep.

"Angel, I need you to call me back. I promise we can fix this. I've worked it out with Smoke. We'll smuggle you on the jet—"

If you're satisfied with your message, hang up, or press one to re-record it.

"*Shit!*" I huff through gritted teeth and press one.

Beep.

"Baby, please. I need you. Just call me back."

<hr />

Nine p.m. and twenty-three calls later.

Hi, this is Ivy. I can't come to the phone right now, but if you leave your name, number, and a message, I'll call you back.

323

Beep.

"Goddamnit Ivy—call me," I demand.

By the thirtieth attempt, or thirty-sixth because I'm not really counting, my phone lands in a spectacular crash against the far wall. I rub a hand through my hair. If I could just talk with her, I can fix this. I just need her to pick up the goddamned phone.

I blow out a breath and pace the room. The phone is surprisingly intact...except for the face. The glass is cracked like a spider web but functional. So, I posture my finger to dial again.

I've tried sweet Leo, stern Leo, cheerful Leo, pissed as hell Leo. I flip a coin to see if I'm going for domineering Alpha Leo this time, or *at-the-end-of-my-rope,* begging Leo. I opt for the latter and press to connect.

But it only rings once, and I deflate with a sigh. "An eye for an eye," I mutter bitterly.

She blocked me.

CHAPTER 48
Leo

Trinity tracks me down like the bloodhound she's become. "You're not answering your phone," she says.

"No."

She joins me, and we stare at the clothes on my bed. A tailored black suit, a custom shirt, and a handsome, expensive pair of Italian leather shoes that cost more than my first car. Tomorrow is *Erede al Trono*...again. And this is the custom-made suit I'd worn nearly a month ago.

I look down at them, disgusted.

"You're really doing this?" Trinity asks.

I've put this off long enough. "Yup," I say, nodding.

I collect the clothes and shoes and march to the side of the house. The trash bin is about to get a mouthful.

Trinity holds open the lid as I throw it in. "I hate that Ivy can't come," she says.

Fucking Andre. My emotions get the better of me, and I

slam the lid shut. I dust my hands and meet Trinity's wide eyes. "What?" I ask, mildly unnerved.

"Nothing." She smiles and links an arm with mine.

We wander along the lake. I can't remember the last time Trini and I did this: shuffled our feet on the gravel pathway. I stare off, aimlessly.

"Do you miss her?" Trinity asks.

Miss her? Understatement of the century. What gave it away? My three-week beard? Or perhaps it's me wearing the same outfit for five straight days.

"Why not remove the sun and ask if I miss it?" I retort, irritated. I iron out my mood, determined not to take out my anger on Trinity. She's the one person, maybe the only person, who never deserves my wrath.

"It's not the same," she begins to say. "The bond that Ivy and I have is as if we're sisters. Wherever she goes or whatever she does, nothing will break our connection. But you...you could really lose her, Leo."

What the hell? "I know," I snap a little harder than I mean. But I can't help it. There's a knife lodged deep in my chest, and it's as if Trinity dropped by to twist it.

She looks up at me, doe-eyed. "What's the plan?"

Plan? Ha! As if there's enough free will in me to devise a plan. This is Aunt Grace's prediction, except my duties to the D'Angelos aren't a choice. They're my oath. My commitment. I gave my word to Antonio, and I can't break that vow.

Instead of answering Trinity, I pretend I didn't hear her and keep walking along. That's when I get a dainty little elbow hard in the ribs. "Ow!"

She shoves me in the chest. "Why aren't you going after her?"

Is she fucking kidding me right now? "Because I gave your father my word."

"Yes," she nods. "To protect the D'Angelos. And somewhere out there is a D'Angelo who needs you way more than I do."

It takes me a moment to come to terms with what she's saying.

"I'll be fine!" she shouts, exasperated. With her hands on my collar, she stares me down. "Listen to me, Leo. I'll be fine," she repeats with her big, blue eyes and sweet, compelling grin.

I clasp both her hands with a squeeze. Is she saying what I think she's saying? "Trinity, you understand if I leave, I'd be quitting. For good."

She stares me down. "And if you don't quit, I'll have no choice but to fire you."

Warmth fills my chest. Delirious, I chuckle. Trinity will be fine. Look at her. If I don't go, she really will fire me. She's a fucking boss. I kiss her on the cheek. "You sure?"

She nods. "At least if you quit, you get to pack."

"True." I laugh heartily as tears collect in her eyes and mine. I brush her bangs from her face. "You say the word, and I am here. Okay?"

"Okay," she says, wrapping a tight hug around me. It's the longest hug of my life. "And Leo..."

"Yes?"

"You'd better hurry. Hunter quit half an hour ago."

"What?"

Trinity cradles my cheeks. "You should really check your phone."

❦

The trip to North Carolina was first class all the way. Chauffeured Bentley to the airport. Private jet. But that's where Trinity and I agreed the D'Angelo hospitality had to end. If I was cutting ties, I was cutting all of them. Especially the biggest one—Smoke. I look down and stare at his text.

Answer your fucking phone!

I set down my bag and wait for my Lyft. When the phone rings again, I hesitate for a moment, then answer. "Hello?"

"Did you have to pick today of all days to do this?"

I feign innocence. "Do what?"

"There are movers at your house. Where are they going?"

"Storage. Until I've sorted everything out."

"Don't do this. Not now. Come back, and you can lose the remainder of your mind tomorrow."

"Have you ever heard the saying that if you love someone, set them free?"

I imagine the vein throbbing in his forehead. "What the fuck does that mean?"

I chuckle. "It means I'm leaving. For good."

My statement shuts him up for all of three seconds. "If you're not here, and Enzo fights my claim, he'll win."

"No one, not even Enzo, wants the wrath of Trinity." I rub my side, still sore from her elbow. "And even if that happens,

328

the two of you will just have to bust out the yard-sticks and measure your dicks."

"Goddammit Leo, I don't have my father, and I want you here." His booming voice softens. "Please."

That should be enough, right? A small request from the man who was there for me when my wife was clinging to life on a ventilator. Except that it's not. I wasn't there for her until it was too late. I won't make the same mistake twice.

If God has heard my prayers and the stars have aligned, I just might have one more shot with Ivy, and nothing will screw that up. "No."

"You can still make it," he says, blatantly ignoring me. "Get back on the jet. Ivy will understand."

As the Lyft pulls up, I heave my US Navy duffel to my shoulder, and dust off my hands. I take a good, long look at my palm and smile. My love line is calling. "Maybe she would understand, Smoke. And maybe I've annihilated my chances with Ivy, but for once in my life, I'm following my heart. She's what I want, and I'm going after her."

"I chose you over each of my brothers, Leo. To stand in place of my father."

The Lyft driver looks over expectantly with an impatient shoulder shrug. The jet is on standby, idly waiting. I send it off with a salute. "I choose Ivy. You see, Smoke, the last time I chose you. That choice was a colossal fuck up I intend to rectify."

Smoke disconnects the call—no doubt smashing his phone in the process—while I bask in the warmth of the bridge I just burned down.

CHAPTER 49

Ivy

I don't need to look at the calendar to know what today is. It's Smoke's big day, *Erede al Trono*. Different day—same old heartbreak. Centuries of D'Angelos have handed down their heritage, one heir to the next. Like a Yeti sighting or Halley's comet, the passing of the D'Angelo torch happens only once a generation, and I am missing it.

"Come to family dinner night." Aunt Grace is upbeat and chipper as she wraps me in a hug. Before I moved to Chicago, I never missed an Everly family dinner. Not one. But now, I've missed four. It's because dinner means sharing your day over a hot meal, laughing over pie, and slowly working our way from the kitchen to the living room for a game of Jenga.

All of a sudden, I hate Jenga.

Considering that I have no job and my day consists of yoga and moping, there's not a whole lot to share. I shake my head.

"Please," she begs, hands clasped.

No. Dinner is too risky. The weight of my broken heart is far too heavy not to drag down the entire Everly clan with it, and I won't let that happen. "I'm still in flannel pajama pants, and my hair hasn't been brushed," I say, pointing out the obvious. "You go on. Have fun."

"Brooke is bringing a guest." Aunt Grace's tone is 100 percent pure honey.

I point a finger at her sweet sadistic face. "That's evil. Baiting me with Brooke and a new boyfriend?"

Aunt Grace rubs a shoulder against mine and spills a little tea. "She says they're just friends."

Just friends? Right. Brooke has been dating since she was in pink rubber band braces, and in all that time, the only guys she's ever brought home are the serious ones, all of them the quote-unquote *just friends.*

With two fingertips, she lifts my chin until my eyes meet her light green ones. "I could tell everyone it's a pajama party. One call and the Everlys are all in."

My sad face lifts to a smile. "You just want an excuse to wear that bunny onesie."

"It's a unicorn, just like the one that singer wore. Come with me, and we will kick everyone's butt in a twerking contest."

Aunt Grace knows every trick to lift my spirits, but the truth is, I don't want to be cheered up. I want to be my unshowered and stinky self, wallowing in a tub of Ben & Jerry's and heartbreak, licking my wounds in peace. "I love you for trying to make me feel better. And for owning a unicorn onesie, but rain check on the twerk off."

She pulls me in for a tight squeeze. "Next weekend, I'm holding you to it." Her kiss is tender on my cheek. "I'll be back in a few hours."

"I'll be here." Just me and my misery.

I follow her out and wave as she drives off. Early evening is alive with cricket chirps and rustling eucalyptus leaves. The scents of wild honeysuckle and earthy citronella wrap around me, inviting me to take a seat on the porch to soak them in.

Half an hour flies by, and when the low hum of a truck makes its way up the drive, I already know who it is.

His boots crunch hard on the pebble driveway and spur a flurry of butterflies in my chest. "Hey," he says, his thick southern accent as welcoming as the large dinner plate he hands me.

A cool breeze kicks up, and I shiver. His leather jacket blankets my shoulders in an instant. I snuggle into it and smile up at him.

He looks down sternly. "So, this is where you've been hiding out."

I peel the tinfoil from the plate and avoid his eyes. "I'm not hiding out."

"Uh-huh," he says, not buying my big, fat lie. "Mind if I have a seat?"

"I'd like that," I say, smiling. I scooch over, giving him room to sit.

CHAPTER 50
Leo

Old habits die hard. I had the Lyft driver let me out exactly one-quarter mile from Aunt Grace's house. I made it the rest of the way on foot. Just me, a bag of clothes, and Mr. Whiskers. It's time he went home to his mom. A knot forms in my stomach as I wonder if I'll be joining him.

The second I step around a thick collection of evergreens, it's Ivy. Alone on a patio, sadder than I've ever seen. She's lost weight, and her eyes look as though she's been crying. I ache for this woman, but maybe I deserve to ache. To hurt. To feel real pain. Ivy is hurting, and I caused that.

Fuck, what if she's better off without me?

An engine in the distance rumbles louder as it approaches. A truck closes in, and I do what any respectable stalker does. I duck into the nearest shrubs.

The truck parks and a man steps out. "Hey," he says as he steps toward her and hands her a plate. Even with his back facing me, his frame, height, and obnoxiously perfect hair are all too familiar. *Fucking Hunter.*

The second she shivers, he's got his jacket around her. "So, this is where you've been hiding out," he says. I glare.

"I'm not hiding out."

"Uh-huh." I can only imagine the boyish grin on that bastard's face. "Mind if I have a seat?"

When she invites him with, "I'd like that," I see red. I'm a footstep and a half closer to them when I stop. The man turns around to sit, and it is not Hunter. It's Wade Everly, the sheriff. "You need to quit skipping dinner," he scolds her.

"I will," she promises as he holds up something fried and offers her a bite. From here, I can't tell if the fried food is chicken or okra, or perhaps gizzards, but at least she's eating.

"Gracie says you're going back to work at Sparrow Assisted Living."

Ivy shakes her head. "Maybe down the road, but not now. Derrick's having a tough time getting over me. I think he proposed."

"Proposed?" the sheriff and I ask in unison.

Derrick has one job to do, and it isn't fucking this. That's it. I'm deep-frying Derrick's balls and feeding them to him.

"But my friend, Angie, lined me up with an interview day after tomorrow. But I think I'm in way over my head with that one."

"What is it?"

"A project pitch for a non-profit—the Delphi Group. They're looking for studies to invest in. She said she called in a favor and mentioned the work I've done with people who are nonverbal. They agreed to meet with me."

"Sounds perfect."

Ivy growls adorably. "It sounds like a disaster. I have to present an idea for them to sponsor, which I don't have. I also don't have a degree, business experience, or the first clue about how to be my own boss."

He kisses her temple. "Have faith. If your friend believes in you this much, you must be doing something right. Plus, it keeps you from thinking of him."

"Who?" she asks as if pretending not to know.

"Who indeed..." He takes a breath. "The man who's caused all the commotion in your heart. Gracie says you're barely eating or sleeping."

Ivy stays silent. She and I are two souls floating through the same netherworld. Trapped somewhere between mild despondence to suffocating misery.

"Do you love him?" the sheriff asks from out of fucking nowhere. I crouch down and struggle to listen.

She shrugs, and my heart falls out of my chest. "It doesn't matter," she replies.

I spy in disbelief. *What does she mean it doesn't matter? Why?*

"Why?" Wade Everly asks.

"Because he has to stay in Chicago, and I have to stay here." I'm half a second from jumping out of the shrubs like a surprise stripper from a birthday cake when Ivy continues. "It's for the best," she adds.

I stop mid-step.

"I need someone I can give my whole heart to, and for that someone to give me all of his in return."

The sheriff waves a chicken leg at her. "And that's not Mr. Heartbreak?"

Can I just say that I hate the nickname?

Ivy sighs. "I don't know. When I needed a dress, he made a deal for Ricardo Ricci to make it."

"The famous fashion designer?" he asks, surprised.

Ivy nods. "And when he found out I was spending my paycheck on Aunt Grace's meds, he paid for them out of his own pocket."

"Remind me later to set you straight on who should be paying for my sister's meds." He bops her on the nose with a drumstick and takes a bite.

She rubs her nose, smiling. "He does so many beautiful things for me," Ivy laments.

"Sounds like a real bastard." They chuckle.

"Ivy," he says, "I know you. A little distance wouldn't keep you from going after what you really want. Gracie wouldn't tell me too much about your relationship, so answer me this. Did he let you down?"

She nods sadly. "Yes," she sighs, and it's a kick in the gut.

"Do you forgive him?"

Does she? I step closer, waiting on bated breath for her response.

Eyes full of tears, she answers softly. "Yes." I sigh relieved. *Thank fuck.*

The sheriff reads my thoughts. "Then what's holding you back?"

She looks up and searches the sky for answers. "I don't know. A million things. I trust him...foolishly, idiotically trust him, but I don't think he'll ever trust me."

"Maybe he just needs to get to know you better."

Ivy's laugh is weak. "The man knows more about me than God almighty. The only thing he hasn't managed to figure out is why I smell of oranges and vanilla." *She's got me there.* My chuckle is echoed by the sheriff.

I've heard all I need to hear. I do trust her. She has to know that. I take a few determined steps, ready to tell her, but stop as soon as I hear her name.

"Lori, his wife, passed a few years ago. I would never want to change his feelings for her. But I guess I hoped there was enough love in his heart for us both. I'm not sure there is. He's too walled off. I'm not sure I can ever really reach him." Her focus fixes on the night sky. "What good is reaching for a star you'll never touch?"

The sheriff looks around, then nudges her back into the house. "It's getting cold. Let's go inside." They do, and I follow their movements, window by window, as they make their way through the spacious house. Ivy swaddles herself in a blanket and lies back on the sofa. I'm not sure where the sheriff's gone. Maybe to the kitchen.

I watched her a million times before, but this time is different. This time, I know the truth. I own her. The problem is, she doesn't know that she owns me.

A lone tear finds its way down her cheek, and I know that words are meaningless. I can't fix this by talking to her. I know Ivy. She'll be thinking about everyone else, and for once, I need her to know there's someone thinking of her. Only her.

But I can't just tell her. I have to show her. Prove beyond a shadow of a doubt that I'm the man who will stand by her side.

I'll never reject her or abandon her. That nothing and no one will ever come between us.

"Freeze," the sheriff demands, his voice low as a gun cocks at the back of my head.

I drop my bag and raise my hands.

Fuck.

CHAPTER 51

Leo

With my hands raised in surrender, I speak with familiar camaraderie. "Hey, Officer Everly." I smile and twist my head to face him. "It's me, Leo Zamparelli. Remember?" My voice lifts hopefully.

He proceeds to cuff and frisk me. I take it that's a no. "Turn around," he says. I do. "I remember you," he says flatly. His friendly flash of recognition vanishes. "I don't recall trespassing being part of our discussion. Let's go."

I shuffle along as he grabs my bag and dumps it into the cab of his truck. I slide into the passenger seat as directed. "I can explain. I just wanted to talk to Ivy."

He starts the ignition. "In these parts, we're not too keen on letting stalkers chit-chat with their victims." The truck rolls away.

"I said I *wanted* to talk with Ivy. Past tense. Just drop me off anywhere."

His eyes flick to me. "I'm not an Uber. The only place you're going is the county jail."

What? "Look, call your sister. She'll vouch for me."

He ignores me.

"See," I hold up my cuffed hands. "I can even dial for you."

His eyes stay fixed on the road ahead as if he hasn't heard a word. It isn't until I recite her number and go into how she changed my life by reading my palm that he comes to a screeching stop on the side of the road.

Finally, he calls her. "Put Gracie on," he says. "I've got some guy here who says you'll vouch for him though I can't believe you'd vouch for a peeping Tom." *Pause.* "Said his name is..." he struggles for a beat. "Souparetti."

"Zamparelli," I correct. "Or Z. Or Leo," I fumble in a rush. "Leo Zamparelli, Chief of Security." Fine, former chief of security, but he doesn't need to know all that.

He eyes me and listens intently. "Uh-huh." *Pause.* "Uh-huh." *Another pause.* I give him my most innocent grin. "Well, he claims to be a chief of security." He squints hard. "Security guard, huh?"

Flabbergasted, my head falls in my tightly cuffed hands. *I can't fucking believe this.* "Sure, put him on," I hear him say. His eyes move to the road. With the receiver pressed against his head, I can't make out any of the mumbling, so I wait. After an eternity, he closes the call. "Will do, thanks." He disconnects.

I look at him, certain that all hope is lost.

"I'll give you two options," he says matter-of-factly. "I can call Ivy right now and have her vouch for you."

Knowing Ivy, she's so determined for me to forget about her, a restraining order would cross her mind. "Or?" I ask, weighing my options.

"Or I can cart you off to jail."

There's nothing to think about. Resigned to the inevitable, I deflate in a sigh. "Jail," I reply with a small prayer for soap on a rope and a private cell.

CHAPTER 52

Leo

"Where are we?" I ask as we pull up a private driveway. Half a dozen cars are parked before a large wooden cabin.

"Where you'll be spending the night." He kills the engine and leads me up to the warmly lit entry. Potted red geraniums give the rustic surroundings a woman's touch. "We're home," he hollers into the house.

Home? A large shepherd gallops over as the sheriff uncuffs my hands. The dog sniffs me for a second and sits. I pat him on the head. "Nice dog."

"He isn't mine," he replies and heads into the other room.

A New York-style taxicab whistle pierces the air and the shepherd bolts to follow it. I look up to find Hunter peering around the corner. "So, you'd pick jail over Ivy." He smirks like an ass, but his bro hug is welcoming. "Ivy was right. You are a martyr." The dog returns, gluing himself to Hunter's side. "What are you doing here?" he asks.

"What am I doing here? What are you doing here?"

Hunter says nothing and simply glances at the dog. There's a cluster of white patches along his chest, and the missing fur on the top of his right paw is unmistakeable. "Is that—"

Hunter shushes me discretely. "This is *Brooke's* dog," he says slowly and deliberately. "Ivy's best friend, Brooke. She adopted him and trained him in medical response." He nudges me to play along, and I do, knowing he'll catch me up later.

"I see," I say with an understanding nod. "What's his name?"

"Hunter," a sweet voice calls out from the other room. The dog hurries back in.

I scratch my scruff, confused. "Is the dog named Hunter, or was she calling you?"

"Both," he chuckles and claps my shoulder. We head through the house to the dining room. The table for eight is filled with enough food for an army. My stomach growls, letting everyone know it's been a while since I've eaten.

"Well, if it isn't my favorite security guard." Grace reels me in with a comforting hug, and boy, did I need that. "Have a seat. Eat your fill. And explain to me why you'd rather spend a night in the clinker than say hello to Ivy."

I do some serious damage to the crispy fried chicken and mountain of grits and lay it all on the line. "Because I've only got one shot to make this work, and Ivy has it in her head that we're better off apart."

"Why?" Brooke asks me with those green, scrutinizing Everly eyes.

My head falls back, chin to the sky. "Where do I begin?"

Hunter chimes in, helpful as always. "You investigated her, had her followed, stalked her, assumed she was working for the enemy, threw *me* at her, and dumped her. Repeatedly." He chomps on the only healthy food at the table—a piece of celery. "Did I get everything?"

"Thorough as usual," I chide.

"But," he adds, pointing at me with the celery stalk that should be a garnish, "you also kept the investigation from the D'Angelos, and went out of your way to protect her until we knew the truth." He chuckles low. "Did you really try to kill Enzo over her toy? Mr. Muskers?"

"First of all, his name is Mr. Whiskers. Get it right. And no, I never tried to *kill* Enzo. If I tried to kill him, the butthead would be dead."

Hunter feeds a slice of carrot to the dog he's pretending isn't his. The dog chomps happily, then rests his head in his lap. "I heard you shot up his favorite chess pieces for Ivy."

"I was extracting information," I explain and pop a hush puppy in my mouth.

"Who's Enzo?" Grace asks.

Wade pours me a tall glass of sweet tea. "Enzo D'Angelo?" His eyes volley between me and Hunter. "The notorious Chicago mob boss-billionaire. He's that slippery bastard who's been on the FBI's watch list for years." We simply shrug. The sheriff cocks a brow. "You went up against him for Ivy?"

"I'd go up against anyone for her."

Grace takes my hand and turns it over so my palm faces her.

Wade rolls his eyes. "Here we go."

"*Shh!*" Grace studies my hand and commences with my reading. I'm not ashamed to admit, I want to hear what she has to say. "Are you sure you want to do this?" she asks cautiously.

I study my palm and smile. Maybe she really is psychic.

"What are you going to do?" Brooke asks, wide-eyed and fascinated.

At this point, everyone—even Wade—stops eating and patiently wait out my reply.

"Whatever it takes to get my girl back."After a slow sip of tea and wondering if it'll be enough, I add, "Even if it kills me."

CHAPTER 53

Ivy

I spent all day and night preparing the presentation for the Delphi Group, which seemed to justify the whole *not-sleeping-because-of-Leo* thing. As presentations go, it turned out terrific considering I pulled it out of my ass. Well, that and all those textbooks I poured over.

They're looking for projects to invest in, and I've got one. Angie. She and I have worked together for years, and her faith in me means more than the project. If I focused my research around her and the others at Sparrow Assisted Living, I could make this work.

With my project in hand and a bellyful of butterflies, I arrived at the Institute for Research, Delphi Division. "You must be Ms. Palmer," the receptionist greets me cheerily. "I'll show you to the conference room."

I'm seated before three people that Angie filled me in on. Dr. Lisa Ackroyd, the chair of the counseling program and internationally acclaimed psychologist. Her work has graced every major scientific research journal, and she was once featured in TIME magazine as one of the most influential people of the year. Her effortless elegance and quiet power instantly make my palms sweat.

Beside her sit two colleagues equally as impressive: Dr. Delaney and Dr. Phillips. Dr. Delaney is a researcher from their psychology branch who was once up for a Nobel Prize, and Dr. Phillips is an internationally renowned lecturer on trauma recovery whose TED Talk has tens of millions of views and is still climbing.

I wring my hands as I swallow the hard lump of reality lodged in my throat. I'm so out of my depth, it's pathetic.

Dr. Ackroyd searches the paperwork. "I don't see your letter of reference."

Crap. Angie didn't mention a letter of reference. "I'm sorry, I don't have one." I quickly add, "with me at the moment, I mean. But I can get it back to you today." Maybe Derrick will be good for something.

"What is your specialty?" the man asks, his accent thick and scientific.

Seeing as I don't really have that either, I make one up. "Working with people who are nonverbal." They smile and nod. I exhale, relieved.

They each thumb through the pages of my proposal. "Your research proposal discusses working with several residents at a local assisted living facility," the chairman says. "One, in particular, named Angie." It sounds like a statement, but it's really a question. "You don't mean Angie Everett, do you?"

A small bead of sweat falls from the back of my neck, cutting icc against my nerves. "Yes, is that a problem?"

"This is so typical of her." She rubs her temple.

"What is?" I question her, confused.

Dr. Ackroyd puffs out an exasperated breath. "I'm afraid that would be a conflict of interest. I couldn't possibly sponsor a project that involved my mother."

"Your *mother*?" I've worked with Angie for years. Thanksgiving. Christmas. Her birthdays. I've never seen this woman. Not once. "Sorry, I don't recall seeing you there."

Her patience wears thin. "I'm a little busy," she snarks. "I'm also afraid this meeting is over. Unless you have another proposal?"

Embarrassed, I flush. It took me nearly thirty-six straight hours to come up with this one.

I open my mouth to apologize for wasting their time as several hard bangs hit the conference room door. Leo barges in, carrying three large boxes. "Excuse the interruption."

In a navy blue suit, crisp white shirt, and hair gorgeously disheveled to just fucked perfection, he breezes across the room. The man steals my breath with his entrance, and I'm stunned silent and senseless.

Leo doesn't make eye contact with me. Instead, he marches to the members of the committee. I shrink in my chair.

Before each panelist, he sets down a box. "Sorry, I'm late." From his pocket, he produces a letter and hands it to Dr. Ackroyd. "Ms. Palmer's letter of recommendation by Dr. Mason D'Angelo." *Smoke?*

Dr. Ackroyd momentarily glances at the letter before she frowns. "This is all well and good, but Ms. Palmer doesn't seem to have a research project."

He straightens his suit and stands tall, his back straight as an arrow. He isn't menacing in his stance. If anything, he's proud. "She does now." He flashes me a knowing glance. "I'm Ms. Palmer's research project."

CHAPTER 54

Ivy

"What are you doing?" I whisper, panicked.

"Giving you everything you want." His hand slides to my cheek, cradling it. "I'm giving you me. No walls. No defenses. No strings. Just me."

His hand falls away as he stands before the committee. "I did a little research on the Delphi Group. You're looking for new, exciting, and interesting ways to analyze the mind and study,"—he air quotes—"the human experience."

They nod in agreement. "That's right," Dr. Ackroyd says.

He unloads the boxes. From one of them, he produces a bright blue journal and points to the cover and the year. "At some point in our lives, we all experience death. On this day, I experienced seven. I'm a former SEAL, in case I didn't mention it." He loses himself in thumbing through the pages. "This is the intimate account of the men I lost. Fathers, husbands, sons. Each of their deaths was tragic, torturous, brutal, and slow. I—" Leo clears his throat. "I was the sole survivor. The journal is titled *Survival of the Fittest*. Each page represents a day that year. Because for every day after that, all I wanted to do was die."

The panelists sit straighter and grow intrigued. Leo is their shiny, new lab animal, dancing for their affection. For me.

I feel sick to my stomach and wrestle back a tear. "Leo, you don't have to—"

"There's also this one." He waves the thick, leather-bound book high for his audience to see. "It's one thing to kill in combat. It's another thing to torture a man to death. But I did it. Not that I'm a serial killer or have a particular thirst for blood. Just a man who occasionally needs a little information. You see, a swift kill does no good in these cases because people will tell you anything to avoid losing their life." He pauses, consumed with pain. I touch my hand to his, but he pushes me away. "I needed the truth, and the truth takes time."

Whatever fears the panelists have morph. They begin taking notes. One pulls out a phone. "Do you mind if I record this?"

"What?" I ask, stunned.

"By all means," Leo says with a practiced grin. "But no names since most of my work has been for the mob."

I dart for the journal and Leo lifts it out of reach. "Don't worry. This is for the greater good. Scientific research. Whatever I say is 100-percent confidential." He winks at Dr. Ackroyd. "Isn't that right, Lisa?"

The daughter of the year nods. "Yes."

Leo reveals another journal. "Let's keep going, shall we? I've had over a dozen therapists, psychologists, and shrinks. The first was in the military where I was diagnosed with dissociative PTSD. The last recently retired. I've logged hundreds of conversationless hours that I'll never get back." He frowns. "The point is that if you want to unlock the mind of a sociopath, then what are you waiting for? Here I am, and Ivy Palmer's your key."

He holds up another enticing journal, waiving the perfect carrot at them.

I snatch it away. "Stop it, just stop. I withdraw my project."

"No, she doesn't." The command of his voice is deep and stern. Determined. We stare off, his eyes red and desperate, mine burning with tears.

Leo is right. These are his journals, harboring his most private thoughts. I could pluck any one of them up and read up on Leo's thoughts that day. See his truest self. A warrior. An enforcer. A hero. A villain.

"This is me, Ivy. This is who I am." His warm thumb strokes my cheeks and wipes more of my tears. "You deserve a man who will do anything...*give anything*...to be the man in your life. I need you to know that man is me." He addresses the committee. "Ms. Palmer knows how to get in touch with me."

<hr />

In less time than it takes for Leo to leave the room, the panelists have descended on the books like vultures on the carcass of a deer. Leo's life open for them to shred apart.

The room spins and I'm dizzy and sick. *Leo.* I have to stop him.

I charge out of the room, but he's already at the elevator at the far end of the hall. "Wait," I say too softly. I suck in a breath and shout, "Wait!"

I rush to him as he meets me in the middle. All the emotions that dominated his steel-blue eyes have suddenly drained. "Oh," he says as if forgetting something insignificant. From his blazer, he tugs out one last journal. A small one with no date. Just a black heart scrawled on the cover. "Here."

"I'm not taking it—"

He closes the distance between us and presses the small book to my heart. "Here. It's yours."

"Leo, please—"

Tenderly, he presses a finger against my lips. "I'm ready to give you everything you ever asked for. My thoughts. My heart. My soul. All of me. No walls. No questions. I need you to read this so you understand."

"Understand?"

He cradles my cheeks and kisses me. I shudder in his hold. "Understand that there's only you. I'm yours, Ivy Palmer. Promise me you'll read this."

"I promise," I say, my voice shaky.

He leaves one last kiss on my lips. "Call me once you do."

CHAPTER 55
Ivy

Three seconds.

That's exactly how long it took me to return to the committee members and stop this mistake. I gather up all the journals. Dr. Ackroyd clings hard to the last one. "He's the perfect specimen."

Who's she telling? "Let go of the journal."

"You don't understand. A lifetime of surveys and interviews would never get us this data. You'll be world-famous overnight. We'll sponsor your project. Whatever you want. Just leave the notebooks with us." Her plea is compelling and desperate.

"If you were trusting me to do the research, then why would you need the notebooks?"

"Evidence, of course," she says, barely masking her patronizing tone. "In case someone questions your work."

"Which means you'd give up his name."

She laughs it off. "Obviously. But only if the research is challenged. It hardly ever happens."

"But that chance goes up because he's a former member of

the military and a mob enforcer, right?" My grip stays on the journal, tight. I summon the strength of the D'Angelo bloodline and produce a deadly glare. "Let. Go."

To my surprise, she does.

With the strength of a thousand tigers—aka Leo—I haul the heavy boxes out. When I nearly trip over my own feet, the two other doctors have the decency to help.

"Stop being a butthead, and go visit your mother. She's an incredible woman," I shout back as the door shuts.

I make my way to my childhood hideout—an isolated stretch of sandy beach that always let me breathe and think. My fingers trace the heart on the cover of the notebook in my hand. I flip to the oldest entry and read.

Dear Diary,

I love the way Lori laughs when I spill a glass of wine or burn the grilled cheese. It's funny that she can still get me to laugh, even when my mind is elsewhere.
It's been days and Antonio is still missing. He's more than an employer to me. He's been like a father. I offered to work longer hours during our search and told Lori that this might be my last dinner with her for a while.
It means I'm probably putting off our anniversary. I think

she understands—hope she understands—but between me running late and burning dinner, I'm pretty sure it wasn't her who just forgave me. It was the half-bottle of merlot she guzzled while she waited.

As soon as we find Antonio, I promised her, we're off to Mexico.

I look back at the date. Four...almost five years ago. I know the pain that's in store, and I want to go back to that Leo and hold him. I scan through more entries and stop at this one.

———

Dear Diary,

I forgot her birthday again. Instead of crying or yelling, she settled on her usual weapon of choice—the silent treatment.

Too bad for her, the silent treatment works both ways, though I'm pretty sure it kills me more.

———

His entries are fewer and farther between with the passing years.

———

Dear Diary,

It's our four-year anniversary, but it doesn't feel like I'm married to the love of my life—it feels like I'm chained to a stranger.

I sent her a dozen roses and an apology. She wants a man who will remember the important things. I want a wife who understands.

Maybe my world was demolished by a tragedy. Maybe while she was getting her hair and manicure done, I was washing the blood from my hands and praying to God we didn't lose Trinity.

Before I can say a word, my pillow is on the sofa.

I turn lemons into lemonade.

At least she's stopped yelling. Maybe I'll get a few hours of sleep.

———

I think of Leo going through all of this alone, and my heart squeezes from his pain. This is why his walls are up. Why he never talks. He can't.

I force through several more entries and stop here.

———

Dear Diary,

Today, Smoke made me his chief of security. And Lori asked for a divorce. I told both of them the exact same thing.

I'll do whatever you need me to do.
And in both instances, I feel nothing.
Nothing but numb.

———

The tears I've been fighting are hot along my cheeks. I don't want to keep reading, but I force myself to, taking heartbreaking steps until the very last page.

I promised I would read it, and I owe it to him—to us—to follow through. I force my way through several more entries and stop at the last page. Here.

———

Dear Diary,

Today the doctors told me Lori wouldn't make it…and neither would her child. Still, I wasn't prepared.
I thought there would've been time. I thought I could fix us.

How could I not know she was three months pregnant? This far along?
Where was the morning sickness? The dizzy spells? A swollen belly. Something. Anything. All I needed was one goddamned sign.

They told me it was a girl. When Lori's parents asked me to name her, I did. A name we always used to talk about.

Amelia.

I don't understand how it can hurt so fucking much when that precious baby girl wasn't even mine, but it does.

I said my last goodbye and forgave her. Forgave her for leaving me. Forgave her for dying. Forgave her for finding so much love in another man's arms.
The son of a bitch died on impact, so I even forgave him.

They say it is better to have loved and lost than never to have loved at all.
They lied.

"Leo," I say softly to the wind. Tears shower the page, and my heart squeezes. He went through all of this. Alone.

I close the book and hug it close to my chest. He's right. He gave me everything I needed.

He gave me all his raw, honest, vulnerable pieces.

He gave me him.

CHAPTER 56

Ivy

T lie on my side, drawing hearts into the sand as I hug my knees to my chest and wait. It's been nearly an hour since I sent my text, and the sun is setting fast. What if he's lost? Or hasn't read it?

Or what if he isn't coming?

A feather-soft throw blanket smooths over my shoulders, covering me. My heart flutters as I look up. Leo is dressed in a white T-shirt and jeans, his hair messed to *no-fucks-given* perfection, and his blue eyes piercing. "Hi." His voice is tender and deep.

"Hi."

We stare at each other, and I'm not sure how I managed without him. I don't notice the basket in his hand until he sets it at my feet. "Sorry, I took so long. I was helping your family with dinner when you texted."

Cautiously, his body moves next to mine. We sit and watch the last rays of the sun dance across the water. "I was worried you might miss this."

He chuckles and slips his hand in mine. "You didn't give me much to go on. Your text said *find me*."

"So, what took you so long?" I face him and my breath catches.

His lips brush against mine. "I'm furious with you," he whispers.

"I know." I sigh with a shudder. "I can never return to Chicago," I whisper back.

"I know," he says.

A low hum ignites the way it always does when our bodies are this close.

Our foreheads touch and the energy between us melts the world away as he says, "I missed you."

God, I missed him, too. For the first time in a long time, I can breathe.

His kiss is cautious at first, as if testing the waters—testing us. His stubble is longer than before, and it's feels like I'm kissing a stranger. Or maybe it just feels that way because for the first time, I'm kissing the real him. Pure, unadulterated Leo. And holy hell, can this man kiss.

His tongue glides inside slow and controlled. In and out. It doesn't matter that we're out in the open on a beach, his length is rigid and my body aches for him. The more he kisses me, the stronger I need him. Before I know it, I'm wrapped around him in a straddle, locking him in my hold.

Leo breaks away. "Wait," he says, shaking his head.

"Wait?" I pant, breathless.

He chuckles. "No more one-night stands."

I comb my fingers through the thick curls of his hair. "No more one-night stands," I agree.

This time, when Leo kisses me, his sweet tenderness gives away to lust and ownership and need. We tear each other's clothes away with the occasional *rip*. He dips one finger inside my heat, slowly invading me. "Fuck, you're wet."

I climb on top of him as our bodies line up. His hands on my hips, he slides me on him and forces me to take all of him at once. *Fuck*," he breathes. My legs spread wider, and with the next thrust, he fills me completely.

We ramp up from sensual love-making to raw, possessive, carnal lust. "So deep," I moan, almost incoherently.

"Take me deeper," he demands, as the last rays of sunset fade across his skin.

His fingers stroke my pussy—his thumb on my clit—and I can't hold back. All the feelings I've denied him surface. When my body takes all it can from Leo, stars explode across the sky. I come. And then he comes.

And nothing exists but us.

We kiss, hold each other, fuck, and make love, slipping in and out of sleep until the sun comes up.

In his groggy-Alpha state, he buries his face in my neck. "You're mine," he says, dominant and possessive.

His.

Tender kisses make their way along my neck. "Do me a favor?"

I giggle. "I'm so afraid you'll want me to skinny-dip with you."

He lifts himself over me, blanketing me with the heat of his skin. His smile is mischievous and way too sexy for this early in the morning. "I used to be a SEAL. Ice cold water is never a problem."

"I'm a southern girl who can't swim. Ice cold water is always a problem. Request denied."

His laughter fills my entire soul. "Fine, then how about you marry me?"

A swarm of butterflies rise from my chest as my breath carries me away. I rub the sexy stubble along his jaw and ground myself in this moment. "What about your vow to protect the D'Angelos?"

He rolls beside me, tangling our bodies together. "I intend to keep it, my secret D'Angelo." His smile lights my world. "I vow to love, honor, adore, and protect you, Ivy..." He kisses away all my tears as I well up with emotion. "For the rest of my life."

We wrap around each other. "You are my life, Leo."

He kisses me. "And you are my world."

Epilogue

LEO

Three years later

"Should I call the authorities?" I murmur in my sleep. "I sense a violation in progress." Her gentle touch stirs my cock, and I'm not sure if that's her finger or her tongue. I peel open an eye and peek beneath the covers. *Mmm.* It's her tongue.

Her mouth takes me in and hums along my length. *Maybe* she mumbles with her mouth full.

Not that it matters, but I glance over at the clock. "It's five in the morning."

Her voluptuous curves make their way on top of me. She settles that insatiable wet pussy in position and feathers her lips along mine as she whispers. "Was that a complaint?"

I flip her to her back and spread her legs wide. "Definitely not." As soon as the throbbing head of my dick connects, I drive home. Her moans grow louder. "They'll hear you," I mutter, and latch on to a breast.

I thrust hard, *harder*, and I swear to God if she whimpers

any louder, I'll have to smother her with a pillow. "Turn around," I demand as low as I can.

And oh, my fucking God, with her gorgeous ass in the air and her pussy glistening from the night light, I'm about to blow. It takes every ounce of willpower not to smack an ass-cheek, but *fuck*. It's too risky.

"More," she begs. Damn her, she knows I can't resist it when she begs.

I lick her, feed on her, bury my tongue between her legs until her body quivers from the rushed orgasm. She heaves into the pillow. "You're not done yet," I promise, whispering into the smooth skin of her back.

"Hurry," she pants.

"Yes, ma'am." I'm hard as stone and my wife is soaked in her own come. *One quick fuck*, at your service.

I plow into her as she pushes back against me. It's a rhythm like our heartbeats. It's us. No matter if we're slow and steady, or lust-filled and rushed, we are tethered. Connected. Somehow, our on-again, off-again one-night stand became love.

I grab her hips and pump hard and fast. Her back arches, and her knees spread wide. I chase my climax until the bed bangs against the wall. "Leo—" She giggles and tries, and fails, to contain her own landslide of an orgasm.

"God, baby. Yes!" I come with so much force, I collapse on her. Holy hell, we were loud, but God was that worth it.

"Ten minutes?" she muses.

I kiss her sweet plump lips. "I give it five." I rush through cleaning us up, and playfully toss a pajama top at her head as I jump into the bottoms.

The door begins to open, and I jump into bed. I do a light snore for added effect.

Tiptoes creak along the floor until a finger pokes at my nose. I pop open an eye.

Giggles erupt. "Daddy!" my little girl squeals. I see my sweet Bella Trinity has dragged her brother in tow to join the pajama party. As usual, little Mason has Mr. Whiskers clutched in his hand.

In under a minute, they're on the bed, nestled between us. "Ro sham bo?" my sweet wife offers. She thinks I'm terrible at it. *Eh*, I always let her win.

I ball my hand to a fist, and our fists bob to the beat—rock, paper, scissors. I do rock because I know she's about to pick paper. We kiss. "You always let me win," she smirks with a pout.

"I do not," I scoff, kissing that luscious pout and collecting the kids. "Come on. Daddy's making waffles while we let mommy sleep."

I scoop them in my arms, and dip both of them upside-down. They giggle wildly as she kisses their heads. "Love you," she says and rolls back to sleep.

And I love you, Ivy Zamparelli. With all my heart.

Epilogue Two

LEO

W hen the phone rings, the Chicago number has me smiling wide. I prop my feet comfortably on the desk, pick up the corded phone, and answer with authority. "Sheriff's office."

"Congratulations, Sheriff Zamparelli," Smoke says.

"Sheriff Z. to everyone here."

Smoke huffs a laugh. "Thank God you won. Otherwise, I'd owe Enzo a fuck-ton of money. He demanded a recount."

"I won by a fucking landslide." *Thanks to Wade's endorsement.* "Enzo definitely owes you."

"It's a little more complicated than that. Turns out, he'll end up owing you."

I hang my head. "Could you not attempt to bribe an officer of the law his first day on the job?"

"More like tying up a loose end." He pauses. "Derrick."

Sparrow Assisted Living. A sweet spot for money laundering. The D'Angelo's get their money washed while the residents get all the care they need. And it gives Ivy a job she loves while doing it all on her terms.

Her terms means she works with the residents while Derrick manages the money—under close D'Angelo supervision, of course. Instead of reporting to Derrick, they both report to Smoke. Which means Ivy runs her show the way she wants.

It also means that she manages her own schedule and the kids come with the territory. What can I say? Our little ones are an insane hit with the staff and residents alike, and with number three baking in her belly, her office expansion is already underway.

The down side? This deal keeps the assisted living center umbrellaed beneath D'Angelo Holdings—which is Enzo's dirty little swim lane. Fingers crossed he won't want to conduct inter-rogations on site, though if push came to shove, we do have some open rooms by the deaf residents. "What does he have in mind?" I ask.

"He sold it."

As zen as I try to be under the circumstances, I lose my shit. "We had a fucking deal, Smoke. One call from me, and Officer Ross Friendly will cite you with everything from jaywalking to speeding. You know, indecent exposure is a 72-hour hold that makes you real popular in the cell."

"For fuck's sake, Leo, calm down. It's a gift. All the same terms, but ix-nay on our take. He needed a legitimate non-profit and the new owner had an interest."

I sit up in my chair, fingers steepled to my chin. "I'm listening."

"Trinity is now calling the shots."

"Yes!" I hush with the receiver smothered to my chest. It's a big commitment for Trinity. It means she's feeling confident and might brave more trips out here. I speak back to the receiver. "My wife will be ecstatic. Hell, we're all ecstatic." I check my watch. It's getting late. "Are you still flying down tonight?"

"Yes, but I'll be returning to Chicago sooner than expected. Enzo and I have a lead on our father's disappearance."

A lead? "If you need anything. Access to our databases. Or if you need to delay coming out—"

"No," he insists. With Ivy in her second trimester, nothing could keep Smoke from all the big appointments. Tomorrow, we find out the baby's sex. Considering Smoke has delivered both my kids and wants to be here for the third, sharing these beautiful milestones with him has only brought us closer.

That and I hear the D'Angelo brother betting pool is somewhere in the six figures, and Smoke has his money on a girl.

"We can't wait to see you. I hope you brought your buffet pants. She and Aunt Grace have been busy baking."

A long silence edges on, and I wonder if I lost him. Then, he says, "I envy you." His words are as full of heartfelt sincerity as they are heaviness. As if what I have is somehow out of his reach.

Smoke gave up his entire world to care for Trinity and chase down the mystery of what happened to his father. Why can't some of my good fortune rub off on him? I'm not asking for much. Just a miracle...Smoke finding happiness, peace, and love.

"The kids can't wait to see you. And spoiler alert, Ivy, Brooke, and Aunt Grace might have a friend joining us all for dinner tomorrow night."

"A friend? As in a date?" His grumble is priceless. "Not again."

"Don't worry. Hunter and I have calibrated our watches. At exactly twenty minutes into the meal, there will be an emergency and we will rush you out."

"Appendectomy?"

"We feel a brutal case of the runs would be safer. She'll probably be disgusted and repulsed by you, and you'll be thoroughly embarrassed."

"Can't wait," he smirks.

I pause and broach the subject cautiously. "She's actually very nice. The two of you might hit it off."

Silence.

"I didn't forget the life you lead," I tell him honestly. "But a wise man once told me baby steps. One night won't kill you."

He puffs out a breath. "Famous last words." There's a brief silence, but I can tell, he's thinking. "I'll do my twenty minutes. Nothing more."

"Just tossing you a life preserver."

"Leo, you and I both know no matter who you set me up with, it won't work."

"Why not?"

"For starters, I prefer my life preserver be in Chicago. A woman who understands the world I live in. Someone who needs no explanations and keeps secrets like a vault. And while you're making Christmas list notes, I'd love a virgin sacrifice with the body of Aphrodite and the heart of a mafia queen."

"If Aunt Grace was listening, she'd recommend a vision board."

"And if Enzo was listening, he'd recommend a hooker. I'll

do the date for twenty-minutes, but I'm not getting my palm read and I'm not manifesting a woman."

A knock sounds at my door. "Listen, Smoke, I'd love to keep helping you conjure a virginal fem-bot mob queen, but I've got a reporter waiting."

"Reporter?"

The trace amounts of concern in his tone make me chuckle. "This isn't Chicago. The reporter in question is a seven-year-old student from Brooke's class." The young girl and her mother smile at me through the glass door. "Good news, Smoke. The reporter's mother is just your type," I tease.

That has him laughing. "Her *mother* is a virgin?"

"She's a defense attorney with the balls of a mob boss. With her clientele, keeping secrets is all in a day's work."

"Why does a long-distance relationship with a member of the court sound like hell in the making? And for the record, at no time did I request balls on a woman. Keep looking, sheriff."

"Will do. Safe travels. See you soon, Smoke." I disconnect the call and wave them in.

The little girl rushes up to me with her hand fully extended. "Hi, I'm Sarah," she says, her wide smile revealing a tooth missing. "School reporter," she announces proudly.

I smile back and shake her hand. "Sheriff Z., at your service."

Thank you for reading SINS of the Syndicate! I hope you love Leo and Ivy as much as I do.

And get ready for Smoke's Story!
1-Click Book #3 in the series
>> SINS: The Debt

Need another angsty billionaire romance?
1-CLICK>> MARKED

Eight years ago I nearly died.

And it wasn't that I didn't remember her.

I didn't recognize her. There's a difference.

She was a kid.

And I was a soldier...

Two seconds from deploying with her brother for our third, and final, tour.

One I wasn't sure I'd be coming back from.

She thinks I don't remember.

That kiss was beautiful. Innocent.

It kept me alive when I thought it might be my last.

How could I ever forget?

So, shove me off all you want, country girl.

Because you've just landed in my sights,

And you're about to be mine.

SCROLL AHEAD FOR A SNEAK PEEK >>

How about something a little Ruthless?

Power plays are hard.

Trying to one up the stranger who banged me senseless last night?

Definitely harder.

Get RUTHLESS WARS Now>

"Tons of chemistry and passion ... Highly addictive" ~*Goodreads Reviewer*

Join Lexxi's VIP reader list to be the first to know of new releases, free books, special prices, and other giveaways!

Free hot romances & happily ever afters delivered to your inbox.
https://www.lexxijames.com/freebies

Marked

BOYS OF BISHOP MOUNTAIN

Chapter One
JESS

Have you ever believed that if you wished for something hard enough, you could make it happen?

I did. It all started when my mom used to say, "Never underestimate the power of a wish." Then she'd hold the fluffy-white dandelion in front of me as my cheeks puffed with air. "Blow, baby girl!"

And I would. Wasting a universe of wishes with reckless abandon on books, candy, and toys. It's like slots for toddlers: The more you wish, the more chances you have of one of those wishes coming true.

It took a few years before I got serious. Doubled-down on just one wish. What was it Hannibal Lecter said? We covet what we see every day? Who knew the words of a fictional psychopath could ring so true?

And see Mark Donovan, I did.

My brother's best friend. Yeah, try not seeing him. Dark, carefree waves that melted down to eyes that changed with his mood. Golden caramel at his happiest. Moody winter green when he was brooding.

He was it. My first big wish. My first epic fail.

Every night for a month, I wished I would grow up to marry him. And then I did the unthinkable. With my little-girl outside voice, I said it. "I am going to marry you." Said it straight to his beautiful boy face.

Considering I was six and he was twelve, it went over like a loud fart in a packed church. What started with a wince morphed into uncontrollable laughter, culminating in Mark doubling over on the floor.

Oh, that last part wasn't from laughter. It was from my angry little-girl fist jabbing a full-force punch square at his balls.

This cautionary tale taught me two things. First, boys apparently can't breathe without their balls. And second, wishes aren't meant to be trite or trivial. If only a few wishes are meant to come true, make each one precious. Make them count.

When my dear, sweet parents made their way to heaven—a pain so raw, it hurt just to breathe—I had faith. For every dandelion I plucked, I wished messages could make their way up through the clouds, delivered by the wind.

I wished Nana Winnie was as happy as a lark, cutting out crazy patterns for her latest quilt. I wished our old Labrador retriever, Saint, was with them, running fast and free to catch a Frisbee from my dad. I wished every time I sang to the clouds, my mom could feel the love I poured into every note. Knew how much I missed her. Missed them all.

When my brothers moved away, lured by the military, I

wished them back. Brian showed up the next day, the Rock of Gibraltar by my side ever since.

How? I have no idea. Considering he's a sniper at the beck and call of the Army, I can't imagine how he worked that out. But we both knew it couldn't last forever, and the lifeline he cast me was beginning to strain.

In five short days, he returns to the other side of the world, and the last thing he needs to worry about is me.

So, today's dandelion is for a job. Not just any job. Just a small promotion that keeps the lights on and cements me in place, home on Bishop Mountain.

On my day off, and armed with the fluffiest dandelion I could find, I close my eyes and imagine my mom holding it out. My small smile makes way to a gust of breath. I blow all my fears and doubts away, letting the feather-soft wisps fly free on a breeze.

One wish. One shot. And one man who can make it all happen.

Chapter Two

JESS

"Have you seen Tyler?" I ask, standing a respectable distance from the customer side of the bar.

Anita frowns as she side-eyes me while flipping a shaker with finesse. "I thought you were off."

I shrug. "I am." Though I have no idea why. I pause for a beat. "But I wanted to pick up my check." I can't help my envious stare at her nametag. ANITA MAE, BARTENDER.

She nods, her smile knowing. "And call dibs on my job?"

I scrunch up my face. "Too obvious?"

"Uh, it's called initiative. You're a Bishop. I'd expect nothing less." She notices the space I've created between me and the bar. Bartending in the great state of New York at eighteen? Totally legit. Taste-testing even one drop of alcohol? Not so much.

And as I am the last of the Bishop children to work in this establishment, let's just say I don't want to be the one to eff it all up with the liquor authority.

"You're not a kid anymore, Jess. Step on up!"

380

Proudly, I do. With a lighter, she demonstrates a technique called *flaming an orange peel*. With the strike of a match and the flick of her fingers, a fireball showers the drink, then vanishes behind a small trail of smoke.

"Doesn't that burn?" I ask.

She shakes her head. "You're not really lighting the peel as much as spraying the orange oil against the flame into the glass." She walks me slowly through the motions. "See?"

I nod. Rumor is, her promotion is in the bag, which leaves her job up for grabs. It's a long shot, but I've been practicing. Thank God for YouTube.

She peers over thick-framed glasses. "Master this trick. People eat it up, and the tips flow like water." She gestures grandly to the wall of liquor and art-deco accents. "This will all be yours someday."

Fascinated, I glance around. "There's so much to learn."

She tosses a small notebook on the glossy wood. "Here. You want the job? Memorize this."

Flipping through, I realize it has to be fifty pages of customized cocktails from the *Adirondack Sunset* to *Donovan's Deadly Twist*. But when my gaze hits *Bishop's Breeze*, I pause, and my eyes well up. I expected it to be a drink created by Brian, Rex, or Cade—any one of my brothers—but it's not. It was written by Henry.

Henry James Bishop, my father. My fingers skim across the page as I inhale pride and exhale sadness. Vodka. Lemon. Honey. Club soda with a splash of Moscato. I choke up. I can almost see him making it for mom.

Anita's warm hand covers mine. "Anything I can do?"

Rewind time. Stop them from getting in that car.

"No," I say softly. *Not unless you can bring my parents back.* It takes a breath before the pain subsides and a few blinks to dislodge an annoyingly stubborn tear.

"Lunch?" she says kindly.

I decline with a hopeful grin. "Rain check?" Considering I'm blowing all my money on my gift for Brian, I will absolutely take a free lunch IOU.

Sharp, jabbing pains erupt in the lowest point of my gut. *Not now.* I suck in a breath to stave it off. A hard pinch comes again, a tight twist. I hug both arms against my belly, wrestling the pain away, grateful that Anita's too busy to notice.

"Hmm . . ." She fills a thick glass mug with whatever's on tap. "Tyler?"

She thinks for a moment while I try not to double over in pain. Or cry out "*Mercy*" to the gods of pain.

Month after month, my periods are ten times worse, and over-the-counter medications are barely making a dent. With any luck, the extra-extra-strength medication I got at the drugstore will kick in any second now.

While I bite my lip like a bullet, Anita ponders on. "Tyler . . ."

Maybe it's the repeated knife jabs to the gut talking, but if one more person says they haven't seen Tyler Donovan, I'll throw down like a toddler. I'm two seconds from unceremoniously face-planting onto the questionably clean floor, arms and legs flailing about in full-on meltdown mode.

Anita sets a pink-and-purple drink at the pickup station and a mug of beer next to it before sliding her glasses to the tip of her nose.

"So, you have to see Tyler?" she sings suggestively. Or hopefully. I swear, the woman is vying for the official title of Cupid.

The knife jab below the belly subsides to a dull ache enough for me to play along. "Obviously, because Tyler knows how to make a girl truly happy."

She gives me the hairy eyeball. "You're lucky you're legal," she says, smirking as she waggles her brows.

"All I need is a few minutes alone with him. Just me and Tyler so he can"—I deadpan— "pay me." I lower my voice and clasp my hands in prayer. "And pitch him a dozen reasons for why I'd be perfect for your job."

By her outrageous yawn, she's underwhelmed. "Boring." She leans in confidentially. "Moment of truth . . . which one?"

"Which one what?"

"Which one of the Donovans melts your butter?"

Which? How can she ask me that? I mean, they're all friends with my brothers. *Which* makes it weird.

Wide-eyed, Anita smiles expectantly as I think it through. Anything to take my mind off the pain, though it's eased up enough that I'm no longer tasting blood from my lower lip.

Ignoring my childhood faux pas of a wish, I run through the list.

There's Tyler, who's inherently sexy because he has my paycheck. He's the older, wiser, kinder of the Donovan brothers. His sandy-blond waves are always as carefree as his soul, and his twenty-seven-year-old smile warms you from the inside out. One day in the not-too-distant future, this business will be his kingdom, an attractive quality that the vagina of every eligible bachelorette in the tri-county region has zeroed in on.

Hunk-worthiness? A ten and a half. On the date-worthy

LEXXI JAMES

scale, I can't even go there. He's almost paternal. Or a really hot uncle you hope will find his forever match. Whenever I come in, he's always checking to see how I'm doing and if I've eaten. Thanks to this place, I have.

Then there's Zac, the youngest and three years older than me. A young McDreamy in his own right; his looks are totally wasted. The man has been my BFF since forever ago, but he never dates. Between studying at New York University and launching his own mogul career, you'd think the man was thirty-one, not twenty-one.

Over summers and holiday breaks, he returns to Saratoga Springs to shake things up. Moving the inventory system from the caveman era into the next millennium. Shifting the ordering to the cloud and ensuring it takes everything from Venmo to Bitcoin. And launching a spruced-up website with candid shots that always manage to blow up Instagram, which he often credits me for.

Every chance I get, I snap outrageous photos and videos, and at Zac's insistence, they've posted every single one. Food photos. Tyler clowning around, serving a bachelorette party in nothing but a black apron. Well, he had shorts on, but you couldn't tell from the front. Even simple things like Anita plopping dry ice into drinks at Halloween.

Zac says I have raw talent. I call it an obsession with Mrs. D.'s food.

Zac will forever be my biggest cheerleader and best friend, but something more? Let's just say our one and only test-the-waters kiss was all we needed to be eternally friend-zoned. Plus, I'm not sure he'll ever settle down. Core-of-the-Earth-level

384

hotness? A thousand percent. A compulsive workaholic? Ten-thousand percent.

And last, but not least, there's Mark. The very same Marcus Evan Donavon my child mind thought I could marry. Silly girl. I couldn't possibly marry an ass, and make no mistake, that man is an ass.

As if reading my thoughts, Anita asks, "Ooh, is it Mark?"

Heat flares up my neck to my cheeks as I scoff. "Mark? Mark hates me."

"He does not."

"He even gave me that stupid nickname."

Anita coos at me. "It's adorable."

My palm is affronted before I am, and it flies in her face. "Don't even."

Her hands raise in surrender as she smartly backs up a step. "Okay, okay. Just saying, he's not terrible on the eyes."

When Anita gets googly-eyed for Mark, I gag. She grabs a ticket and pulls a highball from the shelf to work on her next drink.

All I can think is . . . Mark? Really?

I mean, to look at, yes. Agreed. If Mark had a mute button, he'd be the perfect man. The problem with him—or rather, the biggest problem with him—is that his looks far overshadow his tiny, little pea-brain. That and his two-sizes too-small heart.

Have you ever seen a man too beautiful to exist? Sure, in and of itself, it's not a reason to hate him. What I hate is that Mark wields it like a weapon. Whenever he walks into a room, I feel the need to dispense chastity belts with reckless abandon.

Again, I'm not talking about your garden-variety good looks, as in he looks great in a pair of jeans with an insta-swoon dimple that could launch a thousand ships. I'm talking about a legs-locked, knees-weak, heart-stopping level of sex appeal that would stand out in a sea of Hemsworths. The irony is that with all that heat, Mark is too cold.

Anita pops the cork on a bottle of Moscato and works on a Bellini. "Well, if your heart's set on Tyler or Zac, you're SOL. I just remembered that Tyler isn't here. He and Zac went fishing with their dad before Zac returns to school."

I nibble my lower lip again, worry twisting my gut.

"Nope. Don't do that," Anita says, frowning.

"Huh? Do what?"

She waves an accusatory strawberry-margarita painted fingernail in my face. "That thing where your brows pinch so hard, they nearly touch. Trust me, you're too young to start with the permanent angry line." She wipes down the bar. "You worried about Brian leaving?"

"No," I lie, lifting a defiant chin. "Brian has been here long enough. Having him take care of me since my parents—"

My mouth dries, sand filling my throat before I can say the words. I breathe through it until words come out.

"Anyway, the military gave him all the leave they could. I'm an adult. I've graduated. I'm a big girl, and my brother's a big boy. We can take care of ourselves." I say this out loud at least a dozen times a day, because any day now, I'll believe it.

Anita places a bowl of mixed nuts between us and pops a few into her mouth. "Then what is it?"

Deflated, I sigh. "I have five days to get Brian his going-away gift before his deployment."

"That should be plenty of time."

"I need to be able to afford it first. It costs my entire paycheck."

She lifts a brow. "All of your paycheck?"

I nod. "Along with the engraving, yes. I caught him drooling at the jewelers over some stupid-expensive tactical watch. After an insane amount of searching, I found a pre-owned one, but I have to pick it up today. The owner already has other buyers." I'm about to show her on my phone, but my battery's already low, and I still need to use it to find this guy. Wiggling my fingers at her, I say, "Give me your phone."

Anita hands it to me, and I pull up the Laney Jewelers website, then scroll to the right photo. With a two-toned whistle, she approves.

I smile. "And then hopefully, I'll have time to get it engraved before Brian leaves."

"You mean Brian and Mark. What, no gift for his bestie?" she teases.

My lips quirk as my narrowed eyes respond for me.

"Hey, if push comes to shove, girl, I've got you." She holds up a paring knife. "Seriously, how hard can it be to scratch two Bs on the metal band?"

"What I had in mind is a little more than his initials, and this watch is worth weeks of my life," I say indignantly as I lower her knife-wielding hand. "As skilled as you are with slicing and dicing, how about we leave the pretty letter carving to the experts." I tap the counter, not sure what to do. "Who can I get my check from?"

"You can get it from Mark."

"What? Mark's here?" My brows pop up as the name of my

arch-nemesis rings through the air. Or is it just nemesis? "Mark never comes here. And why isn't he fishing with everyone else?"

Smiling, she shrugs. "Mrs. D.'s working out the details for the Whitney wedding. I guess he's filling in."

"Perfect." I let out a frustrated sigh. "Any idea where he is?" Anita shakes her head as I slide off the leather stool. "I guess I'll stop looking for Tyler and hunt down Mark."

"Hang on." She fishes cash from the tip jar and hands it to me.

Blinking, I stare at her. "What's this?"

Her hands grab mine, shoving the bills into it. "A bunch of tourists went all out at brunch. Take it. I don't want you not to have a paycheck. You'll be working this side of the bar soon enough."

Emotions overwhelm me as I stare down at the twenties, tens, and fives. This isn't just how Anita is. It's how everyone is here. Always looking out for me when I suspect it least and need it most. Everyone here cares for me. In return, I have to care for them back.

Counting it quickly, I split it right down the middle and toss half back in the jar. "Thanks," I say, rushing out of there before I'm a blubbering puddle in the middle of the floor.

Sternly, I wipe my cheeks and make my way down the hall. I can cry when I'm at home. That's what showers are for.

Scowling, I mutter under my breath. "Yoo-hoo . . . Satan. Come out, come out, wherever you are."

Where Tyler and Zac are wholesome goodness wrapped up in sunshine and smiles, Mark is the polar opposite, ready to fight, run, or fornicate at a moment's notice. His brothers are easygoing sails on tranquil waters, while Mark is a storm.

And those eyes. Shamefully, I've stared at them more than once.

Some men were meant to build castles while others were born to slay dragons. That's Mark. A hot-blooded fighting machine who can't turn it off. It's what makes him the best. And the broodiest.

When Brian entered the Army, Mark rushed in after him, besties since their stupid blood oath in the fifth grade. Seriously, how deep did they need to cut? They both required five stitches each. But that was them. Two beautiful idiots pridefully counting every last scar.

It's the reason why no matter how hard I try, I can't avoid Mark. Like my brother's shadow, he's always around. A personal tormentor, ready and eager to strike at will.

I pop my head into the break room. A few waitresses are eating a late lunch and gossiping about customers.

Gasping, Kara looks up at me. "I thought you were off," she says, offended at my very presence. "Tyler said you needed a personal day." Her eyes roll to a resentful stop. "Must be nice."

Why would Tyler tell them that? I ignore her, and not just because Kara's an ass, but because convincing Kara that Tyler is wrong would be as fruitful as convincing Mark I should be a bartender. There's no point. It'll never happen. But I still need to pick up my check. "Have either of you seen Mark?"

"Oh my God," Starr says as she whips back her pink hair. "Is Mark *Danger Zone* Donovan here?"

Kara claps and squeals like a seal, while I rub my temple, praying that the migraine she just spurred up goes away. High-pitched and hopeless, she carries on. "He's so lickable. I heard he now holds the record for the most confirmed kills."

Confused, I stare. "How does that make him hot?"

She smirks. "You wouldn't understand." She scans me up and down before dismissing me with her eyes. "You're too young."

"I'm only a year younger than you, Kara."

She scoops her breasts into her crossed arms, forcing cleavage that even her overstuffed push-up couldn't tackle. "There's a world of difference in a year."

Perhaps to a dog.

"Trust me," Starr says. "His brothers are princes, but Mark Donovan is a full-fledged demi-god." She licks her spoon suggestively. "I've got something that sharpshooter can aim at."

She sucks her finger, amplifying the point. I dry heave and leave the room. Only God knows where that finger's been.

Kara calls after me. "Tell him we're looking for him, too, okay?"

Their giggles echo wildly as I shake my head. *Sure. Why not? Because maybe if I offer two semi-virginal sacrifices to your demi-God, he'll give me that promotion I desperately need.*

"Jess?" I hear Mark say. His deep, gravelly voice flows effortlessly down the hall, though I don't see him.

As I approach his office, the door is ajar. I slide a hand on the handle, pausing as soon as I hear, "What about her?" Because Mark isn't talking to me, he's talking *about* me.

The door is cracked ever so slightly, an obvious invitation to listen in. His heavy footsteps move farther away, and I nudge the door a hair, wide enough to peer inside.

Framed by the large picture window at the other end of the office, Beelzebub stands in all his glory: dark blue jeans, crisp white shirt, and chestnut-brown hair mussed to perfection. The million-mile stare he sports is fixed somewhere off in the distance as he presses the cell phone to his ear.

It's wrong of me to stare. But I can't not stare. I mean, it's hardly the first time I've seen Mark Donovan. It's just the first time I've dared to unapologetically stare at his ass.

He shifts in place, and the move is hypnotic. Did he bulk up . . . his butt?

I knew he did some heavy lifting, but this is ridiculous. I mean, once, when traffic was blocked, he and Brian lifted a fallen maple to the side of the road. By themselves. So, yeah, I get it. Muscle mayhem. But now, his arm bulge alone has his shirtsleeves within an inch of their lives. It's as if he graduated from bar-belling trees to tanks.

"What?" he snaps indignantly.

I shouldn't hang on his every word, but I do. Who's he talking to? Is someone complaining about me? Because I've been crushing it. Taking double shifts. All smiles. Amped up like an Energizer bunny. Nobody works as hard as I do, and not just for the tips. I have the Bishop legacy to maintain.

And yes, I may have mixed up an order here and there, or spilled one tiny little kid's milk. But I fixed every last mistake. And the *milk spill Boomerang clip* the kids posted got a ton of love on TikTok. Granted, the putrid dairy after-smell was wafting about for weeks, but thankfully, it's gone. Almost.

"No. No way," I hear Mark say, chuckling. I frown hard. I know that laugh. That's his evil laugh.

It's the laugh he had when he and Brian set a rope snare and trapped me in it, which, in my defense, I was eight. It was also the laugh that accompanied that nasty bowl of foul-tasting jellybeans and his insistence that girls couldn't eat them. He knew what he was doing. Throwing down a double-dog dare in the face of the female race. Well, I ate every last one. And whoever decided that vomit and boogers were palatable should be shot.

He also had that very same annoying laugh when he came up with that stupid nickname—

"Choir Girl?" he says with a scoff.

Fire fills my face as my grip on the door handle tightens.

This is the same man who tosses nicknames like *babe* or *princess* at every walking vagina in town, but for me, I'm simply Choir Girl. I mean, sure, I was in the church choir. And not just because everyone there was nice or that they handed out cocoa and cookies after every performance, which I lived for, but because Mom was there, too. It was our space as much as anyone else's.

"Me with Choir Girl?" He says it as if disgusted. By this point, I'm already inappropriately one foot in the office and charging straight at him. But Mark doesn't notice and just keeps going.

"Not with a ten-foot pole," he says with another scoff, and half of my heart shatters as he goes from being cold to cruel. "Make that a hundred-and-ten-foot pole. She's too"—he pauses for a moment for just the right word, the wheel in his mind landing on—"Jess."

Seriously? It's bad enough that he's banished me like a dwarf planet in my own brother's solar system. Why talk about me at all? Oh, that's right. Because he's Mark.

I bite my cheek, my face burning with more emotions than I can count. Frozen with indecision—to leave or to knee him in the groin—I blink away my stubborn tears just as he turns around. "Not even if the fate of mankind was dependent on my dick connecting with her vag—"

His mouth snaps shut, and I narrow my eyes.

He hangs up. For the longest second in history, I stare down the first man to make my *Vow to Hate for All Eternity* list. And that's not just my period talking.

"Jess," he says with a huff, annoyed. "Ever hear of knocking?" He walks over to his desk.

He did not just say that. *Ever hear of not talking shit behind someone's back, butt-munch?*

My mouth falls open, and I can feel every last one of my freckles catch fire. "Oh, I'm sorry, Your Royal Highness. Is that the proper etiquette? Knocking so I don't disturb you being an asshat?"

"Asshat?" His steps stop cold. He spins, facing me. "Well, this asshat happens to be your boss for today, Jess. That is, if you were working, which you shouldn't be. How about you come back tomorrow?"

Is that why Tyler told me to stay home? Because of Mark? When I could've used those tips? I feel my anger rise to a dangerous high as I stand my ground. "How about you give me an apology?"

When he rolls his eyes, I poke him in his dumb, stone-hard chest. *What am I doing?*

His eyes dart to my finger, then to my eyes. "I—" I take a breath, my chin defiant. "I deserve an apology," I snap.

He edges closer into my space. "Haven't you heard? In life, you never get what you deserve, Jess. Only what you can negotiate. Move it along, Choir Girl."

Again with the name? "Make me," I say in total stupid-

brazen disregard for my stand-in boss. But I can't back down. Instead, I step up to him, toe-to-toe. I'm keenly aware of the childishness of my action considering the man has, oh, I don't know, a yard of height on me.

My stare-down is feeble, pathetic, really. I blame his eyes. They're gold now—charged and deadly—like some wild exotic cat I'm stupid enough to be in a staring contest with.

Two knocks chop at the door.

"Come in," he barks.

"Hey, hey, hey." Brian's voice is too familiar to both of us, but neither of us budges. My brother wraps a casual arm around me as if the death-glare crossfire isn't happening at all. He pulls me back and leans over to Mark. "I thought we had a talk about this."

I whip my head to Brian. "A talk about what?"

"Nothing." Mark's reply is quick. Too quick. He retreats behind his desk. *Coward*.

I turn my attention to Brian, breaking down his resolve with my angriest angry eyes. "What talk?"

He shrugs, his guilty smile on full display. "Nothing," he says, rushing me out of the room with both hands on my shoulders. "Mark and I need to chat, sis. See you later."

Before I get too far with a protest, the door slams in my face.

"*Argh.*" I stomp my foot. I still need my check. Maybe if I'd taken Anita up on that lunch, I wouldn't be consumed with hangry rage. Between my hunger and my period, there's only one solution: full-blown annihilation. Crazed, I plow down the door, guns blazing.

"Why'd you hang up on me?" Brian asks Mark.

"What?" I glare down my enemies, Tweedle Dumb and

Tweedle Asshat, trying to make sense of why Mark's dick and my vag would ever come up in their conversation.

What the hell?

When Anita asked me about Mark, did I say, *"Me? With the dildo of the century? Not even if my vagina was on fire and his dick was the only way to put it out."* Wait, that came out wrong. And of course, I didn't. At least, not with my outside voice.

Instead of being a half-decent person, Mark clasps his hands and cocks his head in that arrogant way he always does. "Remember our little talk about knocking, Jess?"

It's as if his balls are begging to be kicked so hard, they lodge in that vacant space where his brain should be.

Fire licks at my good senses. I'm so ready to hand him that perfect ass of his on a platter, but the second I open my mouth, he adds, "I'd hate to see you lose your job for something as trivial as manners."

Stunned, I stare. *He'd really fire me over this?*

And what about Brian? Instead of standing up for me, my idiot big brother is just standing there. Like a big, dumb oaf, he's doing nothing but warning me with his eyes and a slow shake of his head.

Brian's right. I know he's right. He's leaving in a few days and taking this worthless sack of shit with him.

I should stay calm because I don't want this job, I need it. And not even for the money. Without it, I'm more or less alone. Rex is stationed in New Jersey. Close, but never close enough. And Cade is away in some god-forsaken part of the world that feels as unreachable as the moon.

Tears threaten fast. Too fast. As soon as he says, "Well, what do you know? Even choir girls have manners," no-holds-barred atomic anger wins.

I see the stack of checks on the desk, miraculously in alphabetical order. Mine's right on top. I snatch it up and stuff it in my pocket.

"Go to hell, Mark Donovan." And once again, when faced with the most beautiful man I've ever seen, my brain snaps in two, and I do the unthinkable. "I. Quit."

Pulse racing, I rush out of the room, determined not to cry like a girl or beg for my job. How did today end up like this?

I should've spent today planning the sendoff of the century for the brother of the year. Instead, I'm stuck spending the better part of it finding a new job and hating the both of them.

Asshat, one.

Choir Girl, zero.

Chapter Three

MARK

A fist of fucking titanium flies from out of nowhere and slams me square in the chest. "Ow." My tone is pure *what the hell?*

It's true, I know better than to pick a fight with Jess. And I am technically the grown-up. Well, with her being eighteen and all, I guess she's a grown-up too. But I swear to God, that woman gets under my skin like lava-coated chiggers. Or maybe it's the guilt.

Brian and I know the price of his extended leave. It was a deal with the devil. Saying our next mission will be dangerous is like saying the Pope sometimes prays. There's a good chance we'll never see our families again, and the last thing I needed was to face off with Jess and her big, blue, soul-searching eyes. Hell, I can't even bear to look my mother in the eye.

Guns blazing, Brian lays into me. "You fire my sister five days before our next deployment?"

I didn't fire her. She quit. But with Brian glaring me down, there's no use arguing that technicality. Flustered, I point a finger at him. "This is your fault."

"My fault?"

"For giving me the fucking third degree and accusing me of making a play for Jess. Which she overheard. Thanks a fucking heap."

"Ah." He flicks a speck of dust from the desk. "How was I supposed to know you'd have that conversation with the door opened?"

I wave both arms in the air. "Now you know. And Jess was eavesdropping. *Again*. Her own bad habit brought this on."

Brian gives me a *don't fuck with the Bishops* face. "I can't have your back if things aren't square with Jess."

I rub at the ice pick driving into the base of my neck. "Well, technically, she quit."

When Brian hits me this time, he doesn't hold back. The man packs a punch like a battering ram. "Fix it, fucker."

I look at him as if a dick sprouted from the top of his head. "How? You know your sister. She's earned every last flaming strand of that red hair of hers. Fuck, we haven't spoken in years, and this is our reunion." I huff and lift my chin to the sky. "She hates me."

He shrugs. "Well, considering your first conversation in years is to threaten her job, her hating you seems validated."

"Is it my fault you made me say I wouldn't make moves on your sister with my outside voice?"

"Is it my fault you'll hump everything from a hydrant to a lamppost, and it wasn't exactly a stretch?"

I gesture at the door. "Clearly, you had nothing to worry

about." I adjust my pants from behind the desk. *Yeah, that's a bald-faced lie.*

"Clearly." Brian shakes his head. "You can't talk to her like she's twelve. She isn't."

Duh. One look at her ass told me that.

I remain stone-faced as Brian continues to lambast me. "You don't understand. Jess is stressed, too. With all the shit she's going through—" He clams up.

My ears perk up. "What's she going through?" I ask, tiptoeing as I pry.

He shakes it off. "Nothing. Just, *er*, woman stuff."

Enough said. The last thing I need to hear about is the world of Jess's uterus, though it does explain her flying off the fucking handle. With Jess, Moody is her middle name. Plus, with how full her breasts are and—

Where the fuck did that come from? I scramble to wipe the image from my mind. *Can we change the subject already?*

Brian drones on. "She's not a child anymore. And you're only filling in for the day, dickwad. Don't make me call your mommy on you."

"I know she's not a child."

While the very full-grown woman was busting my balls, it took every sheer ounce of willpower to avoid staring at those full, pouty lips. *Fuck*, she can't come back here. At least, not while I'm here. This is my funeral in the making.

Hmm. I think it through. Because I also can't *not* bring her back. Brian would murder me—*Saw* movie style.

I offer a solution. "She can consider herself on paid vacation until we leave. This way, the two of you can spend some time together."

And she'll be far the hell away from me.

Brian socks me again. Playfully, this time, but considering he gave it all he had the last round, I wince. "I guess you'd better find her and tell her that."

My eyes shoot wide. "You're her brother. Why don't you find her and tell her?"

"Because it's not my mess. It's yours. And we have our entire next mission to clean up after each other." He winks, the smartass, and heads for the door. "You know my baby sis would love to tend bar," he sings at me on his way out.

I throw a stress ball at his head. And miss.

He chuckles. "And they call you a sharpshooter," he calls out as he closes the door behind him.

Fucker.

I scroll through my phone until I find Jess's number, filed under "CG." I shoot her a text and wait her out.

Can we talk?

An hour later, after a thorough review of Zac's new inventory system, I check my phone. Still no response from Jess, so I try again.

I really need to talk to you.

By the time I've finished reviewing next month's menus with the staff, getting the seating arrangements for the Whitney wedding changed to accommodate nearly two hundred people instead of one hundred people, and reconciling the accounting for the month, my brain is fried.

I blow out a breath. Not a word from Choir Girl.

So, I do the unthinkable. I apologize.

Sorry I was an asshat. Please call back.

A text pings back, but the small surge of relief is instantly snuffed out. It isn't Jess. It's Brian. Even his text looks unhinged.

Did you talk to Jess???

Brian sends me a screenshot. Her phone finder app has her pinned on possibly the worst street in Albany. Without even speaking to him, I know Brian's about to lose his shit. Hell, my heart's beating out of my rib cage, and I'm half a breath away from losing my own shit.

What the fuck is she doing there?

Keep calm, I tell myself. If I'm panicked, Brian will panic tenfold.

I lock my voice into casual mode and call. "I've texted her several times. She hasn't returned my texts, but that's nothing new, considering her nickname for me is sometimes Satan. Have you tried calling her?"

"Yes, dumbass. Tried that first. I'm heading that way, but I'm home." The Bishop home is buried in a southwest pocket of Adirondack Park—at least an hour and a half from Albany. His voice rises, unnerved. "I need you to—"

"I'll take care of it. I'm leaving now."

I grab the nearest keys and rush out the front, nearly plowing down Anita. "Sorry, I'm in a hurry."

"Wait." She blocks my path. "Did Jess find you?"

"Yes," I grumble, irritated. Now I just need to find her.

"Oh, good. I know she was worried about getting that watch for Brian."

Impatient, I mutter, "What watch?" as I move around her and make my way to the truck.

Anita keeps pace, shoving her phone in my face. "This watch."

I check out the price tag. All her paychecks for two months wouldn't cover that watch. "How is she paying for a four-thousand-dollar watch?"

"She isn't. Some guy is selling his old one."

Of course. Because that's what people do. Sell four-thousand-dollar watches for a fraction of the price. It happens every day.

I get in the truck, slam the gas, punch the dashboard, and shout, "*Fuuuck!*"

<hr />

Ready for more of Mark Donovan & Jess Bishop?
1-CLICK NOW>> MARKED

About the Author

Lexxi James is a best-selling author of romantic suspense. Her feats in multi-tasking include binge watching Netflix and sucking down a cappuccino in between feverish typing and loads of laundry.

She lives in Ohio with her teen daughter and the sweetest man in the universe. She loves to hear from readers!

www.LexxiJames.com

THE DOODLER MURDERS

THE DOODLER MURDERS

UNSOLVED MURDERS OF SAN FRANCISCO

KILLER CRIME
BOOK EIGHT

ALAN R. WARREN

COPYRIGHT

House of Mystery Publishing

Seattle, Washington, USA

Vancouver, British Columbia, Canada

First Edition

ISBN (eBook): 978-1-989980-80-4

ISBN (Paperback): 978-1-989980-82-8

Cover design, formatting, and editing by Evening Sky Publishing Services

BOOK DESCRIPTION

The Doodler Killer was a serial killer responsible for at least sixteen murders and three assaults of gay men in San Francisco between 1974 and 1975. He was called a doodler because he drew pictures of his victims before killing them. The term "black" was also given to him by some media because the survivors of his attacks described him as an African American. The Doodler Killer is still unidentified, and the case has never been brought to justice. The killer met his victims in casual settings such as gay restaurants or bars. He would draw cartoonish pictures of his victims and present his drawings to them to start a conversation, hoping to convince them to have a sexual encounter. While the Doodler Killer was active, the police believed there were two other active gay serial killers in the San Francisco area as well. Five drag queens were murdered in the Tenderloin district, and another six men were murdered in what they called the "leather community." Police now

thought they were dealing with a third serial killer of gay men with The Doodler. Little did they know that all of these murders, though different in the victim type and the murder method, were actually being committed by the same killer.

CONTENTS

PREFACE

One of the most common questions in gay-related murders is how they differ from heterosexual murders.

If you were caught performing a homosexual act in the Victorian Era, they would say you were "sexually insane" and commit you to an insane asylum. By the early 1900s, most countries decided it was more of a deviant act, something you shouldn't do. They would put you in a regular prison instead of an insane asylum if caught. By doing so, homosexuality became a crime, not as severe as murder, but more on the level of crimes such as theft, burglary, or arson.

A stunning example of the treatment of homosexuals in society is that of Alan Turing. Turing was a British mathematician, cryptanalyst, and computer scientist during World War II. In 1939, he joined the Hut 8 team. There, he solved the German Enigma code, which was considered the turning point for the Allied Forces winning the war against the Nazis.

So, what did society decide to do with one of its heroes?

Alan Turing was a homosexual. In 1952, when he was 39 years old, he started a relationship with Arnold Murray, who was 19. Shortly after the couple began seeing each other, Turing's house was robbed. After the police investigated the crime, they discovered that the thief was Murray and that Turing and Murray had been acquainted. It was also found that the two men had been involved in a sexual relationship. Both men were charged with gross indecency. Turing later pleaded guilty to the charges and was convicted. He was given a choice between imprisonment or conditional probation. What were the conditions he had to meet?

Turing had to undergo physical and hormonal changes designed to reduce his libido. He received several injections over one year, which feminized his body. During that year, he became impotent and grew breast tissue. Along with his body changes, he had his security clearance removed and lost his job with the British Intelligence Agency. He tried to move to America, but they denied him as he was then a convicted felon.

On June 7, 1954, Turing committed suicide in his home by ingesting cyanide. His housekeeper found him with a half-eaten apple lying beside him in his bed the following day. It was hypothesized that he had doused the apple with the cyanide. An inquest later determined that he had committed suicide.

When society forces one of its citizens to be sterilized for being homosexual, one considered to be among the

best and a war hero, why would they care about other homosexuals being murdered or hurt?

It didn't end there.

Even after homosexuality was legalized in 1967, it was still considered a sickness or illness in the medical community that needed curing. Almost like alcoholism, only the general public looked at alcoholics with sympathy. After all, they were still pleasing people, and it was just the alcohol that made them do bad things. It was the Christian thing to do to help them. Most alcoholics weren't even arrested for driving while drunk or starting a fight in a public place. They were merely told to go home and sleep it off; if they kept on fighting, they were put in the drunk tank by the police for a night.

Whereas, if you were having or attempting to have sex with someone of the same sex as yourself, you were a pervert. It was considered wrong, disgusting, dirty, and perverted behavior. It was also judged as something you didn't need to do.

Why would someone want to have sex with another of the same sex?

The public didn't know what to do with homosexuals after they were no longer considered criminals or insane. At least with alcoholics and drug addicts, there were treatments for their problems; after all, they just needed not to do it!

So, what would they do when they couldn't arrest these homosexuals or put them into the local mental institute? History repeated itself, and they turned it over to the religion of the day to handle.

In the past, when "dealing with" the Indigenous

people of North America, the church and state decided that to "civilize the savage," they had their children forcibly extracted from the reserves they were imprisoned on and taken to Catholic schools to learn how to be "good Christians." Only now, many years later, an astounding number of unmarked graves are being discovered all over Canada, where Indigenous children were buried after their deaths at these residential schools. We do not even know the names of these children or why or how they died. Despite this atrocity, they believed they were successful in those cases with people they didn't understand, and they figured they would be successful in handling the gay population with the same iron fist.

So, keeping up with societal tradition, Evangelicals developed a new program to cure homosexuals. It was called "Exodus." In other words, they intended to "Pray away the Gay." They convinced several young gay men and women that the devil's influence made them believe they were gay and could fix their "problem" if they turned their lives over to the Lord and worked through the Exodus program. If they did, they would be cured, and they would be able to live healthy, productive, straight lives. As with so many other religious plans to remedy what didn't need healing, it left many young gays confused, in despair, and committing suicide.

A significant component of the books in this series will include an individual analysis of the killers. In some

cases, the question of who the murderer was about will be examined – whether the murderer was about the person they desired or the person at the heart of the murder. From the killers' outlook, was their reason for committing murder different because of their sexual orientation? Or was the murder about the act of desiring them?

The answer to this question is entirely different when the victims are gay. After all, like any other minority group or class of people in the World, that fact creates a reason for some to want to kill them. The sexual component is complex, so it will take several examples. Some cases involve both the killer and the victim being homosexual. In these particular cases, we can see quite a few similarities to that of heterosexual murderers. We will find emotional perspectives to be the major causes of the murders. The motive could be anything from jealousy to unreciprocated love or the actual murderer unable to find love due to mental issues or social circumstances. But most importantly, in all those cases, the type of love, albeit homosexual or heterosexual, is only the affection of such devotion.

INTRODUCTION

The Doodler Murders book focuses on 1970s in San Francisco, United States. This decade was known for everything from the political scandal of Richard Nixon and "Watergate," to the feminist movement with Gloria Steinem and the wave of a new style of music called "disco." But in addition to these controversies and movements, America was also becoming known for its significantly increasing crime in cities. The highest crime rate in the country was during the 1970s – the beginning of the decade saw an increase of 11% in 1970 alone. Along with crimes, corruption within law enforcement was exposed. Also, urban decay peaked when some of America's largest cities, including New York, Atlanta, Boston, and Chicago, lost more than 10% of their population.

Random violence and crimes weren't the only things on the minds of the people who lived in the cities. There was something much more sinister. Crimes committed by a person who would plan them out to the last detail.

Someone so skilled that they would get away with their crimes for sometimes even years. That someone had the attention of the media, police, and public. That someone was dubbed by law enforcement "the serial killer."

Serial Killers weren't exactly a brand-new thing that started in the 1970s, but they became something that happened more often than ever, especially in the United States. The 1970s would be the peak decade in history for the number of serial killers in America. The news from different major cities in America was warning people to be careful from such killers as John Wayne Gacy in Chicago, Ted Bundy in cities across four states, including Florida, David Berkowitz, a.k.a. "The Son of Sam" in New York, the "Hillside Stranglers" in Los Angeles, and of course San Francisco's most famous "Zodiac Killer."

Even major religious cult-like groups flourished in the 70s. Such as Jim Jones, who took his followers down to Jonestown, Guyana, where they all committed suicide. And Charles Manson, who led his family to commit one of California's most famous murders: the murder of actress Sharon Tate, who was pregnant at the time the Manson Family brutally killed her.

But amongst all the notoriety of such events and brutal murders, there was one that was never talked about and is still very seldomly mentioned. The media dubbed it the "Black Doodler Murders" or just the "Doodler Murders."

The Doodler Killer was a serial killer responsible for at least sixteen murders and three assaults of gay men in

San Francisco between 1974 and 1975. He was called a doodler because he drew pictures of his victims before killing them. The term "black" was also given to him by some media because the survivors of his attacks described him as an African American.

The Doodler Killer is still unidentified, and the case has never been brought to justice.

The killer met his victims in casual settings such as gay restaurants or bars. He would draw cartoonish pictures of his victims and present his drawings to them to start a conversation, hoping to convince them to have a sexual encounter.

While The Doodler Killer was active, the police believed there were two other active gay serial killers in the San Francisco area as well. Five drag queens were murdered in the Tenderloin district, and another six men were murdered in what they called the "leather community." Police now thought they were dealing with a third serial killer of gay men with the Doodler. Little did they know that all of these murders, though different in the victim type and the murder method, were actually being committed by the same killer.

So, why didn't this serial killer create the same impact that the others were making at the time? One answer could be that since the gay community is such a small percentage of the population, it flew under everyone's radar. Also, because the sexuality of the gay community defines them, it's conceivable that people underestimated the likelihood of them being a victim of serial murder. Perhaps it was ruled out. Or perhaps they pushed the fact that they had a new serial killer

specifically targetting gay men aside in their minds and focused only on the known serial killers they might be victims of. But maybe the reason why the Black Doodler Murders didn't get much fanfare just goes a little deeper than that.

PART I

BACKGROUND

SAN FRANCISCO IN THE 1970S

L argely, San Francisco was considered a city of tolerance where groups that ordinary American people viewed as radical seemed to headquarter. The city captured the attention of many young people of the era, who would flock in droves to find their newfound Mecca. Many of these groups sought their right to live free among the others without persecution – a place where they could live, work, and love their families while having equal rights to other groups like the LGBT, hippies, feminists, and minorities.

The only thing was, with the city gaining the attention of the country and the rest of the world, it also attracted many outcasts, and the drug and sex culture exploded. The downtown area became full of sex shops, adult movie theatres, sex workers, pornography, and drug culture. High-rises were being built around the downtown, like the Transamerica Pyramid, which changed the landscape from a stretching city of home residences to rows of skyscrapers reaching the sun.

Like in the previous books of this series, we begin by looking at the background or climate towards gay people in the city and country where the crimes happened. San Francisco had become well-known as a liberal place in the '70s. But that didn't mean everything was great for minorities and gay people. It means that the city was moving in the right direction towards giving equal rights and freedoms to all its citizens much faster and further than any other American city at the time.

Several growing pains were still involved with these changes or attempted changes. After World War II ended, African Americans moved to San Francisco by the thousands after hearing about the city's free policies. However, the reality was that the same attitudes existed in corporations such as banks and law enforcement agencies like the police.

The San Francisco Police Department (SFPD) had fewer than 150 minorities working for them in 1973. Among those minorities, there were only six inspectors and eight sergeants. In April of that same year, a few black officers on the police force filed a civil rights lawsuit to try and end the discrimination inside the department. The lawsuit was a significant turn of events, not only for getting equal rights for black people wanting to join the police force and have an equal siting but for what followed the lawsuit.

Previously, the police force had mainly been run by Irish Americans, who were all white, and the police union decided they would fight this lawsuit. The decision to fight the lawsuit caused an automatic divide in the force, leaving most minority officers ignored and

unable to go out on social activities among the white officers. Some officers became hateful and frustrated, which led to threats of violence toward minorities. The tension only worsened as the lawsuit continued over time.

When a police force becomes so divided that officers will not work together and, in fact, hate each other, how can you expect them to focus on the crimes of the area they are supposed to be protecting? Throughout the criminal cases investigated by detectives, the top conversations were always about the lawsuit and racism.

More tension in the race division occurred after John V. Young of the SFPD was shot and killed by members of the Black Panther Party. Then, by the Spring of 1974, the city became aware of the "Zebra Killings," which resulted from a group calling themselves the "Death Angels," who set out to kill who they believed were the white devils responsible for enslaving black people throughout the years. They aimed to kill as many white people as possible to achieve status within the Black Muslim Brotherhood. In the same year, Patty Hearst, newspaper heiress and daughter to Randolph Hearst, was kidnapped from the Berkley part of the city by the Symbionese Liberation Army (SLA). Later, she would be filmed robbing a bank with other members of the SLA using an M1 carbine rifle, eventually leading to her arrest for being part of the group and not being kidnapped. Her trial is where the term "Stockholm Syndrome" came from. The psychological condition was her primary defense.

Tensions were pushed to the brink when, in August

1975, most of the SFPD went on strike because the city did not give any police officers raises in their pay. A month later, Sara Jane Moore, one of Charles Manson's disciples, tried to assassinate then-President Gerald Ford in front of the St. Francis Hotel.

With the city's police in such a state and crime out of control, gay people wouldn't stand a chance. Being gay had just become legal in the courts only six years before this lawsuit. So gay people were considered even less than most minorities. Public opinion was that being gay was another strike against a person.

When the SFPD spokesperson publicly stated that he wouldn't hire anybody who was gay to be on the police force because he considered gays to have a lower moral standard. He believed they were more likely to commit crimes because of their nature and were too unstable to be a police officer. Based on his words, how do you think the SFPD would treat a gay person?

In 1971, San Francisco hosted one of the largest anti-war protests where people demonstrated their rage about the US's involvement in the Vietnam War. An estimated 150,000 protesters took part. There were several violent conflicts with police, and over one hundred people were arrested.

In 1970, a gay postal worker was fired for "moral incompetency," so he sued them. In November of that year, he won and was given his job back. His win would inspire others to follow his lead and do the same at any chance they could when someone was wronged.

PART II

THE MURDERS

GERALD EARL CAVANAUGH

O cean Beach outlines six miles of San Francisco city along the Pacific Ocean, where crowds of people grab a quick break from their noisy, hectic city life in the daytime. The waters are usually lined with surfers and tourists visiting the San Francisco Zoo.

In the early hours of Sunday, January 27, 1974, a couple who lived in the North part of the city, working

late-night jobs, one as a server and the other as a bartender, needed to unwind after a hectic Saturday night at work. After getting back to their apartment, the two decided they were too wound up to get any sleep, so they decided to take a walk along the beach. It was a typically mild evening at 54 degrees, cloudy, and a slight breeze made the night perfect.

They got to the shore within a few minutes of arriving at the beach, and both took off their shoes to walk in the shallow part of the water. About ten minutes into their stroll, one of them noticed a big pile of sand about ten feet from the shore. It didn't look like a sandcastle or some sand structure, though. It looked like something was buried there. They both stepped out of the water and started walking towards the mound. They could see what looked like the bottom part of a long coat poking out of the sand and felt something weird was happening.

When they got to the sand pile, one of them started brushing off the sand at the top. An arm fell out and hit the ground. They both screamed and ran back towards the water. The scream caught the attention of another couple sitting on a log further down the shore, and one of them stood up to try and see what had happened and yelled across, "Is everything okay?" Not hearing an answer, they both got up and slowly ran toward the mound of sand.

The four argued about what they should do, and finally, two of them decided to go to shore and find a phone booth to call the police while the other two waited by the body.

"Police! Police!" the caller yelled into his receiver. The 911 phone number was launched in California in 1972, but most people still didn't use it. Often, they would dial "0" and ask the operator to connect them to the police. So, when the station officer answered the phone, the caller wasn't sure he was connected to the police.

"Yes, sir. This is the police. What can I do for you?"

"A dead person might be on or at the beach across Ulloa Street. Just follow the street right down to the water," the caller hung up then. They ran back to the others waiting by the body and, being nervous, decided to leave the scene, return to their homes, and not get involved. This conduct was common back in the 1970s when people didn't want to get involved in a crime or assault. It wasn't that long ago that in the early hours of March 13, 1964, a 28-year-old woman, Kitty Genovese, who was returning home from her job as a bartender, was raped and stabbed at her apartment building entranceway in New York. Later, it was discovered that thirty-eight witnesses to her attack, both hearing and some even seeing it, but not one reported the crime to the police that night. That crime would become known in New York as "Genovese Syndrome" or in the rest of the country as the "Bystander Effect." Research on this event found that some of the witnesses to the crime tried to contact the police, but they could not get involved for various reasons. The story still resonated throughout the country. When news channels and papers at the time asked people around the country, "If they would help out to stop a crime if they saw it happening," most

responded that they wouldn't help and gave the reason because they didn't want to get involved.

The police knew that this part of the beach close to where the body was found was famous for gay men who would meet at some bathroom. So that must have been the first thing that entered their minds. Two officers arrived quickly, realizing a dead body was piled in the sand and called it in. After taking the statements of the four who discovered the body, they roped off the scene, and the homicide unit arrived.

The body was that of a male who was stabbed seventeen times. There were defensive wounds on his left hand. He was five foot eight, weighed two hundred and twenty pounds, and balding. He wore typical clothing, including a dress shirt, casual pants, socks, underwear, and a Timex watch. He had $21.12 in cash in one of his pockets but didn't carry a wallet or have any I.D. or driver's license. The *San Francisco Sentinel* would later run a picture of Cavanaugh looking for anyone to come forward and give them any information on the deceased man.

It took police three days to identify the body of forty-nine-year-old Gerald Earl Cavanaugh, who had lived in the Tenderloin district, a poor neighborhood. He worked at a mattress factory. He attended a local Catholic Church regularly. Cavanaugh's sister flew in from Montreal to identify his body but struggled because his body and face had been severely mutilated during the attack. Plus, he was found a whole week after his murder.

The medical examiner wrote in Cavanaugh's death report that he was found in a condition of slight rigor mortis and supine position, which means he had been there and dead for at least a few hours before he was found. He was also listed as forty-nine and never married, a periodic statement among police in San Francisco that Cavanaugh was probably gay.

Gerald Cavanaugh moved to San Francisco, like so many others from around North America, to try and find a sanctuary to live his homosexual lifestyle, which was not accepted by most at this time. Later, they would discover that he was a Canadian who had moved to the city, lived illegally and worked for cash. Cavanaugh was born in Montreal in 1923 and, like many young people, joined the U.S. Army during World War II. When Cavanaugh returned from battle, he lived in the Haight-Ashbury part of San Francisco, probably because it was a popular spot for anti-war and government groups and a place to live with some sexual freedom.

According to one of his surviving family members, the whole family, including Gerald, knew there was no way he would live as an openly gay man given the times. So, his moving to San Francisco was the best solution. He could live and work there as a straight military veteran, and whenever he needed to fulfill his urges to be with another man, he could go to the Castro district.

Later, Cavanaugh's murder would be considered the first victim of the notorious Doodle Killer of San Francisco. But in 1974, people in law enforcement thought that gay people were criminals who performed

illegal acts or, at a minimum, considered gay people to be mentally ill and needed to be put in a mental hospital. Some would not care what happened to Cavanaugh.

Cavanaugh's murder received little to no notice in any of San Francisco's newspapers or media outlets, never mind being mentioned nationally. The 1970s was a time when there was much civil unrest, and several gay men were bashed or robbed regularly, with little-to-no recourse. Cavanaugh only received one or two-paragraph mentions in the local paper. And the reports carried no substance. The third and final newspaper report finally mentioned that he had "Homosexual propensities," which did add to the story. But in the wrong way. It was almost as if being gay was an appropriate reason for his murder.

Even in San Francisco, gays had to be very careful of their actions from people around the city. The police were still constantly raiding gay establishments and arresting men for breaking the sodomy laws that were still in place at the time. They did this even if the men were not having sex in the bar or club, but perhaps just being close and kissing. The police were also known to frequently stop men in the Castro, accusing them of having anal sex, even if they were walking to a store or something. If you looked gay, you could be investigated. Back in those days, if you wore Speedos or looked in any way feminine, you'd be investigated. Even teenagers and young men who were out on the weekends looking for trouble, once they had enough alcohol to drink, would go to the Castro and looks for gay men to harass.

It wasn't until city councilman Harvey Milk came along and started using his elected position to try and combat these attacks from police and gay bashers. He knew the police would not help gay men, so he decided it would be best to rely on each other in the community. He had the idea of handing out whistles to everyone. If you were walking anywhere in the Castro and heard someone blow their whistle, you were to run towards it to try and help the person being harassed. Milk also started several community patrols that would walk the streets in Castro at night, using walkie-talkies to talk with each other to try and prevent any attacks.

There's no direct evidence that police knew Cavanaugh was gay. Still, if they had investigated his murder, they would have found several witnesses to him being at gay bars in the Castro district of San Francisco. Not only the night his body was found but regularly for months. The area where Cavanaugh's body was discovered was a popular meeting place for gay men or a spot for two gay men who had met in a club earlier to go alone.

It doesn't matter why the police chose not to investigate this murder or that even after a few more murders in the future occurred, they didn't care because the victims were gay. After all, complete disregard by law enforcement for the assaults on gay people in Castro continued years after the Doodler Serial Killer had stopped his murder spree. Even after Milk, and even as changed as San Francisco became in 1976, it would take at least another generation of police to come along to be more accepting of the lifestyles of gay men.

Could this have been a reason there was no task force set up or direction provided for any real investigation into this murder and many more within the following two short years? I don't think we will know the answer to that question.

JOSEPH "JAE" STEVENS

I t was a blustery Tuesday morning on June 25, 1974, when Karla decided to go for a quiet walk on the shores of Spreckels Lake in Golden Gate Park. She had just been in a fight with her partner and needed to be alone to try and figure things out. The lake was a realtor reserve constructed in the spring of 1904 on the park's north side. The lake was built and used for model boaters, from sailors to speed-racing boats. Feeding birds at this lake or connecting with any wildlife there was

illegal, which was perfect for Karla's walk as anyone there would be there for model boating, creating a sense of isolation for her.

It was an hour after Karla arrived at the lake before she noticed what looked like a woman lying on her back beside a large tree, staring face up toward the sky. She seemed to be very close to the shores of the lake. In fact, so close that the water from the lake was washing up around the women's knees. Karla thought this looked weird, so she approached the woman to try and find out what she was doing. When Karla got within five feet of the woman, she realized a lot of blood was over her chest and mouth.

Karla quickly ran from the lakefront towards 36th Avenue – the route she usually took to walk into the park on her way to Spreckels Lake. This time she was in a panic, already stressed from her previous night with her partner. She found the payphone quickly even though she had never had the cause to use it there. Karla dialed "0" and waited for what seemed like an eternity. In reality, only three rings went through before the operator answered.

"Operator. How may I direct your call?"

"Hello, caller? This is the operator. How can I help you? Are you there? Hello?"

For some reason, Karla remained silent. She couldn't seem to muster up a voice to answer the operator. She realized that she had never screamed when she found the body. She thought she called a name and opened her mouth to yell, but nothing came out. She had to speak! She had to talk! She had to get help!

"Caller, do you need help?"

"Yes." Karla barely whispered out into the receiver.

"Hello! Hello! Caller, what do you need?"

"I need the police." She continued quietly, "There's a dead woman at the lake."

"Stay online, and I'll connect you right away."

Karla explained to the officer who answered the phone what she had found on the shore of the lake. The officer asked her to identify herself, but she remained quiet. After he got the directions to where the body was, the officer again asked for her name and if she knew who the victim was. He repeatedly asked her to identify herself until she finally told him she didn't know anything and couldn't tell him whom she was before hanging up the phone. Karla remained silent.

Police arrived at the scene to find the dead body of 27-year-old Joseph Stevens lying beside a tree. He had been badly beaten and stabbed several times on both his frontside and back. Blood had been on the outside of both Stevens' nose and mouth. When police first arrived, they believed the body was female because of the clothing. After the officers checked for any sign of life, they soon realized it was a man.

JOSEPH "JAE" Stevens, born in Texas, was a relatively famous female impersonator in San Francisco. Jae had recently been named the summer replacement featured performer at Finocchio's, a popular nightclub that was the place to go for any celebrity since the 1930s. Jae did

a terrific Julie Andrews. She actually would sing, not lip sync. She also sang, danced, and performed stand-up comedy. By the early 70s, the club shifted to cater to the tourists who had heard about the club. It caused the local clientele to go elsewhere to escape the looky-loo tourists. The club also became a more conservative-style place to go, which deterred having gay customers as they believed them to be 'too hands-on.'

After a short investigation, police determined that Jae was at the Cabaret Club on Montgomery Street in the North Beach area the night before. They believed she had picked up someone and driven to the park in her car. The two of them probably planned to hook up, and something went wrong. Perhaps she was being robbed, a fight ensued, and she was killed.

Even though Jae grew up and lived in the San Francisco Bay area her whole life, being the only Doodler victim to have done so, she was buried in a graveyard in Concord with no family or close friends around her. Her sister Melissa Stevens Honrath was the one who identified the body.

After Jae's murder, the events that occurred in her family were genuinely horrifying. The family was still living in Concord at the time of the murder, and Jae's other sister, Alma Teresa Stevens, believed she was now haunted by evil spirits that were awakened by Jae's death. About three months after Jae's murder, Alma killed and dismembered their mother, burning her remains in the family's home fireplace. She also attacked her sister, Melissa, with a sledgehammer, beating her over the head until she was dead. Or so she thought.

Melissa survived and went on to have a child. After Alma attacked their family and was arrested, their father died in an office fire.

Alma was committed to an insane asylum and died in 2004. Melissa moved to Europe to escape her family's bad memories and start over. The family's home is now considered haunted by the current owners.

KLAUS A. CHRISTMANN

A little more than a week later, on Sunday, July 7, 1974, Tauba Weiss got up around 6 a.m. and took her German Sheppard dog, Moondance, for their morning walk as she did every day. After arriving at Golden Gate State Park and entering Lincoln Way, Moondance bolted. Weiss immediately chased after her dog, not wanting him to bite someone or get lost. She finally caught up with him to find he was sniffing a man

lying motionless on the beach. Weiss knew he was dead and leashed her dog. They rushed home, where she called the police to tell them what she had discovered.

Inspector Dave Toschi was called in after officers arrived and realized the man had been murdered. Brutally. Toschi had been a detective for about twenty years by then and worked the famous Zodiac Killer case in San Francisco. It was an extremely bloody scene where the man's body had been stabbed at least fifteen times, and his throat was slashed so deeply that investigators believed it looked like the killer was trying to remove the victim's head from his body.

The victim wore typical clothing for the period, including black zippered ankle-length boots, a tan leather jacket, a white dress shirt, polyester flared dress pants, a couple of fashion rings, and a gold wedding band. Still, the body had no identification on him, just as the previous two murder victims didn't.

Among the dead man's possession was a small jar of face makeup, and the coroner noted that the victim's pants had been unzipped and left open at the scene, and he was wearing an orange bikini thong underneath his pants. That, plus being located at the beach, led the officers to immediately guess the dead man was probably a gay person and might have been working as a female impersonator or even a sex worker.

It was the same location as the other victims, all within a few miles apart. So, the police started looking at a possible connection between them. Perhaps there was only one killer. The detective's theory was that probably the killer was enticed into getting involved in a gay

sexual act. Afterward, he felt guilty and killed whom he had sex with to prevent anyone from finding out. If anyone found out, it could ruin their lives by getting them divorced and fired from their job even.

Police released photos of the victim to the local newspapers looking for the public's help in identifying who this victim was. Within days, it was discovered that the victim was 31-year-old Klaus Christmann, who had recently moved to the city and had been staying with a friend, Booker Williams, whom he knew from when they were both in the army in Germany. Christmann had managed a bar that served both gay and straight clientele. It was during that time that he realized he was gay. After hearing about how San Francisco was the place to go if you wanted to live a more open and accessible gay life than anywhere else in the world, he decided to move there.

In San Francisco, he wanted to achieve something better for himself and his family back in Germany. But the last time he was seen was in the dance club Bojangles in the Tenderloin district the night before his body was found. He had arrived from Bamberg, Germany, only three months previously, leaving his wife and two children. His body was returned there to be laid to rest. The family was notified that he had died from a telegram with almost no other information. He had been working for the Michelin Tire Company. His wife wasn't sure that he was gay, even though he was attractive, well-groomed, and carried makeup that might have been unusual then. She also didn't believe that just because he worked at a gay bar, he was gay.

Strangely, Inspector Toschi immediately assumed that Klaus Christmann was gay even though he was married and had two kids, simply because he had a makeup container on his body. The importance of making these kinds of assumptions cannot be stressed enough when it comes to an investigation involving the murder of a gay man. But it came from the top of the police department. The SFPD Director of Personnel, George Eimil, told the *Advocate Magazine* on January 25, 1975, that the department would never hire any gay people to work for them because gay people committed felonies and were of bad moral character. In addition, in October of that same year, the SFPD's Director of Public Relations, Captain William O'Connor, told the *San Francisco Sentinel* that he thought gay people were too unstable to be in the police force.

Like the previous two victims of the Doodler Serial Killer, other than the fact they were gay, there was no connection between them. Just as it was with Fritz Haarmann, the "Butcher of Hanover," who is covered in Book 2 in this series, there was no rhyme or reason for selecting his victims. Later, we learned of Haarmann's choices. They were simply for what the victim had on them: clothing, personal items, or even, some think, the victim's body itself (i.e., meat for eating).

With the Doodler Murders, we never did find out what his purpose was. He was never caught. And the bodies of his victims were not used for any purpose either. After this third victim came to the attention of police, those concerned about a possible killer on the loose in San Francisco didn't consider serial murder.

Each victim was so different in looks and lifestyle that detectives started to believe there were three killers, not one. And people outside the gay community only saw the differences between the three victims. The first one, Gerald Cavanaugh, was your average working-class guy who lived a relatively normal life, appearing to be straight, attending church every Sunday and working a regular job five days a week. The second victim, Joseph "Jae" Stevens, was a man living as a woman or transvestite, who performed in public around the city. The third victim, Klaus Christmann, was also married but worked at a bar serving gay and straight patrons.

FREDERICK ELMER CABIN

The following year everything went quiet on the Doodler Killer front. Perhaps the murders were getting too much attention from all local media outlets and national newspapers. It was enough attention that Inspector Toschi from the Zodiac Killer case was now assigned to find this killer. Whatever the reason, no more murders were discovered until May 12, 1975.

On a Monday morning around 9 a.m., 22-year-old Christopher Griffin decided to take a walk on the beach.

He walked to Ocean Beach from his apartment in Golden State Park, as it was usually the quietest and most isolated area to walk. Within an hour of his walk, he spotted a man he initially thought was sunbathing. When he got closer, he saw that the man was wearing all his clothes. Within a couple of feet from the man, he noticed that the man wasn't breathing and that there was blood on his chest. So much blood that it was soaking through his shirt and jacket. He ran back to the park entryway since he knew some pay phones were there so that he could call the police.

When the police arrived at the scene and saw a dead male who appeared to have been stabbed several times, they realized that it was where the first Doodler victim, named Cavanaugh, was found the year before in 1974. The only thing different about this crime was that drag marks through the sand indicated that the body had been moved about twenty feet from where he was probably killed. The man had been dead for at least ten hours, which led the police on site to conclude that he was perhaps out cruising the beach area looking to have some casual gay sex when he was murdered.

The medical examiner ruled the cause of death was a stab wound directly into the heart, cutting his aorta. He was about six feet tall, weighed about 150 pounds, and wore a blue cord jacket, funky multi-colored shirt, blue jeans, brown socks, and shoes. Both his shirt and jacket were soaked in blood.

Detectives found no identification on the body. So, they ran his fingerprints like the previous victims. This time, they got a hit. The victim was 32-year-old

Frederick Elmer Capin from Port Angeles, Washington. He had been working as a nurse in San Francisco. His fingerprints, kept on file for registered nurses in California, came up for investigators. It was also discovered that he enlisted in the Navy and served in the Vietnam War, receiving a medal of honor for saving four men under fire. He was survived by his grandparents and sister, living in Port Angeles, Washington, at the time of his murder.

HARALD GULLBERG

In June 1975, another hiker, 22-year-old Christopher Griffin, went for a stroll in Lincoln Park and found the dead body of an older man about ten yards off the main trail. His neck had been slashed. His body had been there for a few weeks, and he had maggots and fly larvae on his face.

The coroner reported that the man had had liver cirrhosis, probably from drinking too much alcohol for many years. But he had died from the laceration wounds

in his neck. He was dressed typically, except for wearing no underwear, and his pant zipper was down.

Police identified him as sixty-six-year-old Harald Gullberg, a naturalized citizen, in August 1955. He was originally from Sweden and was a professional sailor.

WARREN ANDREWS

F ifty-two-year-old Warren Andrews was discovered unconscious, lying in a pool of blood, by a hiker in Lands End in April 1975. Andrews had been severely beaten but still alive, so the hiker called the police and ambulance. As soon as he was stable, Andrews was flown to a hospital in Washington State so his family

could be close to him. Sadly, Andrews died of his injuries about seven weeks later.

When the police first investigated the crime, they didn't think of sincere victims for several reasons. Since his death, Andrews has worked as a lawyer for the U.S. Postal Service. His family said that they believed him to be gay but closeted. Even though this murder was a brutal or rage killing in an out-of-view location on the beach, just like the other Doodler murders, there were other things the police didn't think the Doodler Killer would have done.

The primary thing detectives thought didn't fit the Doodler's MO was that there appeared to be a struggle between Andrews and the killer. The fight between them made the killer lose his knife off the nearby cliff edge. As the battle continued, he first grabbed a tree branch to keep beating Andrews with and then a rock to try and finish him off.

Years later, in 2021, SFPD declared that Andrews could have been another victim of the Doodler as he fit the profile. Andrews was a white gay male who was attacked in the same way that the other victims were. He was also left in the same area and in the same way.

OTHER UNSOLVED MURDERS

M urders that happened to gay men in San Francisco started well before the Doodler Killer began his killing spree in 1974. There are many reasons that murder occurs, not just hate murders aimed towards minorities or gay people. I don't think that society generally considered that being gay would be enough reason to be killed, even back in the 1960s. However, many crimes were committed against the gay community. Again, mainly because it was still a crime to have gay sex, and most people looked down on gay people in public. It made it easy to assault and mug a gay man, as nobody would care or do anything about it, even the police, who considered gay people criminals of lower moral standards. Not to mention that most gay men would not risk going to the police and telling them because they wouldn't do anything about it, and it would become a public record that the victim was gay, which could lead to losing their job and family or friends who found out.

When I started working on the Doodler Serial Killer case, I wanted to analyze the city's crime rate at the time in all areas. I was looking for a breakdown of the different types of crimes recorded. The data included serial killers, murders, and assaults of all people, not just gay people. The analysis helped determine how the community treated all crimes and how law enforcement policed them.

Looking back at the crimes committed against gay people, it was hard to determine the reasons for most of them. One reason is the confusion around the classification "Gay Murder." The classification "Gay Murder" is still a problem today in many cities and states that use this term. Law enforcement should instead identify whether a murder involving a gay person is a hate crime or not. In the sixties and seventies, they didn't classify crimes as hate crimes. So, if the attack, assault, or murder was reported, the gay element was usually not mentioned. And the cases would be mixed with others. The police seemed to lump gay-related cases in with drug addicts and prostitutes, who never did receive much attention from detectives. Because gay-related cases were considered less important to police, the details and evidence collected were sparse, and almost no real investigation was done. So, little to no information is available when we review these cases now. Even if we can determine that the victim assaulted or murdered was gay, we have a problem establishing whether it was a hate crime or not. Gay people do get involved in love disputes, drugs, and other things that could lead to murder. All gay-related

murders are not hate crimes. And sometimes, robberies or muggings happen strictly to steal someone's money or possessions, whether they are gay or not. The details of a crime are necessary in every case.

Quite a few articles covering the Doodler Murders would always mention how he had assaulted various numbers of gay men who weren't killed. Still, I couldn't find any information about the victims or what had happened to them. The only factual information I could find was the description given to police of the suspect at the time of the attack. There were no personal details about the victim at all.

The fact that the personal details were sparse seemed strange to me until I discovered that most of the victims involved with the Doodler must have been gay and, therefore, didn't want to report the crime. They didn't want to be labeled as gay because the police would lose interest as soon as they learned it was a gay-related crime. This suspicion led me to start with all murders and assaults committed in San Francisco during that period and try to determine which ones were gay involved and if the Doodler possibly engaged any others. Below is the list of murders.

Eliminated from this list were crimes where the attack or murder was committed using a gun since the Doodler never used a gun during any of his known murders. Also eliminated were the solved murder cases. There would be no point in adding cases where the murder was solved, or the perpetrator was known to the list.

1. Donald Fleming, a 33-year-old gay man, was found naked and murdered in his home in Bernal Heights on May 10, 1967. He had been strangled and stabbed to death with a butcher knife.

2. John Gilleran, a 26-year-old gay man, was stabbed with scissors at his home on Knob Hill on September 21, 1967.

3. Dave Evans, a 39-year-old gay man, was strangled with a towel in his apartment in Noe Valley on October 3, 1968.

4. Joey Ramirez 41-year-old man who was in the air force, never married, and unsure if he was gay, was tied up and strangled in his Tenderloin apartment on October 22, 1968.

5. Franc Blachinger, a 52-year-old gay man, was strangled in a hotel room in the Fairmont Hotel on Nob Hill on February 16, 1969. This hotel was where gay sex workers used to have sex with their clients. Perhaps the killer was someone who bought Blachinger's services.

6. Charles Hedberg, 44 years old, was stabbed in his apartment on June 24, 1969.

7. Louis Brinkmann was a 49-year-old man stabbed with a knife in his apartment on Holyhoke Road on February 25, 1970.

8. Effin Pace, a 29-year-old man, was stabbed to death in his apartment on May 9, 1970.

9. Alfred Trudeau, a 38-year-old U.S. Army, was stabbed on November 6, 1970, in his apartment on Market Street.

10. 52-year-old Lyle Miller was bludgeoned to death with a lamp in his home on January 6, 1971.

11. George Ward was a 21-year-old Vietnam soldier who drowned on February 8, 1971.

12. James Whaley was stabbed to death in his home on April 19, 1972, at the age of forty-five.

13. Edward Ladd died of blunt force trauma at forty-three in his home on October 22, 1972.

14. Carl Pryer was fifty-three when he was stabbed in his home on July 9, 1973.

15. Paul Snyder, 34 years old, was robbed and stabbed to death on Broadway on September 7, 1973

16. Arthur Pindell was robbed and stabbed to death in his home on October 11, 1973, at the age of forty-six.

17. Paul Jankowski was beaten and kicked to death at the age of 50 years old on January 29, 1974.

18. Stig Berlin was 37 years old when he was stabbed in his apartment on February 19, 1974. He was from Europe, and his apartment was a bloody mess.

19. Dan Shepard was 34 years old when he was stabbed on September 14, 1974, in his home.

20. Richard Gonzales was stabbed to death on February 2, 1975. First, he was a witness, then became a suspect in the Tenderloin Murders.

21. Joe Vasquez was born in Mexico and was 23 years old when he was stabbed in his apartment on March 16, 1975. Transvestite. Second of the Tenderloin Murders

22. Thomas August Almli was fifty-three when stabbed on March 20, 1975. Third of Tenderloin Murders

23. The reward for information on the killer. Jose Rodriquez was stabbed to death was a 39-year-old transvestite in a neighboring apartment. This was the fourth of the Tenderloin murders, and this caused the neighborhood to cancel most of their meetings and event because of the murders of transvestites, and they offered $50,000.

24. Warren Andrews was attacked and knocked unconscious by being hit on the head with a rock on April 27, 1975, in Lands End. He went into a coma and died a couple of months later. Lands End was a popular cruising spot for gay men.

25. Dennis Dickenson was 28 years old when he was beaten, stabbed, and probably robbed. He dragged himself to get help and died of his injuries.

26. Jeffery Alfano was 18 years old when he was robbed and killed by blunt force trauma.

27. David Reel was strangled and mutilated in a parking lot after leaving a leather bar in SOMA when he was 31.

28. 32-year-old George Gilbert was stabbed and murdered on Market Street in the Fox Plaza on September 27, 1975.

29. On the lower floor of the Fox Plaza, two attacks occurred; one was stabbed and the other tied up in July 1975. Both were thought to have been done by the Doodler.

30. Claude Demott, formerly in the army and 36 years old, was killed with blunt force trauma and castrated. Demott was a transvestite, and this became the fifth Tenderloin Murder.

31. George Steeples was a 54-year-old who worked as a sex worker and was stabbed by his trick in the Mission District on January 8, 1976.

32. Bruce DeJon, 51 years old, became the sixth Tenderloin Murder when he was beaten with a lamp from his apartment.

33. John Marsalla was strangled and stabbed at age 52 on April 25, 1976. There was a similar butchering of the body as in the previous case.

34. Nick Bauman, known as Granny Goose, was 29 years old when he was attacked and dragged into a basement, where he was beaten to death on May 2, 1976. His testicles had been pulverized.

35. Daniel Silva was knifed to death on September 19, 1976, when he was 50.
36. Grant Dailey was stabbed and cut to death on October 12, 1976, where the knife also mutilated him.
37. Donald Webb was killed in his apartment on December 24, 1976. He was 50 years old.

THE ZEBRA MURDERS

N ot long before the Doodler Murders, there was a different series of murders in San Francisco called the "Zebra Murders." The six-month murder range began in October 1973 and lasted until April 1974. The final tally of victims isn't known for sure, but it's believed to have been as many as seventy-three. The killers were eventually caught and convicted of fifteen murders and the assault of eight others.

Oddly, there wasn't just one serial killer in this particular case, but four. They called themselves the "Death Angels" and consisted of four Black men: Manuel Moore, Larry Green, Jesse Lee Cooks, and J.C.X. Simon. Their targets and victims were White Americans, and their motive was purely racism.

The Death Angels' meetings often talked about how many White men there now were in America compared to Black men, thinking they were outnumbered 5 to 1. Worldwide, it was the opposite. Black men outnumbered

White men 10 to 1. If Black men outnumbered White men and had more land, why did it seem like the White man believed he was superior in America?

The group believed that religious communities, both Christians and Jews, were guilty of spreading their false religion throughout the world and creating the Black slave market. The group thought that Allah was the one true God, and they were the true Muslims of the Earth. As Allah's enemies were White, White people were solely responsible for all crimes against Black people in the country and world. The Death Angels were up to the task of killing the White devils. It was their responsibility to kill four White devils each, and they would receive their reward in the form of a button to wear on their coats when they went to Mecca to show their brother, Mohammed. To be awarded "wings," each Death Angel must kill four White children, five White women, and nine White men. When it all began, fifteen Death Angel members were known. Whenever an angel completed the murders required to achieve their wings, the group would photograph them and draw a pair of black wings on their picture. It was then placed on a board at their meeting place to keep track and give incentives to those who hadn't achieved any kills or not enough.

By October 1973, the killing wave began. As a group, they had already killed 135 men, 75 women, and 60 children or some combination for fifteen members to have achieved their wings. It was later discovered that California's Attorney General had been secretly creating

a list of murders, and by October, they had forty-five on that list. All victims were White, and all suspects were associated with the Black Muslim group.

The first wave of attacks began on the early evening of October 19, 1973, when thirty-year-old Richard Hague and his wife Quita were out for a stroll only blocks from their home on Telegraph Hill. The Death Angels drove beside them in a van, forced them into the back by gunpoint, and quickly drove off. The victims were taken to an industrial part of town, where they were both attacked with a machete. The victims were taken to an industrial part of town, where they were both attacked with a machete and left for dead on a set of railroad tracks after the required pictures were taken to receive credit for killing the two White devils.

Around 11 p.m. that same evening, another couple, the Battenbergs, were out for a drive, and just as they went through an intersection, they noticed what looked like a man staggering on the road, and at first, they thought he was probably just drunk. As they got closer to the man, they saw that he had his hands tied behind his back. They quickly pulled their car over and ran to the man to see if they could help. Richard Hague had survived. The couple soon realized the man had his head cut up badly to the point that the bones on his skull and face were exposed through his cut face. They took Hague to the closest hospital and informed the police of what they had discovered. Later, at the hospital, Hague briefly described the attackers as three young Black men driving a white van to the police.

The description provided by Hague rang a bell with both detectives David Toschi and Charles Ellis, who received a report of another attempted kidnapping just 30 minutes before. Three young kids, 11-year-old Michele Carrasco, 12-year-old Marie Stewart, and 15-year-old Frank Stewart, were walking along the sidewalk in Ingleside when a white Dodge van suddenly pulled up beside them, and two men got out. One had a gun and ordered them to enter the van. They all scattered and ran in different directions. The three returned to their homes and told their parents, who then reported the attempted kidnapping to the police.

A week later, on October 30th, 28-year-old physical therapist Frances Rose was shot in the head and neck and died while sitting in her car, parked near the University of California Extension, where she was taking art courses. Witnesses of the murder said they saw a young Black man sitting in the passenger seat of Rose's car. They heard the two arguing but couldn't clearly hear what they were saying. Suddenly, he shot her several times, jumped out of the car, and ran.

There happened to be two police detectives working close enough to the attack to hear the gunshots. When they rushed to the scene, Rose was still alive then, and she was able to identify her assailant as Jesse Lee Cook. She later succumbed to her injuries. Within minutes Cook was apprehended, still holding the gun with which he shot Rose. Later that night, during Cook's interrogation, he admitted to the shooting. Cook had been released only three months before, from San Quentin, on a conviction of armed robbery. The

prosecution only took four months to convict him of this shooting murder.

The next murder happened on November 9th, when Pacific Gas and Electric Company clerk Robert Stoeckmann was stopped by a man who asked him for directions. Before he could answer, Robert was dragged outside to the property's backyard and shot in the neck. Stoeckmann survived the shooting and even fought with the man, managing to take the gun away from him. When the attacker began to run away, he shot him three times. The assailant was captured and identified as Leroy Doctor, who was convicted of the assault and sent to prison for nine and a half years.

The murders continued through December. On December 11th, Paul Dancik was waiting to use a public phone when two Black men walked up to him and shot him to death. On December 13th, Art Agnos, an aide for the San Francisco assemblyman Leo McCarthy was shot by a Black man while he was having a conversation with two coworkers. Fortunately, Art would survive the attack. Less than ninety minutes later, the same Black man shot thirty-one-year-old Marietta DiGirolamo, who was standing outside in front of a business on Divisadero Street.

On December 22nd, the next group of shootings took place. Nineteen-year-old Neal Moynihan was walking on Market Street and was shot three times by two Black men. It was just two blocks away and five minutes later when sixty-five-year-old Mildred Hosier was shot four times. Witnesses all said the men wore buckskin coats and had a medium complexion. The

same men would continue to shoot random people for the next week shooting seven victims, with five of them dying. They were added to the list of murders as none were robbed of anything, and there seemed to be no other motive.

On December 24th, the last random murder of the year was discovered on Ocean Beach. The only difference was that the body was unidentified and had been dismembered and wrapped in plastic. The remains were placed into a cardboard box. The way the body was cut apart doesn't fit the others, but the police included it on the list.

One of the problems police had in linking any of these murders was that they were all committed with different guns of different calibres. Matching calibers was one of the ways police looked to connect cases and to try and link them together. Police were also faced with the fact that both Larry Green and J.C.X. Simon had never served time or had any kind of criminal record.

The administration of the police department at the time also didn't want to raise any issues relating to politics or religion as being the cause of the murders. They didn't accept the idea of the detectives working the case that the Nation of Islam was the cause of these seemingly unmotivated murders. It wasn't long before the rumors of a possible Black-killing-White motive circulated among law enforcement, and a division ensued.

Tensions between Black and White cops became the norm by early 1974. In the January issue of the magazine *Notebook*, a cartoon that displayed a police

academy graduation class was published. And in that class, Frito Bandito, a Mexican cartoon character used in the Frito Lays potato chip ads on television, Frankenstein, and a gorilla were included. The caption below these characters was, *"I've heard of minority hirings, but this is ridiculous."* Putting such things in print drew a line in the sand between White and Black police.

The killing rampage started again on January 24, 1974, with five more people being shot and four dying. It began that morning when thirty-two-year-old Tana Smith was shot after shopping and was walking home about six blocks. Less than ten minutes later and only eight blocks away, sixty-nine-year-old Vincent Wollin was shot twice in the back while putting garbage in his garbage bins for pick up the following day. Wollin died at the scene. It was his birthday. Eighty-seven-year-old John Bambic was shot two times in the back less than an hour later while standing in the front yard of his house, where he died almost instantly. Only a few blocks away at the local laundromat, forty-five-year-old Jane Holly was doing her laundry when suddenly a man ran in and shot her twice. She also died. A few minutes later, twenty-three-year-old Roxanne McMillan was unloading her dirty laundry from the trunk of her car in front of the same laundromat. The man ran out and shot her twice as well. She survived her wounds.

Also, in 1974, came one of the coldest winters on record for San Francisco. The area was covered with frost and snow, where buses and cars got stranded nightly. For a short time during this cold snap, the murders seemed to stop, but tensions remained. Groups

such as the Black Liberation Army and the Black Panthers had the attention of the American public and, in many cases, were blamed for the murders of white people throughout the city.

Marcus Foster, the superintendent of the Oakland school system and a rising star in politics for the Bay Area, was shot to death in a school's parking lot. A Palestinian grocer, Saleem Erakat, was shot as well. These last two murders didn't fit in with the motiveless murders of Whites around the area, as Foster was Black. It wasn't long before another group, the Symbionese Liberation Army, claimed responsibility for those murders. The rationale for the SLA was that they didn't want the establishment to reform. They wanted a revolution and therefore targeted African Americans trying to change society by getting into politics.

Later that month, during a random stop of a van driven by two White men, Joseph Romiro and Russell Little, who were members of the SLA, the murder weapons that were used to kill Foster were found. This fact led to difficulties in trying to convict both Romiro and Little, as the witnesses told detectives that three Black men shot Foster.

Everything went quiet for a few months until April 1st, when two Salvation Army cadets, nineteen-year-old Tom Rainwater and twenty-one-year-old Linda Story, were shot when they were going to grab some lunch at a nearby restaurant. Rainwater would die while Story survived the attack. Two weeks later, on April 14th, fifteen-year-old Terry White was waiting for a bus to pick him up to take him home and was shot two times.

Just a few blocks away, eighteen-year-old Ward Anderson, who was trying to hitch a ride, was also shot twice by the same men. Both would survive their attacks and be able to describe their attackers.

Two days later, on April 16th, twenty-three-year-old Nelson Shields had just purchased a new floor rug and was trying to make room in the trunk of his car. He was shot three times by what appeared to be the same men. He would die from his wounds.

OPERATION ZEBRA

San Francisco began to see a considerable decline in their tourist industry and entertainment businesses such as nightclubs, restaurants, theaters, and hotels. Even the locals were not going out as much in public as most of the murders happened to people who were out doing things. Even though many other people witnessed these attacks, they kept on happening, and nobody was getting caught. "Operation Zebra" was initiated on January 28th, right after the murder of Marcus Foster. The name "Zebra" came from the police frequency used for their investigation, "Z."

The common patterns the killers used were that, in most cases, it was a hit-and-run style shooting. The killer would walk up on his victim while they were doing some routine everyday task, shoot them a few times at close range, then run or drive away from the scene. The killers almost always used a .32 calibre gun on their victims.

One day after the final shooting, on April 17th,

police started a stop-and-search program. They set up six zones in the city with more than one hundred and fifty officers involved in the operation. In each zone, the officers stopped people, questioned them, and did a basic search of their person to see if they were carrying any weapons. Police only had a few basic composite sketches of what had been described to be by the surviving victims.

Whenever somebody whom police questioned looked like a possible killer, they would fill out an interrogation card which included their name, age, address, social security number and driver's license. Those cards were given to the homicide detectives working on this case, who would call the people in for further investigation. The operation caused massive outrage in the Black community as only Black men were stopped and searched and brought in for further interrogations. The Black Panther Party, as well as the Nation of Islam, called out the investigation as both racist and vicious as well as unproductive. The SLA saw Operation Zebra as a planned offensive against them and viewed it as the beginning of the race war, which they believed was coming.

The police chief at the time responded to the public backlash by comparing Operation Zebra to the Zodiac Killer investigation, where they had only been stopping and questioning White men who were suspects of being that serial killer.

In total, 567 Black men were stopped, questioned, and searched during the operation. Of those men, 181 were brought to police stations for further investigation

and questioning. It was decided that no effective leads came out of it.

Two lawsuits would be filed by the NCAA asking the court to stop the operation, saying that the stop-and-search tactics that police were using were unconstitutional. On April 25, 1974, the court responded with a ruling that agreed with the lawsuit and found the random searches unconstitutional. They violated the rights of young Black men. Police could only carry out such searches when they have probable cause. The likeness of a composite sketch was not enough probable cause to search someone.

Police responded by filing an appeal, which was denied. They then offered a $30,000 reward for any information that led to the arrest and conviction of the person or persons involved in the murders.

Arrests

On May 1, 1974, police arrested seven men for being responsible for the murders committed over the last year. The men were 29-year-old J.C.X. Simon, 22-year-old Larry Green, 23-year-old Manuel Moore, 28-year-old Dwight Stallins, 31-year-old Thomas Manney, 22-year-old Edgar Burton, and 27-year-old Clarence Jamison. However, Stallins, Manney, Burton, and Jamison were released later due to insufficient evidence.

The trial began on March 3, 1975, and lasted 212 days. It saw the testimony of 181 witnesses. The jury only took three days to return a finding that the men

were guilty, and the men were all sentenced to life in prison.

List of Known Victims

1. Richard Hague (30): October 20, 1973, Survived
2. Quita Hague (28): October 20, 1973, Died
3. Frances Rose (28): October 30, 1973, Died
4. Robert Stoeckmann (27): November 9, 1973, Survived
5. Saleem Erakat (53): November 25, 1973, Died
6. Paul Dancik (26): December 11, 1973, Died
7. Art Agnos (35): December 13, 1973, Survived
8. Ilario Bertuccio (81): December 20, 1973, Died
9. Terese DeMartini (20): December 20, 1973, Survived
10. Neal Moynihan (19): December 22, 1973, Died
11. Mildred Hosler (65): December 22, 1973, Died
12. John Doe #169 (28): December 24, 1973, Died
13. Tana Smith (32): January 28, 1974, Died
14. Vincent Wollin (69): January 28, 1974, Died
15. John Bambic (87): January 28, 1974, Died
16. Jane Holly (45): January 28, 1974, Died

17. Roxanne McMillan (23): January 28, 1974, Survived
18. Thomas Rainwater (19): April 1, 1974, Died
19. Linda Story (21): April 1, 1974, Survived
20. Terry White (15): April 14, 1974, Survived
21. Ward Anderson (18): April 14, 1974, Survived
22. Nelson Shields IV (23): April 16, 1974, Died

PART III

THE SUSPECTS

SUSPECTS

During the first years of the murders of gay men in San Francisco, the police had no one detective in charge or overviewing the crimes. It was handled by several police detectives, more as independent murders with no chance of being connected. With this oversight, along with the protective nature of the gay community not to talk about gay men who were trying to keep their sexuality on the down low, there would be no real advancement in any of the cases. But in early December 1976, things would start to change.

LAWRENCE ROBINSON

Fifty-five-year-old Richard Wilson died in his Pacific Heights apartment on December 8, 1976. He had been bound and gagged with ties and shot in his chest at close range with a small caliber handgun. Wilson's apartment showed no signs of being broken into, which led the

police to believe he must have known his killer and let them in the apartment.

Robbery did not seem like the motive behind Wilson's murder. As CEO and Chairman of the Board at Endurance Products Company of San Francisco, he lived very well with many lovely things in his apartment, but nothing was missing. Everything seemed to be in place. The rooms were neat, and nothing looked like it had been rifled through.

That said, the police soon discovered that Wilson had just bought a brand new car, a 1977 Cadillac, which was a deep blue color. But it wasn't in his registered parking spot. The medical report stated that Wilson had been dead for about five days, so the culprit had quite a head start with the Cadillac. When detectives found Wilson's plate number, they put out an all-points bulletin for the vehicle.

During a police raid in the Watts area of Los Angeles, the local police came across Wilson's stolen car. Officers would find two men in the vehicle: 28-year-old Charles F. Vann and 22-year-old Lawrence Robinson. At this same time, SFPD put Inspector David Toschi in charge of this case, and he flew down to interview the suspects. After several hours of interrogation, Vann was released. Robinson was charged with the robbery and murder of Wilson. In addition to being caught driving Wilson's car, he also had several of Wilson's credit cards in his wallet when they first arrested him. The arrest soon became a great marketing strategy for detectives who had, up to now, been chastised by the press and the gay community of San Francisco.

Toschi made a big production of it when he arrived at the San Francisco airport with Robinson in tow, making it sound like there was a definite connection between the Wilson murder case and many of the murders of gay men in the area over the last few years. Robinson's picture did match the 1975 composite sketch of the Doodler Killer. But also in 1977, the police arrested 24-year-old Jacob Stevens in his San Francisco apartment for the August 1976 murder of Bill Wenger. During the investigation of the murder, police had taken fingerprints from the apartment, and Stevens' was among the prints found.

THE FREEWAY KILLERS

To add to the already panic among the residents of Southern California, another group of serial killers came onto the scene who became known as the "Freeway Killers" or "Trashbag Killers." I refer to them as a group of serial killers because three different men killed the same type of young man in the same area and even the same way. Patrick Wayne Kearney, William Bonin, and Randy Kraft were all dubbed "The Freeway Killer," with Kearney being the most prolific of the three, who was thought to have killed up to 43 men. After his capture and arrest, Kearney admitted that he began to kill young gay men in 1962.

Patrick Wayne Kearney

The first murder of which Kearney would be

convicted wasn't until 1968. Kearney's modus operandi was to pick up his victim at either a gay bar or as a hitchhiker looking for a ride somewhere. After taking the men to a secluded location, Kearney would shoot and kill them and then sexually assault their dead bodies. After Kearney finished with his sexual assault, he would dismember their bodies using a hacksaw, put their remains inside a heavy-duty black trash bag, and leave them along the side of a freeway or in a canyon or landfill.

After Kearney's first few murders, he became more comfortable with the process. He often took the body of his victim, after he had already killed and raped them, back to his home. There, he would place the body into the bathtub, drain the blood from the body, and wash them thoroughly, eliminating the possibility of any strong odors that would eventually lead to their discovery. It also helped eliminate any evidence he might have left on his victims.

Kearney was finally arrested after he murdered 17-year-old John Otis LeMay on March 13, 1977. LeMay's remains were found five days later, and after the police found out that he had been in contact with Kearney, they went to his house, searched it, and found evidence of the assault and murder. Kearney was arrested on July 1, 1977, and afterward, he confessed to 28 murders. He was sentenced to life in prison. He confessed and pled guilty to avoid the death penalty. Detectives also believed Kearney was responsible for at least seven other murders, but they have been unable to find enough evidence to get a conviction for them.

. . .

KEARNEY'S VICTIMS

1. Unknown 1 (19): Spring of 1962; driven to a deserted area, shot in the head, & sodomized postmortem.
2. Unknown 2 (16): 1962; driven to the same location as the first victim, shot in the head, & sodomized postmortem. According to Kearney, this victim was the younger cousin of his first victim.
3. Mike (18): shot in the back of the head & sodomized postmortem.
4. George: murdered Dec. 1968 but not discovered until Jul. 8, 1977; shot in the head while sleeping, then put into a bathtub & sodomized postmortem. Police found his skeleton with Kearney's direction after his arrest.
5. John Demchik (13): murdered Jun. 26, 1971, found Feb. 9, 1973; Shot to death.
6. James Fletcher Barwick (17): Sep. 22, 1973; Shot in the back of the head.
7. Ronald Dean Smith Jr. (5): Aug. 24, 1974; Suffocated.
8. Albert Rivera (21): Apr. 13, 1975; Shot in the head, taken to Kearney's house, sodomized postmortem, dismembered, & stuffed into trash bags to be disposed of in various locations.

9. Larry Gene Walters (20): Oct. 31, 1975; Shot, sodomized postmortem, dismembered, put into trash bags, & disposed of in various locations.

10. Kenneth Eugene Buchanan (17): Mar. 1, 1976; Shot in the back of the head, sodomized, then shot 3 more times.

11. Oliver Peter Molitor (13): Mar. 21, 1976, Never found, Picked up while hitchhiking, sexually assaulted, shot, dismembered, & buried in various areas at the Palos Verdes landfill.

12. Larry Armendariz (15): Apr. 18, 1976; Shot in the back of the head, sodomized postmortem, & dismembered.

13. Michael Craig McGhee (13): Jun. 11, 1976; Shot in the back of the head, sodomized postmortem, & dismembered.

14. John Woods (23): Jun. 20, 1976; Shot to death.

15. Larry Espy (17): Aug. 1976; Shot in the back of the head, sodomized postmortem, & dismembered.

16. Wilfrid Lawrence Faherty (20): Aug. 1976; Shot in the back of the head.

17. Randall Lawrence Moore (16): Aug. 1976; Shot in the head.

18. Timothy Brian Ingham (19): Sep. 1976; Shot in the back of the head while asleep. The remains were thrown down a ravine.

19. Robert Benniefiel (17): Fall, 1976; Picked up while hitchhiking, shot in the back of the head, sodomized postmortem, dismembered, & dumped in various locations.
20. David Allen (27): Fall, 1976; Shot in the head & left on the side of the road.
21. Mark Andrew Orach (20): Oct. 5, 1976; Shot in the head.
22. Nicolas Hernandez-Jimenez (28): Jan. 1977; Shot, dismembered, & wrapped in trash bags for disposal.
23. Arturo Ramos Marquez (24): Feb 1977; Shot, sodomized postmortem, & dismembered.
24. John Otis LaMay (17): Mar. 13, 1977; Shot, sodomized postmortem, & dismembered. The murder of LaMay was the crime for which Kearney was arrested.
25. Merle "Hondo" Chance (8): Apr. 6, 1977; Smothered, sodomized postmortem, then dumped off of Angeles Crest Highway.

William Bonin

WILLIAM BONIN WAS ALSO KNOWN as a Freeway Killer because he, too, had committed a series of at least 21 murders of young men also in the Southern California area between May 1979 and June 1980. Bonin would eventually be convicted of 14 of the murders linked to

the Freeway Killer murders. Unlike Kearney, who is serving life in prison, Bonin was sentenced to death and, after spending 14 years on death row, was executed by lethal injection in 1996 at San Quentin State Prison.

Bonin had a slightly different M.O. than Kearney did. Even though he killed his victim and left them on the side of a freeway, he didn't kill his victim before he raped them. But just as Kearney had done, he often picked up his male victim, who was usually hitchhiking. After picking them up and sometime during the ride, he would get them into the back of his van and use handcuffs or a wire cord to keep them prisoner. Bonin would then rape and beat his victims before finally strangling them to death, often using clothing that belonged to the victim.

During the trial, it was also discovered how Bonin enjoyed his victims' torture process and had made them drink hydrochloric acid or slowly drive ice picks into their ears. One of his victims even died from shock as Bonin had slowly been impaling him in several places throughout his body. Because of Bonin's torturing process, he was sentenced to the death penalty.

BONIN'S VICTIMS

1. Thomas Glen Lundgren (13): Disappeared and found on May 28, 1979 in Los Angeles County; emasculated, bludgeoned, stabbed, slashed his throat, and fatally strangled.

2. Mark Duane Shelton (17): Disappeared on August 4, 1979, and found on August 11, 1979, in San Bernardino County; sodomised with various objects and unintentionally killed after he went into shock.

3. Markus Alexander Grabs (17): Disappeared on August 5, 1979, and found on August 6, 1979, in Los Angeles County; sodomised, beaten, and fatally stabbed 77 times.

4. Donald Ray Hyden (15): Disappeared and found on August 27, 1979, in Los Angeles County; stabbed in the neck and genitals, strangled, and fatally bludgeoned.

5. David Louis Murillo (17): Disappeared on September 9, 1979, and found on September 10, 1979, in Los Angeles County; raped, bludgeoned, and fatally strangled.

6. Robert Christopher Wirostek (18): Disappeared on September 17, 1979, and found on September 27, 1979, in Orange County; raped and strangled to death with ligature after being assaulted with a tire iron.

7. Kern County John Doe (15–27): Body found on November 1, 1979, in Kern County; strangled with ligature and died from penetration of the head with an ice pick.

8. Frank Dennis Fox (17): Disappeared on November 30, 1979, and found on December 2, 1979, in Orange County; raped and fatally strangled with ligature after going into shock from sodomy.

9. John Fredrick Kilpatrick (15): Disappeared on December 5, 1979, and found on December 13, 1979, in Los Angeles County; strangled to death with ligature after being flagellated with string.

10. Michael Francis McDonald (16): Disappeared and found on January 1, 1980, in San Bernardino County; mutilated and strangled to death with ligature after being assaulted.

11. Charles Dempster Miranda (15): Disappeared and found on February 3, 1980, in Los Angeles County; raped, beaten, and fatally strangled with a tire iron.

12. James Michael Macabe (12): Disappeared and found on February 3, 1980, in Los Angeles County; raped, beaten, and fatally strangled with his own T-shirt.

13. Ronald Craig Gatlin (18): Disappeared on March 14, 1980, and found on March 15, 1980, in Los Angeles County; sodomised with an ice pick and fatally strangled.

14. Glenn Norman Barker (14): Disappeared on March 21, 1980, and found on March 23, 1980, in Los Angeles County; raped, beaten, assaulted with an ice pick, burned with a lit cigarette, and fatally strangled.

15. Russell Duane Rugh (15): Disappeared on March 21, 1980, and found on March 23, 1980, in San Diego County; strangled to death with ligature and assaulted.

16. Harry Todd Turner (15): Disappeared on March 25, 1980, and found on March 26, 1980, in Los Angeles County; sodomised, bit, beaten, bludgeoned, and fatally strangled with his own T-shirt.

17. Steven John Wood (16): Disappeared and found on April 4, 1980, in Los Angeles County; strangled to death with ligature.

18. Darin Lee Kendrick (19): Disappeared on April 29, 1980, and found on May 1, 1980, in Los Angeles County; forced to drink hydrochloric acid and fatally stabbed in the ear with an ice pick by accomplice Vernon Butts after being chemically poisoned by Bonin.

19. Lawrence Eugene Sharp (17): Disappeared on May 10, 1980, and found on May 18, 1980, in Los Angeles County; beaten and killed by strangulation.

20. Sean Paige King (14): Disappeared on May 19, 1980, and found on May 20, 1980, in San Bernardino County; raped and killed by strangulation.

21. Steven Jay Wells (18): Disappeared on June 2, 1980, and found on June 3, 1980, in Orange County; raped, beaten, and fatally strangled with his own T-shirt

Randy Kraft

THE THIRD MAN, also known as a Freeway Killer, is Randy Kraft, who is believed to have raped and killed up to 51 young men in the Southern California region between 1972 and 1983. Detectives nicknamed him the "Scoreboard Killer" as Kraft had kept a list of his kills on a scorecard, listing 61 entries. The scorecard included coded details about his victims. He was bunched in with the other two Freeway Killers as he, too, left many of his victim's bodies off the side of the state's freeways.

In May 1983, Kraft was caught and formally charged with 16 murders. His trial didn't begin until August 1988, which included 160 witnesses and over 1000 pieces of evidence. In May 1989, he was convicted of all 16 counts of murder and sentenced to death. As of today, in 2023, Kraft remains on death row at San Quentin State Prison.

Kraft's Victims

1. Edward Moore (20): December 24, 1972
2. Kevin Bailey (17): April 9, 1973
3. Ronnie Wiebe (20): July 28, 1973
4. Keith Crotwell (18): March 29, 1975
5. Mark Hall (22): January 1, 1976
6. Scott Hughes (18): April 16, 1978
7. Roland Young (23): June 11, 1978
8. Richard Keith (20): June 19, 1978
9. Keith Klingbeil (23): July 6, 1978
10. Michael Inderbieten (21): November 18, 1978
11. Donald Crisel (20): June 16, 1979

12. Robert Loggins (19): August 23, 1980
13. Eric Church (21): January 27, 1983
14. Rodger DeVaul (20): February 12, 1983
15. Geoffrey Nelson (18): February 12, 1983
16. Terry Lee Gambrel (25): May 14, 1983

UPDATE

In January 2023, the San Francisco Police Department's cold case division released a new forensic sketch of what the Doodler Killer would look like today. Along with the new sketch, they increased the reward that was $200,000 to $250,000 for information leading to the arrest and conviction of the Doodler Killer.

REFERENCES

1. The Doodler: He was a serial killer who sketched his gay victims. We set out to untangle the mystery (sfchronicle.com)
2. Yesterday's Crimes: The Serial Killer Who Stalked Gay Men in the Castro - S.F. Weekly
3. The Doodler: The Truth About the Unidentified Serial Killer (grunge.com)
4. The Untold Story of the Doodler Murders - The Awl
5. The Doodler — Wendy Heard
6. "Views from enforcement officials," *The Advocate*, January 29, 1975
7. https://media.ktvu.com/media.ktvu.com/photo/2018/06/21/ViewScan_0003_1529605859741_5687938_ver1.0_640_360.jpg
8. Probable sixth victim of Doodler serial killer announced by San Francisco police (sfgate.com)
9. Murder By Forgotten Category: The Gay Murders of San Francisco 1968-1982 – quester site (wordpress.com)
10. Slaying link to earlier kidnap try - Newspapers.com
11. SF Woman Found Slain - Newspapers.com

Alan R Warren is a Bestselling Author, the Producer and lead host of the popular NBC Radioshow House of Mystery and Inside Writing, both heard on the 106.5 F.M. Los Angeles/102.3 F.M. Riverside/ 1050 A.M. Palm Springs/ 540 A.M. KYAH Salt Lake City/ 1150 A.M. KKNW Seattle/Tacoma and Phoenix.

His bestselling true crime books in Canada include *Beyond Suspicion: The True Story of Colonel Russell Williams*, which will be featured on CNN's *Lies, Crimes, & Videos* (Season 4), and *Murder Times Six: The True Story of the Wells Gray Park Murders*. In America, his bestsellers include *The Killing Game: Serial Killer Rodney Alcala*, which was featured on several television shows such as *Very Scary People with Donny Wahlberg*, Oxygen's *Mark of a killer*, *Reelz' Killer Trophies*, and soon to be included in a four-part Sundance Channel documentary called *Death's Date*. His bestseller, *Doomsday Cults: The Devil's Hostages*, was featured on Vice's *Dark Side of the '90s*.

His latest series, *Killer Queens*, is a six-part book series covering murders that affect the Gay Community. So far, it includes Book 1 - Leopold & Loeb, Book 2 - Butcher of Hanover: Fritz Haarmann, Book 3 - Grindr Serial Killer: Stephen Port, and Book 4 - Bruce McArthur: Toronto Gay Killer.

KILLER CRIME SERIES

HANNIBAL THE CANNIBAL: The True Story of Robert Maudsley (Killer Crime Volume 7)

Robert Maudsley casually walked into the cell of another inmate, who was sleeping on his bunk facedown. A savage rage quickly took over, and Maudsley started stabbing the back of the man's head. There was blood, pieces of brain, and chunks of hair flying in a fury. After the man went limp, Maudsley grabbed the man's head and held it in both palms and started to smash it against the walls of the cell, so hard that the plaster began to fall off the ceiling.

Nurses and guards had to watch on, not being able to get into the cell, hearing the victim's head crack each time it was smashed against the wall. After Maudsley finished with the attack, he sat the limp body up against the bed, got down on his knees, and started to eat chunks of the brain with his home-made knife.

Robert Maudsley was dubbed "Hannibal the Cannibal" on account of his thirst for eating the brains of his victims. He is

one of the most interesting and thought-provoking murderers in prison. He will be housed in a bulletproof cage, in the basement of Wakefield Prison, England, where Britain holds its most savage, high-profile convicts. He is known to be such a danger to others, even inmates, he lives in a specially designed cell that doesn't allow him any contact with anybody, except for guards that will slide his food through a small hole at the bottom of one of his cells.

Robert Maudsley is deemed to be the 'Most Dangerous Prisoner in Britain.' Even though he only killed one person outside of prison, his remaining victims were claimed while incarcerated. This book reviews Maudsley's life from his tormented childhood, his rage-filled murder outside of prison, and the planned torturous murders of three convicted pedophiles.

In the basement of Wakefield, you might be surprised who else has been housed beside him, and what kind of relationship they have.

KILLER QUEEN SERIES

Killer Queens is a new series of historical fiction books based on true stories. Sources, such as police reports and newspaper articles, are examined to gather as many facts as possible surrounding each case. As with any work of fiction, some creative additions are made when telling these stories, usually within the conversations between the personalities involved. The various sources are the basis of these conversations and, hopefully, make them come alive for the readers to help understand what was meant by those words.

LEOPOLD & LOEB: The Murder of Bobby Franks (Killer Queens 1)

Book 1 of the series focuses on what has been called "The Crime of the Century" in the 1920s United States. At the center of this murder case were Nathan Leopold Jr. and Richard Loeb – two wealthy University of Chicago students who, in May of 1924, kidnapped and murdered 14-year-old Bobby Franks.

With Leopold and Loeb, both males, the dominance shifted from one to the other. Regardless of who held it, the result was the same. They were both very interested in crime and pushing the envelope for the next thrill. The vicious "thrill kill" of Bobby Franks was the bloody result of an intense and unhealthy co-dependent bond between the murdering duo.

As you read the exploration of the case in this book, ask yourself: Would these young men be as vulnerable to their manipulations today? If they couldn't have harnessed and used shame as a control tactic, would they have been as successful at recruiting a criminal counterpart? Finally, to what degree can we hold the prevalent homophobia of this era accountable as a force to bear on this tragedy?

HOUSE OF MYSTERY INTERVIEWS SERIES

The *House of Mystery Radioshow* has been on the air for ten years, interviewing guests knowledgeable in the world's mysteries in science, religion, history, the paranormal, conspiracies, etc. The Interview Series does not attempt to solve these mysteries. Instead, each volume will provide the main points discussed during the show while interviewing the experts. The series will be an excellent reference for researchers and a good overview for those unfamiliar with each case. Links to the podcasts are included.

JACK THE RIPPER: The Interviews (Volume 1)

the HOUSE OF MYSTERY RADIOSHOW presents

JACK the RIPPER

THE INTERVIEWS: VOLUME 1

ALAN R. WARREN
MICHAEL L. HAWLEY

Scotland Yard's "Whitechapel Murder File," in which Jack the Ripper had a starring role, went cold before it could be solved. Yet the fascination with this mystery continues today. Ripperologists passionately debate suspects, opinions, research methods, and theories. Even which victims should be included in the case is widely debated. Astonishingly, the work continues. Today, Ripperologists are still finding new clues in this 132-year-old crime that brings us closer to solving the mystery.

Volume 1 of the *Interview Series*, Jack the Ripper, covers the ultimate "who-done-it" mystery of 1888 London's Whitechapel. The list of credible and diverse thinkers interviewed on the show includes world-renowned historian

Neil Storey, the Godfather of Ripper Research, Paul Begg, Ripperologists, Paul Williams, Tom Wescott, Adam Wood, and Steve Blomer. Michael Hawley contributes his unprecedented scientific approach to the case. Suspect Ripperologists Jeff Mudgett, whose great-great-grandfather was serial killer H.H. Holmes, weighs in, and Russell Edwards, who believes he solved the case through DNA, provides his opinion.

VOICES OF TRUE CRIME SERIES

The *House of Mystery Radioshow* has been on the air for ten years, broadcasting in over a dozen cities in the U.S. It started as a way to interview guests knowledgeable in many of the world's mysteries involving crime, science, religion, history, paranormal, conspiracies, etc. *Voices of True Crime* series is a curated collection of interviews from the show. Each volume focuses on an actual criminal case, or several, providing the background and reproducing the main points discussed in the interviews. This series is an excellent reference for researchers and a good overview for those unfamiliar with the case. Online links to the actual interviews are included.

The MAKING A MURDERER Case: The Interviews (Volume 2)

Volume 2 covers the Teresa Halbach murder case, made famous from Netflix's Making a Murderer documentary series that began airing in December 2015. The House of Mystery Radio Show interviewed several of the key players involved in the case: Ken Kratz, the prosecutor of both Steven Avery and

"The author even had me (who conducted the interview) on the edge of my seat as I was turning the pages as "the Detective""

MURDER TIMES SIX: THE TRUE STORY OF THE
WELLS PARK MURDERS

---

to all the actual interviews are included.

Edward Wayne Edwards committed the crime. Online links involved in Making a Murderer. He asserts serial killer someone who had nothing to do with any of the players part A&E series suggesting that the crime was committed by Cameron. Cameron wrote a book that is the center of a five-murder case brought on by retired Detective John A.

We also examine one of the major theories surrounding this coming early 2023 titled Convicted.

the Making a Murderer series by creating his own docuseries the record on this murder case and expose the inaccuracies in

filmmaker that set out to correct
interviewed Shawn Rech, a
in false convictions. We also
the Innocence Project, an expert
spoke with Laura Nirider from
attorney. For the defense, we
enforcement to the state's
the misconduct of the law
convicted in his first trial brought
Steven Avery was wrongfully
Manitowoc County who, after
Griesbach, District Attorney for
Brendan Dassey, and Michael

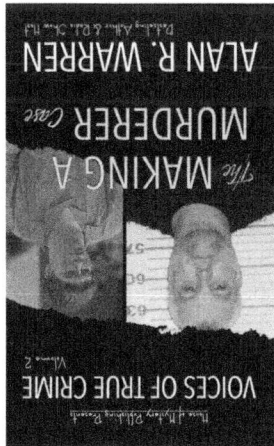

VOICES OF TRUE CRIME

The MAKING A
MURDERER *Case*

ALAN R. WARREN

was trying to unearth the unspeakable truth.

— SGT. MIKE EASTHAM R.C.M.P.

It was a crime unlike anything seen in British Columbia. The horror of the "Wells Gray Murders" almost forty years ago transcends decades.

On August 2, 1982, three generations of a family set out on a camping trip – Bob and Jackie Johnson, their two daughters, Janet, 13 and Karen, 11, and Jackie's parents, George and Edith Bentley. A month later, the Johnson family car was found off a mountainside logging road near Wells Gray Park completely burned out. In the back seat were the incinerated remains of four adults, and in the trunk were the two girls.

But this was not just your average mass murder. It was much worse. Over time, some brutal details were revealed; however, most are still only known to the murderer, David Ennis (formerly Shearing). His crimes had far-reaching impacts on the family, community, and country. It still does today. Every time Shearing attempts freedom from the parole board, the grief is triggered as everyone is forced to relive the horrors once again.

Murder Times Six shines a spotlight on the crime that captured the attention of a nation, recounts the narrative of a complex police investigation, and discusses whether a convicted mass murderer should ever be allowed to leave the confines of an

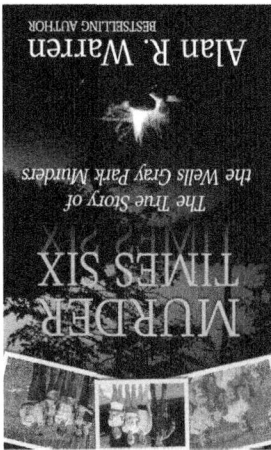

MURDER TIMES SIX

The True Story of the Wells Gray Park Murders

Alan R. Warren

BESTSELLING AUTHOR

institution. Most importantly, it tells the story of one family forever changed.

Printed in Great Britain
by Amazon

47874780R00233